S0-AHM-122

The Woodvilles

The Woodvilles

THE WARS OF THE ROSES AND ENGLAND'S MOST INFAMOUS FAMILY

SUSAN HIGGINBOTHAM

First published 2013

The History Press
The Mill, Brimscombe Port
Stroud, Gloucestershire, GL5 2QG
www.thehistorypress.co.uk

British Library Cataloguing in Publication Data.
A catalogue record for this book is available from the British Library.

ISBN 978 0 7524 8812 7

Typesetting and origination by The History Press
Printed in Great Britain

Contents

Introduction

From 1437, when Richard Woodville, a mere knight, made a shocking match to the widowed Jacquetta, Duchess of Bedford, to 1492, when Queen Elizabeth Woodville breathed her last at Bermondsey Abbey, the Woodvilles trod the boards of the great theatre of fifteenth-century history. Their members married into the greatest houses of England, crossed lances with the finest jousters in Europe, patronised the industry that made it possible for you to hold this book today, fought battles at home and abroad, and helped bring down an entire dynasty. Without them, the history of fifteenth-century England would have been very different.

While individual Woodville family members, particularly Elizabeth Woodville, have been the subjects of popular and academic non-fiction, there has not been (to the best of my knowledge) a non-fiction book that takes in all of the family, save for a self-published book that is largely hostile toward the Woodvilles. Due in part to this situation, myths and unsubstantiated rumours about the Woodville family have flourished virtually unchecked. Readers of historical fiction in particular 'know', for instance, that Elizabeth Woodville orchestrated the murder of the hapless Earl of Desmond, that Jacquetta and her daughter Elizabeth openly practised witchcraft, and that the Woodvilles ran off with the royal treasury during the crisis in 1483 that brought Richard III to the throne. While many of these myths and rumours have been addressed, and demolished, by academic historians, popular non-fiction and fiction has lagged behind, ensuring that for general readers, the impression of the Woodville family remains largely negative. After waiting in vain for a book that would help to set the record straight, I decided to write one myself.

Although the Woodvilles were a numerous family, the reality of researching the fifteenth century means that I have focused on the historically (as opposed to genealogically) best-documented members of the family: Richard and Jacquetta, and their children Anthony, Elizabeth, Richard, John, Lionel, Edward, and Katherine. As numerous books and articles have been devoted to the subject, I have also given short shrift to the great historical mystery of the fifteenth century: the fate of Elizabeth Woodville's two sons by Edward IV.

Because many of the printed primary sources I have relied upon use modern spellings, I have, for the sake of consistency, used modern spelling in all of my quotations here when possible. Likewise, instead of adhering to fifteenth-century spellings of proper names (which in any case were inconsistent, with the surname of the family here rendered as 'Wydeville' and 'Wodeville', among other variations), I have used the spellings most familiar to us today, in general following those used by the *Oxford Dictionary of National Biography*. The new year in fifteenth-century England began officially on 25 March, meaning that a letter dated 24 March 1460, say, would have been written, by our reckoning, in 1461; I have followed the example of most modern writers by giving dates using a 1 January new year. A mark was equivalent to two-thirds of a pound.

⁜ ⁜ ⁜

I would like to thank the many people who have given me assistance and encouragement in connection with this book, particularly Simon Neal for his transcriptions and translations; Hannah Kilpatrick and Kathryn Warner for their translations; Darlene Elizabeth Williams for proofreading; and Karen Clark, Kathryn Warner, and Geanine Teramani-Cruz for their comments on the early draft of the manuscript. As ever, I thank my family for putting up with me. Finally, I owe my deepest gratitude to the latest addition to my household, Dudley, who kindly refrained from chewing up my research materials.

I

The Duchess and the Knight

On 19 January 1460, Richard Woodville and his wife were rudely awakened in their lodgings at Sandwich. Their caller, John Dynham, roused them and their eldest son, Anthony, from their beds, bundled the father and son aboard a ship, and hauled the men to Calais, where they were greeted by their Yorkist enemies: Richard Neville, Earl of Salisbury; his son Richard Neville, Earl of Warwick; and their kinsman, the 17-year-old Edward, Earl of March. By torchlight, the three earls 'rated' the hapless Woodville men. Richard Woodville was a 'knave', a man 'made by marriage', whose father was but a squire.[1]

Whether the Woodvilles replied to this barrage of insults is unrecorded, but in September 1464, the former Earl of March, now King Edward IV, made a surprise announcement to his council at Reading. He had chosen a bride. His new wife, he informed the stunned councillors, was not a foreign princess, but Dame Elizabeth Grey, a widow who happened to be the daughter of Richard Woodville.

It had taken over four years, but the Woodvilles had finally got in the last word.

✣ ✣ ✣

Elizabeth Grey was no stranger to unequal matches. She was, in fact, the product of one, that between Jacquetta, Duchess of Bedford, and Richard Woodville, a knight.

The story of Jacquetta's marriage has its origins, as do so many aspects of the Wars of the Roses, in the English occupation of France. Since 1422, John, Duke of Bedford, a younger brother of the late King Henry V, had served as regent of France for Henry VI, Henry V's infant son. Bedford made a strategic marriage to Anne, the sister of Philip 'the Good', Duke of Burgundy, in 1423. The marriage, though happy, was childless, and when Anne fell ill and died in 1432, Bedford felt the need to remarry quickly. His bride was Jacquetta de Luxembourg, the daughter of Pierre de Luxembourg, Count of St Pol. The groom was a few weeks short of his 44th birthday; the bride was 17. She was, the chronicler Enguerrand de Monstrelet recorded, lively (*frisque*), beautiful and gracious.[2]

Bedford and Jacquetta married on 20 April 1433 at the cathedral in Thérouanne, destroyed in the sixteenth century. In honour of the occasion, Bedford presented the Church of Notre Dame of Thérouanne with a peal of five bells, sent from England.[3] The marriage was performed by the bride's uncle, Louis, Bishop of Thérouanne, who served as chancellor for the English in France and who had made the match. Not for the last time when Jacquetta was concerned, the match was a controversial one, the offended party being Philip, Duke of Burgundy, Bedford's former brother-in-law. Not only had the Duke of Bedford remarried in unseemly haste, the bride's father, a vassal of the Duke of Burgundy, had neglected to ask permission for the marriage. The Duke of Bedford was to remain estranged from the Duke of Burgundy, which happened to suit the interests of the latter at the time.[4]

The Duke and Duchess of Bedford sailed to England on 18 June 1433. Jacquetta's new country was ruled by the 11-year-old Henry VI, who had been king since he was nine months old. While his uncle the Duke of Bedford was regent of France, his other uncle, Humphrey, Duke of Gloucester, was the king's lieutenant and keeper of England. The relationship between Bedford and Gloucester, his younger brother, had long been an uneasy one, and Bedford's journey to England with his bride was no honeymoon or pleasure trip. He had come to answer charges of negligence, likely emanating from Gloucester, and to obtain more funds for the war in France.[5]

Jacquetta settled down to life in her new country. On 8 July 1433, she requested denization, the rights of English citizenship, which Parliament granted her.[6] Unfortunately for the new Duchess of Bedford, her father fell sick and died later in 1433. A funeral service for the duchess's father was held on 9 November 1533 at St Paul's.[7] The following year, the citizens of Coventry presented the duchess with 50 marks and a silver-gilt cup while she and the duke were residing at his manor of Fulbrook,[8] and Jacquetta was made a Lady of the Garter, probably to put her on the same level as Gloucester's duchess, who also sported Garter robes.[9]

In July 1534, the Duke and Duchess of Bedford sailed back to France.[10] The duke's health steadily declined, and on 14 September 1435 he died.[11] Neither of his two marriages had resulted in children, although the duke had two illegitimate children, Mary and Richard,[12] and Jacquetta would later prove to be more than adequate at childbearing.

Bedford had made a will in 1429 naming his wife Anne of Burgundy one of his executors; in his final will, made a few days before his death, he did not entrust Jacquetta with this task. This, as Jenny Stratford suggests, was likely because of her youth; certainly the administration of Bedford's estate would prove to be a lengthy and complicated task.[13] Bedford did treat Jacquetta favourably in his will. She received at least 12,000 *livres* in goods, including, perhaps, a tablet of gold and beryl, made in the manner of a reliquary, garnished with small pearls, and wrought with images of the Trinity, that the duchess later gave to Henry VI.[14] More importantly, Bedford tried to leave his widow a life interest in most of his lands in England, France, and Normandy. For various reasons, including the quirks of English inheritance law and the claims of Bedford's brother, Humphrey, Duke of Gloucester, this proved unworkable, but Jacquetta was by no means left impoverished. Pursuant to her dower rights (a one-third share of Bedford's lands), she was allowed by the king to enter her lands in England and Calais on 6 February 1436 – on the condition that she not marry without royal permission.[15] Michael Hicks has estimated that Bedford's income in England was over £4,000, giving Jacquetta an income of £1,333.[16]

Despite her youth – she was still under 20 – Jacquetta proved tenacious in fighting for her rights. Bedford had left her Harcourt, together with the lordships of La Rivière Thibouville and Le Neubourg, but the council overrode the duke's wishes and granted Harcourt instead to Edmund Beaufort, Duke of Somerset. By the time the grant to Beaufort took effect on 23 December 1435, however, Jacquetta was actively administering her lands at Harcourt. As 'Duchess of Harcourt', she ordered a sale of woods, while at La Rivière Thibouville, she ordered that repairs be made to mills. Beaufort ultimately gained possession of Harcourt in 1537, but Jacquetta continued to press her claim in the courts. She had better fortune with La Rivière Thibouville and Le Neubourg, which she retained until their loss to the French in 1444.[17]

During this time, Jacquetta's lands were not her only preoccupation. By 23 March 1437, she had remarried.[18] She had not sought the king's permission, and her husband was not whom one would have expected.

✣ ✣ ✣

Richard Woodville, Esquire – we shall call him Squire Richard when necessary to distinguish him from his son by the same name – was the second son of John Woodville, who served as Sheriff of Northampton on several occasions in the late fourteenth century as well as in Parliament. He was the offspring of John Woodville's second marriage to Isabel, widow of Robert Passelaw.[19] According to Richard Neville, who 'rated' Squire Richard's son for his low birth years later, Squire Richard was brought up with Henry V.[20] He served in France and in 1423 became the Duke of Bedford's chamberlain. Following Bedford's death, he was appointed Lieutenant of Calais. The following year, he was made constable of Rochester Castle.

Squire Richard was married to Joan Bittlesgate. The couple had two children, named, naturally and confusingly, Richard and Joan. On 18 July 1429, Squire Richard entered into a marriage settlement with William Haute of Kent for William to marry Richard's daughter Joan. Squire Richard gave his daughter a marriage portion of 400 marks and agreed to pay the costs of the wedding, which was to take place at Calais. Joan was also to bring a 'chamber', meaning her personal effects and goods suitable for a gentlewoman of her estate. William, in turn, was to settle a jointure of 100 marks and dower of £40 on his bride.[21] As for Squire Richard's son, he would make his own marriage arrangements.

The first we hear of the younger Richard Woodville is on 19 May 1426. On that day at Leicester, the Duke of Bedford knighted the 4-year-old king, who in turn had knighted a number of other men and boys, including Richard Woodville (whom we may now call Sir Richard). Ironically, one of the other young men knighted on that date was Richard, Duke of York, whose son would marry Sir Richard's daughter.[22]

Although it is sometimes uncertain which Richard Woodville is being referred to, it seems to be Sir Richard who in 1429 served as the captain of 100 men at arms and 300 archers in France, and who on 9 March 1429 received a payment of 100 marks for bringing a payment of wages to Philip, Duke of Burgundy.[23] He was a knight bachelor in the Duke of Bedford's retinue in 1435.[24] That same year, he is said to have been taken prisoner by the French when the English besieged Gerberoy, but he was free by May 1436, when he was serving in the retinue of William de la Pole, Earl of Suffolk.[25]

It was probably in the latter half of 1436 that Sir Richard's thoughts turned from war to love. As Richard was associated with Bedford's retinue, he would have had ample opportunity to make the acquaintance of his new duchess, Jacquetta, but when this happened, or when the couple began their romance, is unknown. All we know is that by March 1437, Jacquetta, breaking the condition that she not remarry without royal permission, had secretly married Sir Richard, the son of Bedford's chamberlain. Monstrelet reported that Jacquetta's uncle Louis and her other friends were indignant at the match, given that Richard, though 'beautiful and well-formed in his person', was much below the social status of Jacquetta and her first husband, but there was nothing they could do about the matter.[26] The last comment is curious; perhaps Jacqueline's marriage had come to light due to a visible pregnancy.

The reaction across the Channel was far more muted, although it is hard to imagine that Squire Richard was less than delighted at the news that his son had landed a duchess as a wife. In the petition the couple brought before Parliament, they claimed that they had 'suffered very great hardship both personally and as regards their property' for their actions, but this language may have been formulaic.[27] In the event, on 23 March 1437, Parliament fined the couple £1,000, but as Lucia Diaz Pascual points out, this was standard practice for noblewomen who married without royal licence. Katherine Neville, Duchess of Norfolk (whom we shall encounter later) would be given the same fine in 1442, as had Margaret, Lady Roos, in 1423.[28]

Once the business of the fine was out of the way, Richard Woodville's career continued uninterrupted. He was made chief rider of Salsey Forest in Northampton on 11 July 1437.[29] In 1439, he was among those troops coming to the relief of Meaux.[30] He was back in France in July 1441, this time coming to the relief of Pontoise.[31]

Richard was active not only on the battlefield but on the tournament field – an avocation which he was to pass to at least three of his five sons. In 1439, he and Thomas Mowbray, Duke of Norfolk, jousted at the Tower of London at Shrovetide.[32] His jousting took on an international flavour at Smithfield in November 1440, where Richard's opponent was Peter de Vasques of Spain. The king, a spectator, cried 'hoo' – thereby bringing the combat to a halt – when the men had finished fighting with their poleaxes.[33]

A medieval wife's primary role was to produce children, and Jacquetta excelled at this task. She and Richard would see twelve of their children live to adulthood; a couple of others died in early childhood. The following handwritten note by Robert Glover, Somerset Herald, to a late fifteenth-century visitation may indicate the birth order of the Woodville children:

> Richard Earl Ryvers and Jaquett Duchess of Bedford hath issue Anthony Earl Ryvers, Richard, Elizabeth first wedded to Sir John Grey, after to King Edward the fourth, Lowys, Richard Erie of Riueres, Sir John Wodeuille Knight, Iaquette lady Straunge of Knokyn, Anne first married to the Lord Bourchier son and heir to the Earl of Essex, after to the Earl of Kent, Mary wife to William Earl of Huntingdon, John Woodville, Lyonell Bishop of Sarum, Margaret Lady Maltravers, Jane Lady Grey of Ruthin, Sir Edward Woodville, Katherine Duchess of Buckingham[34]

No birth dates were recorded for any of Richard and Jacquetta's children, so it is unclear when the babies started arriving. Elizabeth, Edward IV's future queen, is said to have been born in 1437, making her the couple's first child, but the 1437 date is highly questionable. It is based solely upon a portrait, labelled 'Elizabeth Woodville 1463', which states that Elizabeth was aged 26. Elizabeth's circumstances in 1463, as we shall see later, were not conducive to having her portrait painted, however, so it is likely that the label was based on a mistaken recollection of when Elizabeth became queen. It is quite possible, then, that Anthony Woodville, not Elizabeth, was Richard and Jacquetta's first child. Anthony, the first child named in Glover's list, was listed in his mother's 1472 post-mortem inquisition as being 'of the age of thirty years and more', which would put his birth date at around 1442, but the 'more' allows plenty of hedge room and leaves open the possibility that he was born earlier.[35] With other children we are on more sure ground. John Woodville was described in 1465 as being 20 years old, placing his birth year at around 1445.[36] Lionel was described as being in his 29th year in 1482, so he was probably born around 1453.[37] The youngest child was probably Katherine, who is named in her brother Richard's 1492 post-mortem inquisition as being '34 or more', placing her birth year at about 1458.[38] Edward's career is consistent with his being one of the younger Woodville children, as is his name; he was likely named for Henry VI's son, born in October 1453. Although an inquisition post-mortem identifies Richard Woodville as being 35 or more in 1486, which would place his birth date around 1451, his career makes it likely that he fell well into the 'or more' category; he was old enough to require a pardon in 1462.[39]

On 10 June 1440, Jacquetta and Richard acquired a place to house their growing family – the manor of Grafton in Northampton.[40] Squire Richard's brother Thomas had left Squire Richard the hundred of Cleley and land in Grafton, but not the manor itself, which was in the hands of the de la Pole family. Thomas may have been leasing the manor.[41] Squire Richard himself seems to have been primarily associated with the Mote in Maidstone, Kent. It was in Maidstone that he was buried, although his tomb no longer exists.[42] The Mote came into the hands of Sir Richard and Jacquetta sometime after 29 November 1441, when Squire Richard, having made his will on that date, died.[43]

In 1444, Henry VI, now in his twenties, chose a bride: Margaret of Anjou, the daughter of René, Duke of Anjou, and Isabelle, daughter of Charles II, Duke of Lorraine. Margaret was a niece by marriage to the French king, Charles VII, and her marriage was brokered in exchange for a truce. A Frenchwoman like Margaret, Jacquetta had family ties to the new queen: her sister was married to Margaret's uncle, Charles of Anjou. Jacquetta and her husband were among the large party sent in November 1444 to escort Margaret to her new home in England: Alice de la Pole, Marchioness of Suffolk, whose husband William headed the escort, ordered that a boat, the *Swallow*, be reserved for Jacquetta and her retainers. Sir Richard managed with a smaller boat.[44]

Henry married the 15-year-old Margaret on 22 April 1445 in a quiet ceremony at Titchfield Abbey presided over by William Aiscough, Bishop of Salisbury. As Duchess of Bedford, Jacquetta must have been prominent at the queen's coronation at Westminster on 30 May 1445, while Richard Woodville likely was among those jousting at the celebratory tournaments which followed. With the prospect of peace and of a healthy young queen producing a quiverful of children, the future must have looked bright. In fact, Henry's reign had started on a relentless and ruthless path downhill.

For the moment, though, all seemed well. After the death of Henry V on 31 August 1422, his queen, Catherine of Valois, had lived in the household of her young son, Henry VI, until around 1430, when she secretly married Owen Tudor – a match that would put their grandson on the throne as Henry VII – and moved to Much Hadham in Hertfordshire, where she gave birth to a son. Catherine's retirement into private life (she died in 1437) meant that until Henry's marriage in 1445, the court was a male preserve.[45] The arrival of a queen and a kinswoman opened the way for Jacquetta to become a prominent figure at court. The queen's jewel accounts, which survive for 1445–49 and 1451–53, show that Jacquetta's servants received exceptionally generous New Year's gifts. Jacquetta herself received a silver cup costing £35 *6d* in 1447 and a gold tablet with sapphires and other jewels, costing £16, in 1452.[46]

Richard Woodville enjoyed royal favour as well. On 9 May 1448, he became a baron; the origins of his new title, Lord Rivers, have been the subject of much speculation but are unknown. Further honours followed in 1450 when, following his nomination by Thomas, Lord Scales, John, Viscount Beaumont, Sir John Beauchamp, and Sir John Fastolf, he was made a Knight of the Garter on 4 August.[47]

Henry VI's government, however, was lurching toward disaster. A few months after his bride's arrival in England, the peace-loving Henry VI had secretly agreed to hand over Maine to the French and to Margaret's father. The English reluctance at effecting Henry's promise and a disastrous scheme by the English to capture the rich city of Fougères on behalf of Brittany led to a French declaration of war. One by one, English-occupied towns fell to the French or, worse, were surrendered without battle. On 12 August 1450, eight days after Lord Rivers's garter was strapped to his knee, Cherbourg, the last English fortress in Normandy, fell to the French.[48]

The year 1450 was as miserable at home as it was abroad. On 2 May 1450, William de la Pole, Duke of Suffolk, from whom Richard Woodville had purchased Grafton, was murdered as he sailed toward Burgundy under a sentence of banishment. Suffolk, who had taken the leading role in negotiating Henry's marriage to Margaret, was largely blamed for the handover of Maine and the losses in France.

The government was still reeling from Suffolk's murder when an uprising, led by one 'Jack Cade', began in the southeast of England in June. Lord Rivers, along with Viscount Beaumont and Lords Lovell, Scales, and Dudley, were commissioned to suppress the rebellion.[49] Later that summer, Rivers and a number of other men would be indicted in Kent before a commission headed by the Archbishops of Canterbury and of York, Bishop Wainflete, and Humphrey Stafford, Duke of Buckingham, for acts committed while they were pursuing the rebels.[50] Rivers himself, along with Dudley and Thomas Danyell and a force of about 2,000 persons, was accused of assaulting John Miche at Eynsford on 18 June 1450, 'so that he despaired of his life', and of taking away 46*s* 8*d* in cash, along with four pairs of sheets and a coverlet. Dudley later received a pardon. The outcome of the investigation as far as Rivers in concerned is not known, and we cannot tell at this juncture whether Rivers was personally guilty of any excesses, although at the very least he can likely be faulted for allowing his men to run wild. Cade and his men, however justified their grievances against Henry VI's government might have been, certainly did not have clean hands. They had murdered several people, including James Fiennes, Lord Saye, the royal treasurer, and his son-in-law William Crowmer, the Sheriff of Kent. For the amusement of the spectators, the men's severed heads were hoisted on poles and made to kiss each other. Later, Saye's dead body would be tied to the saddle of Cade's own horse and dragged through the streets.[51]

In September 1450, following the suppression of Cade's rebellion, Richard, Duke of York, returned to England from Ireland, where he had been serving as the king's lieutenant. It was an uneasy homecoming, for Henry VI and Margaret had not produced any children and Richard was therefore next in line for the throne. Cade at one point in the rebellion had adopted the name of 'John Mortimer', a name associated with York's family, and the rebels' demands had included one that the king 'take about him a noble person, the true blood of the Realm, that is to say the high and mighty prince the Duke of York'.[52] It was therefore necessary that York defend himself against suspicions of treason. Complicating matters was the return to England the previous month of another duke, Edmund, Duke of Somerset, whose surrender of Rouen and Caen in France without battle had infuriated the English populace. The king, however, did not bear a grudge against Somerset, who soon stepped into the dead man's shoes of Suffolk as the king's chief minister. In turn, York took up the role of the opposition. He was particularly bitter about Somerset's actions in France, which York regarded not only as treasonous but almost as a personal affront. York had been lieutenant general before Somerset, but had not been reappointed, apparently to his disappointment; instead, Somerset had received the post, probably in order to secure his cooperation in ceding Maine, where he held property.[53]

It was during this period that the Commons demanded that twenty-nine persons, including Somerset, be barred access to the king. Lynda Pidgeon has suggested, incorrectly, that Lord Rivers was one of them.[54] In fact, as P.A. Johnson points out, Rivers was one of those men who had been indicted the previous summer but who were *not* included in the Commons' list.[55] Indeed, according to a German envoy, Rivers and Lord Scales accompanied York when he presented his grievances to the king.[56]

For the short term, Somerset was the victor in the rivalry between him and York. He was appointed Captain of Calais – along with Gascony all that was left to the English in France – in September 1451. Lord Rivers, along with sixty men at arms, joined him there in December 1451 and became Lieutenant of Calais soon afterward.[57]

In the spring of 1453, the king and the queen at last had some good news: after over eight years of marriage, Margaret was pregnant. The joy was short-lived. In July 1453, Gascony fell to the French, and a few days later, Henry imploded. For nearly a year and a half, he would be speechless and unresponsive to his surroundings.

While her husband's wits were in abeyance, Margaret at last gave birth to a child, Edward, on 13 October 1453. In a brave show of normalcy, preparations went ahead for her churching, a ceremony which marked a new mother's purification and return to public life. The great ladies of the land, including Jacquetta, were all invited to the churching, which was scheduled for 18 November 1453.[58]

Margaret of Anjou had been raised in a family where women were prepared to take charge when necessary. As it became clear that Henry's illness was likely to continue indefinitely, she prepared a petition asking, as one shocked observer described it, that she 'have the whole rule of this land'.[59] This was a step too far for the English, who in March 1454 instead made the Duke of York the protector of the nation during Henry's incapacity. Somerset had already been imprisoned in the Tower, where he remained without trial throughout York's protectorate. York appointed himself Captain of Calais in Somerset's place, but was unable to secure the loyalty of the garrison, under the command of Lord Rivers and Lionel, Lord Welles, the captain of the castle.[60]

On Christmas Day of 1454, Henry came out of his stupor as abruptly as he had fallen into it. Henry acknowledged his 14-month-old son, ordered the release of Somerset, and ended the Duke of York's protectorate.

Once again, Somerset was in the king's favour. This was not a situation which York could tolerate, and on 22 May 1455, he ended it bloodily. Allying himself with Richard Neville, Earl of Salisbury, and Salisbury's son, Richard Neville, Earl of Warwick, he confronted the king at St Albans. In the street battle that followed, Somerset, probably targeted for death by York's men, was killed outside the Castle Inn.[61]

Henry VI's misfortunes at St Albans seems to have caused him to have become at least partially incapacitated for a time – or at least it suited the interests of the Duke of York to say so. In November 1455, a second protectorate was established. Due to lack of popular support, it was short-lived, ending with York's resignation in February 1456. Meanwhile, with Somerset's death, the way was open to negotiate with the garrison at Calais, and in July 1456, the Earl of Warwick entered Calais as its captain. Rivers surrendered his post. The balance of power, however, was to undergo yet another shift.

Margaret of Anjou had last come onto the scene during her husband's illness in 1453. Her bid for the regency had been unsuccessful, and she had remained largely in the shadows until the time of the second protectorate, when she emerged with a vengeance. It may have been Margaret, described in a letter of 9 February 1456 as 'a great and strong laboured woman [who] spareth no pain to sue her things to an intent and conclusion to her power',[62] who worked behind the scenes to gain support for ending York's second protectorate.[63]

Margaret's first move was to move her household in the spring of 1456 to the Midlands, where Henry's household soon followed her that summer. The effect was to shift the court from the uneasy atmosphere of London to the friendlier locale where Margaret could attract support against any threats to her husband's rule. During the court's extended stay in the Midlands, which would last until November 1457, Margaret often visited Coventry. In May 1457, she saw the city's famous passion plays. Prominent in the queen's party were Lord Rivers and his wife, who along with the Duke and Duchess of Buckingham and their children, and the older and younger Countesses of Shrewsbury enjoyed refreshments provided by the mayor: red wine, capons, pikes, pippins, oranges, ginger, peascods, and comfits.[64] At an earlier visit by the queen, in 1456, the mayor gave Lord Rivers a glass of rose water. The drink, which was thought to have healthful qualities, was duly noted in the records.[65]

King Henry, though much in the shadow of his assertive queen during this period, managed to carry out one of his own objectives. The men killed at St Albans were survived by their angry young heirs, especially Henry Beaufort, Duke of Somerset, who had threatened York and the Nevilles on several occasions and whose escapades had resulted in several watchmen getting killed.[66] To put an end to the hostilities, Henry had summoned his lords and ordered them to hammer out a settlement with the aid of a panel of judges and bishops.[67] To solemnise the agreement, on 25 March 1458, the king, the queen, and the warring lords processed solemnly through St Paul's in what was known as 'Loveday'.

A round of festivities followed Loveday. Lord Rivers was probably past his best tourneying days, but his eldest son, Anthony, along with the Duke of Somerset, jousted in front of the king and queen at the Tower and later at Greenwich.[68]

Henry's longed-for peace was not to last. Historians have assigned various causes, but it is clear that Warwick, stationed at Calais, did not help the situation by turning to piracy in the summer of 1458. Although the English people found the earl's swashbuckling exploits to be endearing, the king and the neutral powers whose ships were attacked were less impressed.[69] In July, Lord Rivers was appointed to head a commission meeting at Rochester Castle to investigate Warwick's attacks on a Hanseatic fleet.[70] As Arlene Okerlund has pointed out, being investigated by a mere baron must have rankled the earl, a man not known for his humility at the best at times.[71]

All-out war erupted in 1459. The events leading up to the renewed hostilities are murky. Contemporary chroniclers, generally sympathetic to York, laid the blame on the queen, as have many historians, but recent historians have been less indulgent toward York and his followers.[72] What seems more likely is simply that York and his followers had determined to seize power. They began their effort in September 1459, when Salisbury left his estates at Middleham and Warwick left Calais with the plan of meeting York at Ludlow. A portion of the royal army intercepted Salisbury's forces at Blore Heath on 23 September 1459. Salisbury won the battle, but more forces were on the way.

King Henry, displaying an uncharacteristic interest in military matters by reading treatises on warfare,[73] proceeded to Ludford Bridge in the Welsh march on 12 October. There he and his men encamped, awaiting battle with the forces of York, Salisbury, and Warwick, who circulated rumours that the king was dead. But fighting against their own king was not something that many men could easily stomach yet, and overnight a number of the Yorkist soldiers defected to the king's side. When those who remained awoke, they found that their leaders had deserted them. York fled to Ireland, leaving his duchess, Cecily, behind, while the Nevilles fled to Calais. With them was York's eldest son, the 17-year-old Edward, Earl of March.

King Henry was then faced with the task of dislodging Warwick from his perch in Calais. The Duke of Somerset was Captain of Calais in name, but he could get no closer than Guines, where he led a series of bold but unsuccessful attacks on the town.

Lord Rivers, stationed at Sandwich, gathered together a fleet to come to Somerset's aid. It was here, on 19 January 1460, that John Dynham made a surprise attack on the fleet and dragged Lord Rivers, his lady, and their eldest son, Anthony, from their beds.[74] The men were unceremoniously hauled across the Channel to Calais, to the amusement of one chronicler, who wrote that Rivers 'was commanded to have landed at Calais by the king, but he was brought there sooner than him liked'.[75] At Calais, they were paraded by torchlight before Salisbury, Warwick, and March, who improved the occasion by taunting the men with their comparatively lowly origins. As reported by William Paston II:

> My Lord Rivers was brought to Calais and before the lords with 800 torches, and there my lord of Salisbury rated him, calling him knave's son that he should be so rude to call him and these other lords traitors, for they shall be found the King's true liege men when he should be found a traitor, &c. And my lord of Warwick rated him and said that his father was but a squire and brought up with King Henry the V, and [afterwards] himself made by marriage and also made lord, and that it was not his part to have such language of lords being of the King's blood. And my lord of March rated him in like wise, and Sir Anthony was rated for his language of all three lords in like wise.[76]

Irksome as this must have been to them, the Woodvilles were fortunate to receive no more than humiliation at the hands of their captors; a few months later, it is unlikely that they would have escaped with their lives.

Jacquetta evidently was spared the journey to Calais, as a contemporaneous letter describes her as being still in Kent.[77] How long the male Woodvilles remained in custody is unknown, but there is no record of them fighting again until the Battle of Towton in March 1461. Meanwhile, Warwick sailed to visit York in Dublin, where the two men may have agreed that Warwick would help York seize the throne.[78]

Officially, however, when Warwick returned to England in July 1460, it was as the king's loyal subject. His protestations of loyalty lost much of their force, however, on 10 July, when Yorkist forces led by Warwick and March encountered the king's forces at Northampton. A timely defection by Edmund, Lord Grey of Ruthin ensured a Yorkist victory. The Duke of Buckingham, the Earl of Shrewsbury, Beaumont, and Egremont were slaughtered, and Henry was taken to London as a captive in all but name.[79]

The next arrival in England was the Duke of York himself, who returned in September 1460, when he began acquiring retainers without referring to the king or even to the regnal year in the accompanying documents, a clear sign that the duke had renounced his allegiance to Henry.[80] Clad in blue and white livery embroidered with fetterlocks, the duke made his way from Chester toward London. On the way, he was reunited with his duchess, who came to him in a chariot covered with blue velvet and drawn by four horses. At Abington, the duke sent for trumpeters and 'claryners' to accompany him to London, gave them banners bearing the royal arms, and ordered that his sword be borne before him.[81]

With 'great pomp and splendour and in no small exaltation of mood', York arrived in October at Westminster Palace, where Parliament had assembled. As one observer wrote:

> [H]e made directly for the king's throne, where he laid his hand on the drape or cushion, as if about to take possession of what was his by right, and held his hand there for a brief time. At last, withdrawing it, he turned towards the people and, standing quietly under the cloth of state, looked eagerly at the assembly awaiting their acclamation. Whilst he stood there, turning his face to the people and awaiting their applause, Thomas Bourchier Archbishop of Canterbury arose and, after a suitable greeting, enquired whether he wished to come and see the king. The duke, who seemed irritated by this request, replied curtly, 'I do not recall that I know anyone in the kingdom whom it would not befit to come to me and see my person, rather than I should go and visit him.' When the archbishop heard this reply, he quickly withdrew and told the king of the duke's response. After the bishop had left, the duke also withdrew, went to the principal chamber of the palace (the king being in the queen's apartments), smashed the locks and threw open the doors, in a regal rather than a ducal manner, and remained there for some time.[82]

Despite the lack of enthusiasm engendered by his bid for the throne, York would not give up so easily, and even began planning his coronation. Dissuaded, he instead submitted his claim to Parliament, which by 31 October had hammered out an arrangement under which York would replace Henry's own son, the 8-year-old Edward of Lancaster, as heir to the throne. York would receive castle, manors, and lands worth 10,000 marks per annum, part of which would be shared with his first and second sons, Edward, Earl of March, and Edmund, Earl of Rutland. Nothing was reserved for Henry's own son, although it may have been intended that he be allowed to succeed to the duchy of Lancaster upon his father's death. The Act of Accord, as it was called, required York, who was older than the king, to swear that he would do nothing to cut short Henry's natural life, but did provide for the eventuality that Henry might abdicate.[83]

The Act of Accord also authorised York to suppress 'rebellions, murders, riots, looting, extortion and oppression' – the unnamed source of such troubles being Henry's own queen. Hearing of her husband's capture at Northampton, Margaret had fled with Prince Edward into Wales, from where she contacted Somerset and her other allies. With every reason to fear for her son's safety if he fell into Yorkist hands, she resisted Yorkist attempts to lure her to London.[84]

As King Henry adjusted to this new state of affairs, Margaret's forces assembled minus Margaret herself, who had travelled to Scotland to seek aid. York went out with his own forces to oppose them. On 30 December 1460, his dreams of the throne ended at Wakefield, where he was killed in battle by forces led by Somerset. The Lancastrians (as it is now most convenient to call them) ordered that the dead duke be decapitated and that his head be placed at Micklegate Bar in York. As a finishing touch, York's severed head was decked with a paper crown.

There had been a notable absence at Wakefield: York's 18-year-old heir, Edward, who had been engaged elsewhere, probably in the Welsh march. He now took up his father's cause. In early February, he defeated Jasper Tudor, Earl of Pembroke, Henry VI's younger half-brother, at the Battle of Mortimer's Cross. This Yorkist victory was quickly followed by a Lancastrian triumph at St Albans. King Henry, who had been dragged along to the battle by the Earl of Warwick, was reunited with his wife and young son. The most significant Lancastrian casualty at St Albans was Sir John Grey, who had been married to Richard and Jacquetta's eldest daughter, Elizabeth. The death of this luckless knight would have undreamed-of consequences three years later.

Yorkist propaganda had painted a lurid picture of Margaret's army as a horde of barely civilised northerners set on wholesale destruction of the civilian population.[85] With Margaret encamped at St Albans, the nervous Londoners were taking no chances. They appointed Jacquetta, the Duchess of Buckingham, and Lady Scales to join a delegation sent to Margaret to beg for mercy for the city – a service which would be remembered with gratitude some years later.[86]

What Jacquetta and the other ladies said to the queen is unrecorded, but Margaret promised to leave the city unharmed. Tragically, from her point of view, she chose not to enter it at all, save for a token force. Instead she returned to the north, leaving London to throw its gates open to the charismatic Earl of March. On 4 March 1461, the earl, just a month short of his 19th birthday, took his seat in Westminster as King Edward IV.

The new king promptly led an army northward to confront the queen's forces. With them by now were Lord Rivers and his son Anthony, who at some unknown point had either escaped or been freed from Calais. On 30 March 1461, in blinding snow, the armies met at Towton. According to the Burgundian chronicler, Waurin:

> Edward had scarcely time to regain his position under his banner when Lord Rivers and his son with six or seven thousand Welshmen led by Andrew Trollope, and the Duke of Somerset with seven thousand men more, charged

> the Earl of March's cavalry, put them to flight and chased them for eleven miles, so that it appeared to them that they had won great booty, because they thought that the Earl of Northumberland had charged at the same time on the other flank, but he failed to attack soon enough, which was a misfortune for him as he died that day. In this chase died a great number of men of worth to the Earl of March who, witnessing the fate of his cavalry was much saddened and angered: at which moment he saw the Earl of Northumberland's battle advancing, carrying King Henry's banner; so he rode the length of his battle to where his principal supporters were gathered and remonstrated with them.[87]

Snow blowing into the faces of Lancastrian troops, good generalship by Edward, and the timely arrival of fresh troops led by the Duke of Norfolk resulted in a Yorkist victory, but at a terrible cost to both sides. By the time the battle and the ensuing rout ended, anywhere from 20,000 to 30,000 men lay dead, some on the snow-covered fields, others in the waters of the River Wharfe. Towton would be the bloodiest battle fought on English soil.

The Lancastrian royal family, Somerset, and a few others, fled to Scotland, while the triumphant Edward IV took the time to send a letter to his mother. William Paston II, who was allowed to read the letter when it reached the Duchess of York, reported that Anthony, Lord Scales – that is, Anthony Woodville – was among the dead.[88] Richard Beauchamp, Bishop of Salisbury, also reported that Anthony had fallen in battle, while Prospero di Camulio, Milanese Ambassador to the Court of France, claimed that Lord Rivers had escaped to Scotland with Henry and Margaret.[89] In fact, Anthony was very much alive, and if Lord Rivers ever made it to Scotland, he did not stay there. On 31 July, Giovanni Pietro Cagnola reported, 'I have no news from here except that the Earl of Warwick has taken Monsig. de Ruvera and his son and sent them to the king who had them imprisoned in the Tower'. This seems unlikely, because before this letter was written, Lord Rivers and Anthony had already made a decision that many other followers of Henry and Margaret made after the slaughter at Towton: they offered their allegiance to the new king. Lord Rivers received his pardon on 12 July 1461, while Anthony's came on 23 July. A third pardon was issued on 8 February 1462 to Anthony's younger brother Richard.[90] On 30 August 1461, Count Ludovico Dallugo, a recent visitor to England, wrote to Francesco Sforza, Duke of Milan:

> The lords adherent to King Henry are all quitting him, and come to tender obedience to this king, and at this present one of the chief of them has come, by name Lord de Rivers, with one of his sons, men of very great valour. I held several conversations with this Lord de Rivers about King Henry's cause, and what he thought of it, and he answered me that the cause was lost irretrievably.[91]

The Woodvilles, once loyal Lancastrians, were now loyal Yorkists. In December 1462, Anthony was among Edward IV's forces besieging Alnwick Castle, held by the Lancastrians.[92]

With the Lancastrian army reduced to a handful of impoverished exiles, Edward set about consolidating his regime. He had another concern as well. For it is a truth universally acknowledged, that an unattached young king must be in search of a wife.

2

The King and the Widow

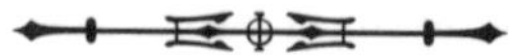

In September 1464, King Edward IV, one of the most eligible bachelors in Europe, informed his council at Reading that he had married. As the councillors waited, no doubt expecting to hear that the king had at last contracted himself with a foreign princess, the king told them that he had married an Englishwoman. The councillors' jaws dropped, and the king in turn dropped his final bombshell: his new bride was no duke or earl's daughter but Dame Elizabeth Grey, the widowed daughter of Lord Rivers and Jacquetta, Duchess of Bedford.

⁜ ⁜ ⁜

For most people in medieval England, years of birth, much less days of birth, were not recorded, and Elizabeth Woodville was no exception. We have only one source for her birth year: a portrait labelled 'Elizabeth Woodville', supposedly dating from 1463 and giving its sitter's age as 26. This would put Elizabeth's year of birth in 1437, the same year her parents were fined for their marriage. The 1437 date is plausible, then, but John Shaw's suggestion that the painting was made in 1463 by the king's own painter, John Stratford, is highly unlikely.[1] First, as Frederick Hepburn has pointed out, this and other extant paintings of Elizabeth appear to be derived from a lost original, so we cannot know what any original label, if there was one, said.[2] Had Elizabeth been on such terms with King Edward in 1463 that he was having her portrait done, she would have hardly needed to ask his friend Lord Hastings for help in 1464, as we shall see later. The possibility that Elizabeth or her parents commissioned the portrait is even more unlikely, given Elizabeth's straitened circumstances in 1463 and the fact that portraiture in

England was very much in its infancy. It seems far more likely that someone labelling the portrait years later (with the modern spelling of 'Woodville') simply was mistaken in his recollection of when Elizabeth became Edward's queen. Thus, while a birth date of 1437 certainly cannot be ruled out, the portrait is not a reliable source, and it is just as likely that Elizabeth was born somewhat later. As for her traditional birthplace of Grafton, given the uncertainty of her year of birth and her father's responsibilities abroad, it is possible that she was born on another one of her family's properties or even in France.

Beyond her first marriage, little is known of Elizabeth's youth. Both Edmund Hall and Sir Thomas More, writing in the sixteenth century, claimed that Elizabeth had served Margaret of Anjou as one of her ladies.[3] At first glance, this appears to be confirmed by the records. An Isabel, Lady Grey, was among the English ladies sent in 1445 to escort Margaret to England,[4] and an Elizabeth Grey, in her capacity as one of the queen's ladies, received jewels from the queen in 1445–46, 1446–47, 1448–49, 1451–52, and 1452–53.[5] 'Isabel' and 'Elizabeth' were often used interchangeably during this period, and it is possible that young Elizabeth Woodville had married her first husband, John Grey, as a child and thus was already known as Elizabeth or Isabella Grey. It is unlikely, however, that the lady named in Queen Margaret's records was the Lancastrian queen's successor. Little Elizabeth would have been a mere child in 1445–46, and therefore rather young to serve in the queen's escort or to receive jewels from the queen. It is far more likely that the person referred to in Queen Margaret's records is Elizabeth, 'late the wife of Ralph Gray, knight, daily attendant on the queen's person', who received a protection on 27 June 1445. Alternatively, Elizabeth Grey could be Elizabeth Woodville's own mother-in-law.[6] It is still possible that Elizabeth did indeed serve Margaret, of course, given the favour her parents enjoyed with the queen, but it is more likely that she did so in the late 1450s, a period for which Margaret's household records do not survive.

A story associated with Elizabeth's youth but now largely discredited is that at some point, she was solicited by both Richard, Duke of York, and Richard Neville, Earl of Warwick, to marry a Hugh John, who was in favour with the two noblemen. As George Smith has pointed out, however, the letters appear more likely to have been directed to a prosperous widow, Elizabeth Wodehille, than to the similarly named Elizabeth Woodville. Moreover, as David Baldwin notes, had Elizabeth Woodville been the prospective bride, the matchmaking duke and earl would have approached her father, not young Elizabeth herself.[7]

Like the date of her birth, the date of Elizabeth's first marriage is unknown. Her spouse was John Grey, the son of Edward Grey, Lord Ferrers of Groby, and his wife, Elizabeth. Sir John Grey was aged 25 or more at the time of his father's death in 1457, putting his birth year at around 1432 and making him a few years older than his bride.[8] According to John Grey's 1464 inquisition post-mortem, Thomas Grey, John Grey's eldest son by Elizabeth Woodville, was 13 or more in 1464, which would put his birth date at 1451, but a 1492 inquisition post-mortem, that of his uncle Richard Woodville, names him as being 37 and more, putting his birth date at around 1455. The latter date seems more probable, in light of this document dated 8 January 1455:

> Letters patent from Richard, Duke of York, Earl of Ulster, Lord of Wigmore and Clare that Richard Castleford, cousin and heir of Richard Castleford, clerk has sworn in his presence that release made of manor of 'Mew & Gyngjoyberdlaundry [Buttsbury]', Essex to Edward Gray, Lord Ferrers, for the settling of a jointure on the son of Lord Ferrers and the daughter of Lord Rivers, is to be disavowed if found to be to the prejudice of Edward Ferrers of Tamworth.[9]

As jointure arrangements were being made for Elizabeth in January 1455, it is probable that she had recently married John Grey or was about to marry him, which would coincide neatly with a 1455 birth date for their first son. This boy was duly followed by another, Richard, whose birth year is unknown.

John Grey's death at the second Battle of St Albans in 1461[10] left his young widow in difficult straits. Her mother-in-law, Lady Ferrers of Groby, had married Sir John Bourchier and was balking at the prospect of allowing Elizabeth to enjoy her jointure of 100 marks, consisting of the manors of Woodham Ferrers in Essex and Brington, and New Bottle in Northampton. Elizabeth and her father were obliged to go to chancery to recover her jointure, and apparently succeeded.[11]

Elizabeth also had the inheritance of her oldest son, Thomas, to safeguard, and this proved a more difficult task, so much so that Elizabeth needed assistance. Although her father had been made a member of Edward's council in 1463,[12] the erstwhile Lancastrian must not have been sufficiently influential to be of much help. Elizabeth, therefore, chose a much more powerful ally: William, Lord Hastings, Edward IV's long-time companion and close friend. On 13 April 1464, Hastings and Elizabeth agreed that her eldest son, or his younger brother in the event of Thomas Grey's death, would marry one of Hastings's as-yet-unborn daughters or nieces. If any lands formerly belonging to Sir William Asteley, Sir John Grey's late great-grandfather, or any of the inheritance of Lady Ferrers of Groby was recovered for Thomas or Richard Grey, half of the rents and profits while Thomas or Richard was under the age of 12 was to belong to Lord Hastings, half to Elizabeth. Lord Hastings was to pay Elizabeth 500 marks for the marriage, but if both of Elizabeth's sons died or there was no female issue on Hastings's side, Elizabeth was to pay Hastings 250 marks.[13] J.R. Lander described the arrangement as a 'very hard bargain' from Elizabeth's point of view.[14]

The arrangement never came to fruition, however, because soon Elizabeth had an even more important ally: Edward IV himself. When Edward and Elizabeth had first met is unknown. It is possible, but purely speculative, that they might have encountered each other on social occasions at court, one possible occasion being the Loveday festivities, when Elizabeth's brother Anthony jousted before Henry and Margaret. The Burgundian chronicler, Waurin, claimed that it was Edward's infatuation with Elizabeth which led to her father's and brother Anthony's pardon in 1461, while Caspar Weinrich, writing from Danzig, claimed that Edward fell in love with Elizabeth 'when he dined with her frequently'.[15] Thomas More, writing years after the fact, claimed that Elizabeth met Edward when she petitioned him to have her jointure returned to her.[16] The traditional, and virtually unshakeable, story has it that Elizabeth, knowing that Edward was hunting nearby, took her two sons and waited under an oak tree in the forest of Whittlebury. When the king came across this affecting tableau of the widow and her little boys, Elizabeth knelt at his feet and begged for the restoration of her children's inheritance, winning the king's heart in the process.[17]

Wherever and however the couple met, both the king and Elizabeth would have liked what they saw. Dominic Mancini describes Edward as captivated by Elizabeth's 'beauty of person and charm of manner', while the author of Hearne's Fragment wrote of her 'constant womanhood, wisdom and beauty'.[18] Her portraits, even if all copies of an original, amply bear out contemporary descriptions of her good looks, although no more than broad generalisations about her appearance were recorded by her contemporaries.

Even her hair colour is uncertain. The chronicler, Hall, writing years after her death, refers in passing to her 'fair hair', which is difficult to confirm from the sliver of hair visible in Elizabeth's portraits.[19] Manuscript illustrations invariably show Elizabeth as a golden blonde, but as J.L. Laynesmith has noted, queens were generally depicted in this manner.[20] What can be dismissed is the famed description of Elizabeth's 'silver-gilt' hair: this appears to be the invention of the novelist Josephine Tey, whose fanciful description was picked up by subsequent novelists and even by popular historians.[21]

For her part, Elizabeth saw a young man 'in the flower of his age, tall of stature, [and] elegant of person'.[22] In 1789, a measurement of his skeleton found Edward IV to be 6ft 3½in; the hair found by his skull was brown, as it is in contemporary portraits.[23] Even if the tall, handsome 22-year-old in question was not the most powerful man in England, a woman might have found it difficult to resist the lure of his bed.

Yet Elizabeth, if two accounts written during her lifetime can be believed, did just that. According to Antonio Cornazzano, an Italian writing no later than 1468, Elizabeth refused to become Edward's mistress and was ultimately rewarded for her virtue by becoming his queen; the virtuous Elizabeth brought a dagger to the meeting, with which she threatened to slay herself rather than to sacrifice her virtue.[24] Dominic Mancini, writing in 1483, has the king wielding the dagger:

> [W]hen the king first fell in love with her beauty of person and charm of manner, he could not corrupt her virtue by gifts or menaces. The story runs that when Edward placed a dagger at her throat, to make her submit to his passion, she remained unperturbed and determined to die rather than live unchastely with the king. Whereupon Edward coveted her much the more, and he judged the lady worthy to be a royal spouse who could not be overcome in her constancy even by an infatuated king.[25]

Thomas More, writing in the next century, omitted the dagger altogether but otherwise gave a similar account:

> [S]he showed him plain that as she wist herself too simple to be his wife, so thought she herself too good to be his concubine. The king, much marvelling of her constance, as that had not been wont elsewhere to be so stiffly said nay, so much esteemed her continence and chastity that he set her virtue in the stead of possession and riches.[26]

Other accounts simply have Edward falling in love, without first hazarding Elizabeth's virtue. Gregory's Chronicle put the matter most succinctly: 'Now take heed what love may do, for love will not nor may not cast no fault nor peril in nothing'.[27] (An alternative view, that Jacquetta promoted her daughter's marriage through witchcraft, shall be dealt with in Chapter 5.) It has even been suggested that Edward married Elizabeth because she had fallen pregnant, leading Edward to 'seize the opportunity for a son and heir',[28] but it is difficult to imagine that the Woodvilles' later enemies would have missed the opportunity to charge Elizabeth with unchaste living had there been the slightest hint that she had indulged in premarital sex with Edward.

Those chronicles that give a date for Edward and Elizabeth's marriage each specify the same one: 1 May. This date is compatible with the known movements of Edward, who was at Stony Stratford the night of 30 April 1464 and could have made an excursion to and from Grafton that morning, as claimed by Fabyan in the sixteenth century:

> [I]n most secret manner, upon the first day of May, King Edward spoused Elizabeth […] which spousals were solemnised early in the morning at a town called Grafton, near Stony Stratford; at which marriage were no persons present but the spouse, the spousess, the Duchess of Bedford her mother, the priest, two gentlewomen, and a young man to help the priest sing. After which spousals ended, he went to bed, and so tarried there three or four hours, and after departed and rode again to Stony Stratford, and came as though he had been hunting, and there went to bed again. And within a day or two after, he sent to Grafton to the Lord Rivers, father unto his wife, showing to him he would come and lodge with him a certain season, where he was received with all honour, and so tarried there by the space of four days. In which season, she nightly to his bed was brought, in so secret manner, that almost none but her mother was of counsel.[29]

Several historians, however, have questioned the May Day date. As David Baldwin notes, 'The idea of a young, handsome king marrying for love on Mayday may have been borrowed from romantic tradition'.[30] J.L. Laynesmith agreed that '1 May is a suspiciously apt day for a young king to marry for love. May had long been the month associated with love, possibly originating in pre-Christian celebrations of fertility and certainly celebrated in the poetry of the troubadours'.[31] Moreover, there are documentary reasons to be wary of the May Day date. On 10 August 1464, Edward signed a document giving Hastings the wardship of Thomas Grey. Wardships were lucrative commodities; if Elizabeth was already married to the king, it seems likely, as Michael Hicks has pointed out, that she would have asked to keep the wardship for herself. Furthermore, on 30 August 1464, Edward granted the county of Chester to his brother George, Duke of Clarence, apparently in his capacity as heir apparent. Such a grant would seem unnecessary if Edward had just married a lady who could be expected to provide him with an heir of his own body.[32]

Whether the couple were married on May Day or later, the scant record does bear out Hall's claim that a priest was present at the wedding. A Master John Eborall, whose church of Paulspury was close to Grafton and Stony Stratford, is said to have offered in 1471 to intercede in a land dispute involving the queen 'supposing that he might have done good in the matter, forasmuch as he was then in favour because he married King Edward and Queen Elizabeth together'.[33] A chronicle known as Hearne's Fragment adds that the priest who married the couple was buried at the high altar of the Minories in London, but leaves a blank space for the man's name.[34]

Whoever performed the ceremony kept it quiet until September 1464, when Edward IV himself announced the marriage to his council at Reading. There is no doubt that the reaction was one of pure shock. English kings had traditionally chosen high-born, foreign virgins for their queens: Elizabeth was an English commoner and a widow with two children. Although Edward III's son Edward, known as the Black Prince, had shocked his family in the last century by choosing an English widow with a tangled marital history, Joan of Kent, for his bride, Joan at least was a granddaughter of Edward I. In any case, the Black Prince had predeceased his father, preventing Joan from becoming a queen consort.

According to Gregory's Chronicle, the king announced his marriage only when his council urged him to find a foreign bride. We can only speculate on Edward's reasons for keeping the marriage secret, although if the couple married after August instead of in May, the delay of weeks rather than of months in announcing the marriage is less problematic. It has been suggested, in light of later allegations of a prior marriage (see Chapter 11),[35] that Edward entered the marriage with the thought of disavowing it once he had accomplished the feat of bedding Elizabeth, but other than a hint in Fabyan ('how after he would have refused her')[36] the chroniclers do not suggest this. Moreover, Edward's subsequent generosity to Elizabeth's family was hardly what one would expect of a man who felt that he had been trapped into acknowledging his marriage.

If Edward had delayed announcing his marriage because he knew it would incite controversy, he certainly was correct. Albrico Malleta, Milanese Ambassador in France, wrote on 5 October 1464 that the match had 'greatly offended the people of England', while the Crowland Chronicler, writing some years later, wrote, 'This [the marriage] the nobility and chief men of the kingdom took amiss, seeing that he had with such immoderate haste promoted a person sprung from a comparatively humble lineage, to share the throne with him'.[37] Dominic Mancini, an Italian observer during the fraught summer of 1483, wrote that by Edward's marriage:

> not only did he alienate the nobles with whom he afterwards waged war, but he also offended most bitterly the members of his own house. Even his mother fell into such a frenzy that she offered to submit to a public enquiry and asserted that Edward was not the offspring of her husband the Duke of York but was conceived in adultery and therefore in no way worthy of the honour of kingship.[38]

As J.R. Lander has pointed out, though, many of the English accounts were written after Edward's relationship with his nobles had soured, when it was natural to look for an explanation of the breakdown and find it in Edward's unconventional marriage. Also to be considered, as Anne Crawford observes, is that while the nobility may have been displeased at the marriage, the average man of the shire may not have minded an English queen, particularly after Henry VI's marriage to Margaret of Anjou had had such disastrous results. The household book of John, Lord Howard, contains a draft letter in John's own hand, addressed to either Lord Rivers or his son, Anthony, in which Howard states that he had spoken to many people in Norfolk, Suffolk, and Essex about the marriage and that only one opposed it.[39]

The person supposedly most offended by the marriage (aside from, presumably, the groom's mother) was Richard Neville, Earl of Warwick, who had been instrumental in helping Edward IV gain his crown. It used to be claimed that Warwick's anger arose because he had been made to appear a fool, having negotiated abroad in good faith for a foreign marriage which Edward knew could never take place because of his Woodville match. Fortunately for Warwick's pride, however, this is not borne out by the evidence. As A.L. Brown and Bruce Webster concluded after examining the records, there is no evidence that Warwick was employed as an ambassador abroad in the summer of 1464; instead, he was in the less glamorous environs of the north of England.[40] His true cause for dissatisfaction probably lay in the fact that Edward had not confided in his close advisers, as a friend of Warwick, John, Lord Wenlock, pointed out in a letter to a French correspondent, and that he had thrown away the opportunity for a strategic marriage.[41]

Elizabeth, however, had been wedded and bedded, so the council had to accept this *fait accompli*; as Wenlock said, 'We must be patient despite ourselves'. There was nothing to do but to smile when on Michaelmas Day, 29 September 1464, the king formally presented his new bride to his subjects, or at least as many of them who could gather in and around Reading Abbey. There 'Lady Elizabeth was admitted into the abbey church, led by the Duke of Clarence and the Earl of Warwick, and honoured as queen by the lords and all the people'.[42] For a few weeks, the couple remained at Reading, no doubt enjoying the usual pleasures of newlyweds.[43]

If the marriage brought Edward neither wealth nor useful foreign alliances, it did bring him a host of new relations, whose futures now became the subject of royal attention. Elizabeth had five brothers, Anthony, Richard, John, Lionel, and Edward, and six sisters, Jacquetta, Anne, Mary, Margaret, Joan (or Jane), and Katherine. Anthony had married Elizabeth, the heiress of Thomas, Lord Scales, who had been murdered in 1460 by London boatmen after holding the Tower against Warwick's men following the Battle of Northampton. Jacquetta had married John Strange, Lord Strange of Knokyn, by 27 March 1450, when the manor of Midlyngton in Oxford was granted to the couple by John's mother, Elizabeth.[44] The rest of the siblings, however, were unmarried, as were Elizabeth's sons.

Edward IV and Elizabeth were still at Reading when Edward arranged the marriage of his new sister-in-law Margaret to Thomas, Lord Maltravers, the heir of Thomas William Fitzalan, Earl of Arundel. The couple were married by 17 February 1466, when John Wykes wrote to John Paston II that Arundel's son had married the queen's sister.[45] Anne Woodville married Henry Bourchier, the heir of William Bourchier, Earl of Essex, around February 1466; on 15 August 1467, she and her husband received lands worth £100 a year.[46] Also around February 1466, Joan Woodville married Anthony Grey, the eldest son of Edmund, Lord Grey of Ruthin, who had deserted to the Yorkists at Northampton and who had been made the Earl of Kent on 30 May 1465.[47] Mary Woodville followed her sisters into matrimony in September 1466 at Windsor Castle. Her groom was William Herbert, Lord Dunster, the eldest son of a Welsh baron, also named William Herbert. The elder William was made Earl of Pembroke in 1468. The marriage indenture for Mary and the younger William was made on 20 March 1466.[48] The grand prize in this marital sweepstakes went to Elizabeth's youngest sister, Katherine, who married Henry Stafford, Duke of Buckingham, a royal ward. Although the anonymous chronicler the pseudo-William Worcester lumps Katherine's marriage as taking place the same time as those of her sisters Anne and Joan in February 1466, Katherine may have been married around May 1465, as she is given the title of Duchess of Buckingham at her sister's coronation that month and played a prominent role there, in the company of her fellow duchesses.[49]

Only one of Elizabeth's unmarried brothers, John, gained a wife as a result of his sister's marriage, but John's marriage generated so much controversy by itself so as to supply the rest. The 20-year-old John's new bride was Katherine Neville, Duchess of Norfolk, who was well into her 60s. The pseudo-William Worcester, who gloomily recorded each of the Woodville marriages, reserved most of his spleen for this match, which took place in January 1465. He called it the '*maritagium diabolicum*' – the diabolical marriage.[50]

Thomas Grey, Elizabeth's oldest son, gained a bride as well – Lady Anne, the only child of Henry Holland, Duke of Exeter, and his estranged duchess, another Anne. The Duchess of Exeter was Edward IV's sister; the Duke of Exeter, who had never got on with his father-in-law the Duke of York, was a staunch Lancastrian who was living in exile abroad. Young Lady Anne had been slated to marry Warwick's nephew George, the son of John Neville, Earl of Northumberland. The queen paid the duchess 4,000 marks for the marriage, which took place in October 1466 at Greenwich.[51]

How controversial were these marriages? The pseudo-William Worcester indicated that the Buckingham marriage was to the 'secret displeasure of the Earl of Warwick' and that Thomas Grey's marriage to Lady Anne was 'to the great and secret displeasure of the Earl of Warwick, for a marriage was previously bespoken between the said Lady Anne and the son of [...] Warwick's brother'.[52] (One wonders how secret Warwick's displeasure actually was.) Warwick, who had no sons and two young daughters, had obvious reasons for resenting the marriage of the wealthy young Buckingham, who would have made an excellent catch for one of his own girls. Moreover, the heirs to the earldoms of Kent, Arundel, and Essex had also been snapped up by the Woodvilles. This would not have been a problem if the king had been willing to let Warwick's daughters marry the king's brothers, George, Duke of Clarence, and Richard, Duke of Gloucester, but Edward preferred to keep his younger brothers in reserve, perhaps, with what must have seemed to Warwick to be maddening inconsistency, for the foreign princesses that Edward himself had cheerfully bypassed.[53] Warwick also had good reason to feel displeasure over the loss of his nephew's bride, although later Edward attempted to rectify matters by promising George Neville to his own firstborn, Elizabeth of York.

As for the Duchess of Norfolk, she was the aunt of both Warwick and the king. First married to John Mowbray, Duke of Norfolk, she had subsequently married Sir Thomas Strangways and John, Viscount Beaumont; the Strangways marriage had been without royal licence. Since Norfolk's death in 1432, she had been enjoying much of the family estates, thanks to her jointure and doubtless to the dismay of the Norfolk heirs. The duchess did not scruple to dower her daughter by Strangways with some of the Mowbray and Beaumont lands.[54] Clearly the point of the match with the duchess was to give John a handsome income, and Warwick may have regarded the match as exploitation of his aged aunt, as suggested by Charles Ross,[55] but nothing indicates what the old lady herself thought of the match. She may have enjoyed the company of the young man, or may have relished the thought of putting yet one more obstacle between her estates and her heirs. Nothing suggests that she was a woman easily cowed. After John's death, a Humphrey Gentille, attempting to settle an account owed to him by John, brought a chancery suit in which he claimed that 'the great might of the said lady' was preventing him from collecting his debt.[56]

One other specific person is said to have resented this burst of matchmaking: the Duke of Buckingham, Katherine Woodville's groom. According to Dominic Mancini, writing in 1483 after Richard III had taken the throne with the aid of Buckingham, Buckingham 'had his own reasons for detesting the queen's kin: for, when he was younger, he had been forced to marry the queen's sister, whom he scorned to wed on account of her humble origin'.[57] While this may or may not be true (no one bothered to record the thoughts of Buckingham, then a mere child, in 1465–66), as J.R. Lander has noted, there are good reasons not to take the comment at face value, given the anti-Woodville propaganda that was being circulated by Richard III at the time.[58] Moreover, as Carole Rawcliffe points out, it is perhaps because of this royal connection that Buckingham was allowed to enter his inheritance three years before he came of age and to recover the lordship of Cantref Selyf, which made him £3,000 the richer.[59] His Stafford relations do not appear to have resented the match: Henry's grandmother, the dowager Duchess of Buckingham, would later play a prominent role at Elizabeth Woodville's coronation, bearing the queen's train.[60] In 1470, the duchess lent the queen money after Edward IV was forced to flee the country.[61] The duchess's second husband, Walter Blount, Lord Mountjoy, and her two surviving sons, Buckingham's uncles, would prove loyal to Edward IV in 1470–71.

As for the families of the other grooms, Michael Hicks has laid great emphasis on the material inducements Edward offered to them.[62] It would surely, however, have been commented upon disapprovingly had the king *not* offered some sweeteners as part of the marriage negotiations. Since none of the spouses, except for Buckingham in later life, is known to have complained of his or her lot, the arrangements must have been satisfactory to those concerned.

Other than marriage, Elizabeth's siblings made some smaller gains from their sister's marriage. John became the queen's master of the horse for which he received £40 per year, while Anne, Lady Bourchier, headed the list of Elizabeth's ladies and also received £40 per annum. Anthony Woodville's wife also served Elizabeth at that salary.[63] In 1468, following the death of the prior of the Knights Hospitaller (the Order of St John of Jerusalem), Edward IV tried to get the order to accept Elizabeth's brother John as his replacement, but the order, presumably not wanting an outsider in their ranks, elected John Langstrother instead.[64]

While the Woodville sisters were being married off, plans were underway for Elizabeth's coronation, which took place on 26 May 1465. The ceremonies began on Friday 24 May, when London's mayor, aldermen, and guild members went to meet the queen at Shooters Hill. From there they conducted her to the Tower, as was traditional. At London Bridge, Elizabeth was greeted by a man dressed as St Paul, most likely a reference to Elizabeth's St Pol ancestry, and by another person dressed as St Elizabeth, the mother of John the Baptist. Mary Cleopas, the half-sister of the Virgin Mary, also stood upon the bridge along with her four sons.[65]

As was customary, the king had summoned a number of boys and men to be made Knights of the Bath, a ceremony which most likely took place on Saturday, following ritual baths and a night vigil on Friday. Among the new knights were Richard and John Woodville, two of Elizabeth's brothers, and William Haute, Lord Rivers's nephew by his sister Joan. The Woodville grooms were also well represented: the Duke of Buckingham, Lord Maltravers, and Anthony, Lord Grey of Ruthin. That Saturday afternoon, Elizabeth rode from the Tower to Westminster, passing through Cheapside and preceded by the newly made knights. Most likely, as did queens before and after her, she wore white cloth of gold and sat in a litter draped with the same material, her hair worn down.

On the following day, Sunday, the king's brother, George, Duke of Clarence, rode into Westminster Hall on horseback, his horse trapped from head to hoof with a richly embroidered cloth garnished with gold spangles. Behind him rode the Earl of Arundel and the Duke of Norfolk (John Woodville's step-grandson), both on coursers trapped in cloth of gold extending to the ground. The three noblemen rode about the hall, keeping the spectators from pressing against the queen as she entered the hall.

Preceded by the Abbot of Westminster and walking under a canopy carried by the four barons of the Cinque Ports, the queen wore a purple mantle and a coronal upon her head. She carried the sceptre of St Edward in her right hand and the sceptre of the realm in her left. The elder Duchess of Buckingham bore the queen's train, while the Bishop of Durham walked at the queen's right hand and the Bishop of Salisbury on her left. Following the queen were the queen's mother and two of Edward's sisters, Elizabeth, Duchess of Suffolk, and the unmarried Lady Margaret.

Covering the path from Westminster Hall to Westminster Abbey was a carpet of ray cloth, upon which the queen walked barefoot (or perhaps in her stockinged feet). Before her walked the Archbishop of Canterbury and other bishops and abbots. Clarence, Arundel, and Norfolk, now on foot, had also joined the procession, along with the 9-year-old Duke of Buckingham, carried upon a squire's shoulders. The king's sisters and Jacquetta still followed the queen, along with Buckingham's little duchess, who like her husband rode upon someone's shoulders. These ladies and the rest of the thirteen duchesses and countesses wore robes of red velvet and ermine, while fourteen baronesses were clad in scarlet and miniver. Seven ladies of lesser rank followed in scarlet.

Having passed into the monastery and through its north door, Elizabeth knelt at the high altar, then prostrated herself while the archbishop prayed. Rising, she was anointed and crowned, then led to the throne.

After the royal procession left the abbey in the same order in which it had entered, the queen was led to her chamber, where she was dressed in a purple surcoat and brought into Westminster Hall to dine, with John de la Pole, Duke of Suffolk (married to Edward's sister Elizabeth) standing on her right hand while she washed and the Earl of Essex holding the royal sceptres. John de Vere, the Earl of Oxford, served the queen her water, while the Duke of Clarence held the basin. The Countesses of Shrewsbury and Kent knelt beside the queen, holding up a veil before her whenever she ate. Each time the queen took a bite, she herself removed her crown, putting it back when she was finished. The Archbishop of Canterbury sat at the queen's right hand, the Duchess of Suffolk and the Lady Margaret on her left.

To cap off the ceremonies, on 27 May, a tournament was held at Westminster. Elizabeth's brother, Anthony, must have surely appeared there, but the honours went to Lord Stanley, who was awarded a ruby ring.

Conspicuously absent from the coronation ceremonies was King Edward himself. This was not a snub but custom; Henry VI had been absent from Margaret of Anjou's coronation, as Henry VII would be from Elizabeth of York's and Henry VIII from Anne Boleyn's. (Richard III was crowned with his queen, as was Henry VIII with Catherine of Aragon; both had married their brides before their own coronations.) It is possible that Edward IV was able to watch the ceremonies unobserved, as would Henry VII when his own queen was crowned.[66] An equally conspicuous absence was that of the king's mother, Cecily, Duchess of York. This may well have been a snub, but the duchess also missed her son Richard's coronation in 1483. The Earl of Warwick was on an embassy to Burgundy. Jacques de Luxembourg, Jacquetta's brother, came to the coronation as the representative of the Duke of Burgundy, which served the doubly pleasant purposes of allowing a kinsman of Elizabeth to see his niece crowned and of lending the event an international cachet.

Lord Rivers is not specifically named as taking place in the ceremonies; probably his rank was not sufficiently high or his role so prominent to merit comment. It is clear, though, that he was a proud father. Later he purchased a romance, *Alexander*, which, he wrote in its inscription, had been bought on the fifth anniversary of the coronation of Edward IV '*et le second de la coronacion de la tres vertueuze royne Elizabeth*'.[67]

3

The Black Legend of the Woodvilles

Soon after her crowning, Elizabeth Woodville would have noticed another change in her life: she was pregnant. The child, another Elizabeth, was born on 11 February 1466 at Westminster Palace. The birth of the king's first legitimate child served to lure even the baby's paternal grandmother, Cecily, Duchess of York, to court, where she and the Duchess of Bedford (smiling hard, one imagines) served as the child's godmothers at the christening at Westminster Abbey. The Earl of Warwick (also smiling hard, one imagines) did duty as the child's godfather. The elder Duchess of Buckingham served as the child's godmother at the confirmation.[1] Over the next few years, Elizabeth gave birth to two more daughters: Mary, born at Windsor shortly before her baptism there on 12 August 1467, and Cecily, born at Westminster on 20 March 1469.[2] The birth of Cecily, the queen's third daughter, prompted a Milanese ambassador to write that the queen 'gave birth to a very handsome daughter, which rejoiced the king and all the nobles exceedingly, though they would have preferred a son'.[3]

It is not for her fecundity in the 1460s, however, that Elizabeth is remembered. Three events that occurred during this period – a churching, an execution, and a trial – have marred her reputation, so much so that they deserve a chapter to themselves.

Following childbirth, a medieval mother was expected to remain in her chamber for about a month, after which a purification/thanksgiving service known as a 'churching' would mark her return to public life. For a medieval queen, a churching was a particularly grand event. An observer from Nuremburg, Gabriel Tetzel, travelling in the suite of Leo of Rozmital, a Bohemian nobleman, happened to be on hand in 1466 to witness Elizabeth's. He reported:

> The Queen left her child-bed and went to church in stately order, accompanied by many priests bearing relics and by many scholars singing and carrying lights. There followed a great company of ladies and maidens from the country and from London, who had been summoned. Then came a great company of trumpeters, pipers and players of stringed instruments. The king's choir followed, forty-two of them, who sang excellently. Then came twenty-four heralds and pursuivants, followed by sixty counts and knights. At last came the Queen escorted by two dukes. Above her was a canopy. Behind her were her mother and maidens and ladies to the number of sixty. Then the Queen heard the singing of an Office, and, having left the church, she returned to her palace in procession as before. Then all who had joined the procession remained to eat. They sat down, women and men, ecclesiastical and lay, each according to rank, and filled four great rooms.[4]

Rozmital and Tetzel went into a separate hall with England's noblest lords 'at the table where the King and his court are accustomed to dine'. There an unnamed earl, quite possibly Warwick, sat in the king's place and was shown all of the honour customarily shown to the king. The breathless Tetzel reported, 'Everything was supplied for the Earl, as representing the King, and for my lord [Rozmital] in such costly measure that it is unbelievable that it could be provided'.

Having finished dining, the earl conducted Rozmital and his attendants 'to an unbelievably costly apartment where the Queen was preparing to eat'. There, Tetzel, watching from an alcove so that his lord 'could observe the great splendour', noted:

> The Queen sat alone at table on a costly golden chair. The Queen's mother and the King's sister had to stand some distance away. When the Queen spoke with her mother or the King's sister, they knelt down before her until she had drunk water. Not until the first dish was set before the Queen could the Queen's mother and the King's sister be seated. The ladies and maidens and all who served the Queen at table were all of noble birth and had to kneel so long as the Queen was eating. The meal lasted for three hours. The food which was served to the Queen, the Queen's mother, the King's sister and the others was most costly. Much might be written of it. Everyone was silent and not a word was spoken. My lord and his attendants stood the whole time in the alcove and looked on.

> After the banquet they commenced to dance. The Queen remained seated in her chair. Her mother knelt before her, but at times the Queen bade her rise. The King's sister danced a stately dance with two dukes, and this, and the courtly reverence they paid to the Queen, was such as I have never seen elsewhere, nor have I ever seen such exceedingly beautiful maidens. Among them were eight duchesses and thirty countesses and the others were all daughters of influential men.

For the Woodvilles' modern detractors, this grand, silent meal, where even the queen's mother and the king's sister were obliged to kneel, epitomises the queen's vanity and the social climber's insecurity. Tetzel's editor, even while acknowledging that silence at meals at the time was not unusual, commented that Elizabeth's 'head must have been turned by her sudden elevation in rank'.[5] This, however, was no ordinary family dinner but a grand occasion for the royal family, marking Elizabeth's safe delivery of the king's first legitimate child. Notably, nothing in Tetzel's account suggests that he found Elizabeth's conduct repellent; he seems to have been merely a fascinated observer, just as he was when he witnessed the unnamed earl dining in royal state. Certainly nothing indicates that the queen was always surrounded by such solemn pomp; to the contrary, Louis de Bruges (Lodewijk van Gruuthuse), visiting the court a few years later, recorded his own account of his visit to the queen's chamber and of the 'pleasant sight' of the queen and her ladies playing games and dancing.[6]

If the queen's churching has fuelled unfair comments about the queen's hauteur and social insecurity, the next episode had led to far more serious allegations against the queen – murder. This story rises from the execution of Thomas Fitzgerald, the Earl of Desmond, at Drogheda in February 1468 under the direction of John Tiptoft, Earl of Worcester, who was Edward IV's deputy governor in Ireland. For reasons which remain murky,[7] Desmond, along with his brother-in-law the Earl of Kildare (who was also named Thomas Fitzgerald) and an Edward Plunkett, had been attainted of treason in the Irish Parliament at Drogheda. Desmond and Kildare, who had attended Parliament, were arrested there, and Desmond was executed several days later. Desmond's brother, Garret of Desmond, gathered together an army. With the help of Sir Roland FitzEustace, who had been accused of urging Desmond to crown himself King of Ireland, Kildare escaped from prison in Dublin and joined Garret's forces. This combined strength forced the hand of Worcester, who was obliged to accept Kildare and FitzEustace back into his favour.[8]

None of this would seem on the surface to have anything to do with Elizabeth Woodville, and indeed, no contemporary – not even Elizabeth's enemies – accused Elizabeth Woodville of having a hand in Desmond's death. In the public outcry in Ireland that greeted the execution of the earl, Elizabeth was never mentioned. Rather, the story of the earl's execution, and Elizabeth's supposed role in it, did not make an appearance until the sixteenth century. The first source for the story is this memorandum allegedly presented to Henry VIII's privy council by James FitzJohn Fitzgerald, Earl of Desmond, Thomas's grandson:

> So it is that this Earl's grandfather was brought up in the King's house, and being well learned in all manner of sciences and an eloquent poet, as the author affirmeth, was in singular favour with his Highness, so far forth that his grace took much pleasure and delight in his talk. And upon a day being in chase a hunting, his Majesty questioned with him, and amongst other things said, 'Sir cousin O'Desmound, for as much as I have you in secret trust, above others, and that ye are a man who doth both see and hear many things, as well in my court as elsewhere abroad, which shall not perchance be brought to mine ears, I pray you tell me what do you hear spoken by me?' To the which he answered his Highness and said, 'If it like your Grace, nothing but honour and much nobility.' The King, nevertheless, not satisfied with that answer, demanded of him again, three or four several times, what he had heard; and willed him frankly to declare the truth, not hiding one jot thereof from his knowledge; whereunto the said Earl made answer as he did before. At the last his Majesty, wading still in that communication as most desirous to grope the full, required him, for that he took him to be not only a man of a singular wit, but of a long experience and judgment withal, and none within this realm in whom he had more affiance, to declare his own opinion, and what he himself thought of him. To the which the said Earl lowly made answer and said, 'If it shall please your Grace to pardon me and not to be offended with that I shall say, I assure you I find no fault in any manner of thing, saving only that your Grace hath too much abased your princely estate in marrying a lady of so mean a house and parentile; which, though it be perchance agreeable to your lusts, yet not so much to the security of your realm and subjects.' Whereunto his Majesty immediately condescended, and said that he had spoken most true and discreetly.
>
> Not long after, the said Earl having licence to depart into his country and remaining in Ireland, it chanced that the said King and the Queen his wife, upon some occasion fell at words, insomuch that his Grace braste out and

> said: 'Well I perceive now that true it is that my cousin, the Earl of Desmond, told me at such a time when we two communed secretly together;' which saying his Majesty, then in his melancholy, declared unto her; whereupon her Grace being not a little moved, and conceiving upon those words a grudge in her heart against the said Earl, found such mean as letters were devised under the King's privy seal, and directed to the Lord Justice or governor of the realm of Ireland, commanding him in all haste to send for the said Earl, dissembling some earnest matter of consultation with him touching the state of the same realm, and at his coming to object such matter, and to lay such things to his charge, as should cause him to lose his head.
>
> According to which commandment the said Lord Justice addressed forth his messenger to the said Earl of Desmond, and by his letters signifying the King's pleasure willed him with all diligence to make his repair unto him and others of the King's Council; who, immediately setting all other business apart, came to them to the town of Droughedda, accompanied like a nobleman with eighteen score horsemen, well appointed after a civil English sort, being distant from his own country above 200 miles. Where without long delay or sufficient matter brought against him, after the order of his Majesty's laws, the said Lord Justice (the rest of the Council being nothing privy to the conclusion) caused him to be beheaded, signifying to the common people for a cloak, that most heinous treasons were justified against him in England, and so justly condemned to die. Upon which murder and fact committed, the King's Majesty being advertised thereof, and declaring himself to be utterly ignorant of the said Earl's death, sent with all possible speed into Ireland for the said Lord Justice; whom, after he had well examined and known the considerations and circumstances of his beheading, he caused to be put to a very cruel and shameful death, according to his desert, and for satisfaction and pacifying the said Earl's posterity, who by this execrable deed were wonderfully mated, and in manner brought to rebel against the sovereign lord and King.[9]

There are a couple of reasons that this memorandum should be treated with caution. First, although Annette Carson and John Ashdown-Hill used the petition to bolster their argument that Elizabeth was indeed behind Desmond's execution, they point out that the editor of the *Calendar of the Carew Manuscripts*, in which the memorandum appears, gives no source for it. They themselves were unable to find the original document.[10] Is it possible, then, that the document is not what it purports to be; was a fabrication foisted upon an unsuspecting editor?

Second, Desmond was in England in 1464, though not on a pleasure visit: he and William Sherwood, Bishop of Meath, had quarrelled, resulting in the killing of nine of the bishop's followers, and both men went to England to put their cases before the king. Art Cosgrove notes that the period that Desmond spent in England cannot be precisely dated, but he was granted an annuity by the king, who was at Woodstock, on 25 August 1464.[11] Edward IV did not announce his marriage to Elizabeth until the end of September 1464. While it is possible that Desmond was still in England in September to be sounded by the king about public opinion of him, there is no proof of this. Nor is there any evidence, other than the allegation in this story, that Edward and Desmond were close friends. Edward had a boon companion, William, Lord Hastings, who would have been a far likelier candidate to canvas public opinion if this was what the king wanted. No doubt the king's mother would have also been happy to pass along any negative feedback about her son's unconventional marriage.

Carson and Ashdown-Hill also point out that James FitzJohn, the author of the memorandum, was Desmond's grandson and could have heard the story of Elizabeth Woodville's involvement in his grandfather's execution from close family members.[12] This is certainly possible, but it does not explain how the Desmond family in Ireland could have learned of the quarrel between Edward and Elizabeth and of Elizabeth's underhanded use of the privy seal, a scenario which somehow escaped the attention of all of the English chroniclers and all of the Woodvilles' enemies.

The memorandum also conveniently ignores the arrest of the Earl of Kildare, which took place at the same time as Desmond's for reasons no source has ever attributed to malice on Elizabeth Woodville's part. Clearly, including Kildare's arrest would have undermined the memorandum's claim that Desmond's arrest and death were motivated by Elizabeth's private spite rather than by the political situation in Ireland. Finally, the memorandum's statement that Edward IV, shocked by Desmond's execution, caused the Lord Justice (i.e. Tiptoft) to 'be put to a very cruel and shameful death' is a gross error, despite Ashdown-Hill and Carson's attempt to gloss over it as merely a popular misconception.[13] Tiptoft was not executed until 1470, and it was not the exiled Edward IV but the Earl of Warwick, then governing for the restored Henry VI, who ordered Tiptoft's death. Attributing the execution order to the right man would have undercut the memorandum's claim that Edward IV was outraged by Tiptoft's (and supposedly Elizabeth's) actions.

The second source for Elizabeth's involvement is the *Book of Howth*, also from the sixteenth century. It reads:

> John Typtofe, Earl of Worcester, being Lord Lieutenant in Ireland, the queen, King Edward's wife, did hear say and credently was informed that the Earl of Warwick and the Earl of Desmond was greatly offended and also was grieved with the marriage of the queen, and said openly that better it were for the king to follow his friends' counsel, which went about to prepare for him a convenient and a meet marriage, not inconvenient for his estate, rather than to marry a traitor's wife, which thing at length said they were assured should come to an evil end and a success. The queen, offended with these sayings, often did move the king thereof, which little he did regard, considering it was spoken for the very love they bare to their assured friend and prince.
>
> When that the queen did so perceive that the king did make no more account thereof, she sought all the means she could to bring the earl of Desmond to confusion. She feigned a letter which the king should have sent to the Earl of Worcester, being in Ireland, and she, resting with the king in his bed at night, did rise before day, and conveyed his privy signet which was in the king's purche and did assign the letter withall, and after went to bed: within which letter was the earl of Desmond should have been apprehended and taken, and his head struck off as sample of other which rebelliously would talk of the queen as he did; which in fact was done accordingly, and so executed at Dublin, then being called thereunto for a parliament for the foresaid cause.[14]

Having claimed that the Earl of Worcester then proceeded to execute two of Desmond's sons, the *Book of Howth* concludes, 'After that the king did hear thereof, being much offended therewith, did send for the Earl of Worcester and, for that and other thing[s], did cause the said Earl to be executed'. As with the memorandum quoted earlier, the *Book of Howth* falsely claims that Edward IV executed John Tiptoft; it also erroneously states that Desmond was executed at Dublin. Again, we are left in the dark as to how the Irish writer learned of Elizabeth's nocturnal signet-stealing while no one in England observed this; again, no mention is made of the arrests of other men, probably because such information would unduly complicate matters by suggesting that Desmond was the victim of events in Ireland rather than of any wrath of the queen.

There are other reasons to doubt the Desmond story. While Edward may have been taken by surprise when Tiptoft executed Desmond, there are no signs that the king was displeased with Tiptoft's actions more than temporarily. The pseudo-William Worcester states only that Edward was 'initially displeased', and, as Cosgrove notes, it is 'difficult to find any manifestation of that displeasure'.[15] To the contrary, as Tiptoft's biographer R.J. Mitchell points out, Edward served as godfather to Tiptoft's son, who was born on 14 July 1469, and gave a gilt cup as a christening present. When Tiptoft, having remained loyal to Edward during the debacle of 1469, was recalled to England in 1470, Edward 'pressed upon him offices and grants of lands and wardships as never before, and, in short, showed every sign of delight in welcoming him home'.[16]

If Edward was 'initially displeased' with Tiptoft following Desmond's execution, there is no sign at all that he was displeased with Elizabeth, as one might reasonably expect a king to be with an upstart queen consort who had gone behind his back to order the execution of one of his subjects. Indeed, in his will of 1475, Edward IV named Elizabeth as the first of his ten executors and referred to her as 'our said dearest Wife in whom we most singularly put our trust'.[17] Even though seven years had passed since Desmond's execution, being tricked by Elizabeth in such an outrageous manner was not the sort of breach of trust that would have been easily forgotten with the passage of time.

Finally, when Warwick executed Tiptoft in 1470, Edward IV was in exile and Elizabeth Woodville in sanctuary. Earlier that year, in suppressing a Warwick-inspired mutiny in Southampton, Tiptoft had acquired a thoroughly unpleasant name for himself by his horrific treatment of the dead bodies of the executed rebels: following the men's deaths by hanging, drawing, quartering, and beheading, the bodies were 'hanged up by the legs, and a stake made sharp at both ends, whereof one end was put in at buttocks, and the other end their heads were put up one'. Warkworth claimed, 'and ever afterward the Earl of Worcester was greatly behatede among the people, for the disordinate death that he used'.[18] Given this popular hatred, Tiptoft's execution in 1470 would have been an excellent time for Warwick, by now an open enemy of the Woodville family, to have tied Elizabeth's name to Tiptoft's by mentioning her complicity in Desmond's execution. His failure to do so suggests that there was no complicity to mention.

The two sixteenth-century accounts in question, then, are hardly reliable sources on which to base a charge of murder against Elizabeth. In the last century, however, Paul Murray Kendall, a biographer of Richard III whose fervent admiration for his subject is matched only by his contempt for the Woodvilles, claimed to have found corroborating evidence in the form of a 1484 letter of instruction by Richard III. The letter in question was addressed to Thomas Barrett, Bishop of Annaghdown (rendered as 'Enachden' in the letter), who was to make diplomatic overtures to the new Earl of Desmond, James Fitzgerald, along with other Irish nobles and gentry. In this case, Richard III wanted to obtain the earl's oath of allegiance; he was also particularly concerned that the earl had abandoned English dress in favour of Irish garb.[19] The bishop, Richard wrote, was to offer James his regrets for the execution of his father sixteen years earlier:

> Also he shall show that albeit the father of the said earl, the king [i.e. Richard] then being of young age, was extorciously slain & murdered by colour of the laws within Ireland by certain persons then having the governance and rule there against all manhood Reason & good conscience, yet notwithstanding that the semblable chance was & happened within this Realm of England as well of his brother the duke of Clarence as other his nigh kinsmen and great friends, the king's grace always continues and has inward compassion of the death of his said father, and is content that his said cousin now earl by all ordinate means and due course of the laws when it shall lust him at any time hereafter to sue or attempt for the punishment thereof.

The Woodvilles, as we shall see, were alleged by some to be behind the execution of George, Duke of Clarence, in 1478. Seizing on this, Kendall, relying on the words 'semblable chance', interpreted the letter of instructions to mean that 'those responsible for [Desmond's death in 1468] were the same ones who had wrought the ruin of the Duke of Clarence (i.e. the queen and her kindred)'.[20]

Kendall's interpretation (followed by Ashdown-Hill and Carson) wreaks violence upon the English language: the phrase 'semblable chance' means 'like chance' and simply cannot be interpreted to mean 'same people'. Moreover, far from suggesting that those who procured the death of Clarence were the same who procured Desmond's death, Richard unequivocally states that Desmond was murdered 'by colour of the laws within Ireland by certain persons then having the governance and rule there'. These 'certain persons' could not be Elizabeth or any other Woodville, none of whom had the governance and rule of Ireland. Richard's reference to the Duke of Clarence, if it was anything other than simply a display of fellow feeling toward a nobleman who had lost relations due to political turmoil, was most likely simply an appeal to sentiment, as Clarence, who was born in Dublin, had been a popular figure in Ireland.[21]

Richard also authorised the younger Desmond to bring to justice those responsible for his father's death. In building their case for Elizabeth's guilt, Ashdown-Hill and Carson find this to be significant. Stating that there was 'even an underlying sense that Richard is encouraging James to take action', they muse, 'we are left to ponder against whom the king had it mind for James to proceed. [...] Edward IV and John Tiptoft, Earl of Worcester, were themselves dead. Elizabeth Woodville, on the other hand, was alive'.[22] This rather ingenuously ignores the fact that although Worcester and Edward IV were dead, there might well have been underlings still alive to face the consequences of their masters' actions in 1468.[23] Moreover, if Richard did indeed want Desmond to take action, and believed that Elizabeth Woodville was the person responsible, it would have easy enough, and eminently sensible, for him to say so. Although it is true, as Ashdown-Hill and Carson point out, that the letter was only to be used as a memorandum of 'talking points' for the bishop's guidance, it is quite detailed, as they themselves acknowledge.[24] Surely, if Richard, who was not given to mincing words when it came to the Woodvilles, believed that Elizabeth Woodville was the person behind the elder Desmond's death, he would have made certain that his envoy remembered to mention this point, instead of trusting it to memory.

Indeed, if Richard believed Elizabeth to be guilty of murder, why did he not proclaim this fact to the country at large? In the summer of 1483, Richard III was engaged in a smear campaign against the Woodvilles.[25] Had there been evidence, or even simply a belief, that Elizabeth had orchestrated the murder of Desmond, Richard would surely have emphasised it, as it would have fitted in beautifully with his claims that Elizabeth and her kindred intended to murder Richard himself.

In the end, having received carte blanche from Richard to bring his father's killers to justice, the younger Desmond did nothing, as far we can tell. He certainly did not proceed against Elizabeth for his father's death, although Elizabeth during Richard's reign was at her most vulnerable.

The story that Elizabeth procured Desmond's death, in short, rests on mighty shaky ground.

This brings us to the affair of Sir Thomas Cook, for which some backtracking is necessary. The year 1466 had proven a good one for Lord Rivers, who in addition to gaining a royal granddaughter was appointed treasurer of England on 4 March 1466 and was created Earl Rivers on 25 May 1466. Another office, Constable of England, followed on 24 August 1467.

Meanwhile, time had not sat still with the Lancastrian royal family. Henry VI and Margaret of Anjou had a small but determined band of supporters, who had continued to cause trouble for Edward IV after the carnage at Towton. Henry Beaufort, Duke of Somerset, had been defeated and executed at Hexham in 1464, and Henry VI himself, after a year of wandering through the north of England as a fugitive, had been captured and sent to the Tower of London in 1465. Margaret of Anjou had gone to France, where she and her young son maintained a poverty-stricken court at one of her father's castles, Koeur. There, she and her loyal followers waited on their chances, stirring up what mischief they could against Edward IV's government and making contacts inside England. One castle, Harlech, was still in the hands of Lancastrian forces. Jasper Tudor, Earl of Pembroke, Henry VI's half-brother, was making plans, with funds from the French king, Louis XI, to go to its aid.[26]

It was in this tense atmosphere that a Cornelius, a servant of a Lancastrian stalwart named Robert Whittingham, was arrested in June 1468 for carrying letters on behalf of Margaret of Anjou. Upon having his feet burned, the unfortunate Cornelius named names, including John Hawkins, a servant of Lord Wenlock. Hawkins in turn implicated Sir Thomas Cook, a wealthy draper who had previously served as London's mayor. He had been made a Knight of the Bath before Elizabeth Woodville's coronation. Cook was tried for treason but was convicted only of concealing a Lancastrian plot against the government, which allowed for a conviction only of misprision of treason. He was fined 8,000 marks.[27] As Hawkins and another man, John Norris, were convicted of treason and hanged, one could consider Cook a lucky man in suffering only in his purse, especially when the autumn brought more arrests and executions of suspected Lancastrian agents.[28]

This was not, however, how the author of the *Great Chronicle of London* saw it. According to the author, who most likely was Robert Fabyan, a former apprentice of Cook, his master was the victim of the greed of Jacquetta Woodville, who was determined to acquire a valuable tapestry which Cook had refused to sell to her. Because the jury refused to find Cook guilty of treason, the story goes, Earl Rivers and his wife contrived to have Sir John Markham, the presiding judge, lose his office.

As is so often the case with stories about the Woodville family, the reality is rather different. The tapestry was indeed seized, but as Livia Visser-Fuchs and Anne Sutton point out, Fabyan does not report that Jacquetta acquired it, only that she had coveted it.[29] It is possible that when Earl Rivers and his agents seized Cook's goods pending trial, as was customary, some property was skimmed off the top, but this was hardly uncommon.[30] As for the hapless John Markham, Sutton has noted that Cook's trial took place in July 1468, and Markham was still being appointed to judicial duties as late as November 1468. By 12 December 1468, he had resigned; a warrant appointing his replacement in January 1469 indicates that he had left his post due to 'his great age and debility' and 'by his desire and special request'. He was 69 at the time.[31] It is possible, of course, that Markham was encouraged to resign, but there is nothing to confirm this or the Woodvilles' involvement in it. It may also be, as Eric Ives has suggested, that Markham:

> had failed in the essential duty of the chief justice, namely to give the crown the judicial outcome it wanted within the limits of due process. Deprived of the king's confidence he felt he had to go, with a face-saving excuse and a decent interval before a successor was appointed.[32]

A sequel to this story is Elizabeth Woodville's attempt to obtain queen's gold from Cook. This was an ancient prerogative which allowed a queen consort to collect a sum equal to one-tenth of a voluntary fine, and payable in addition to the fine itself. Like any other government prerogative, this was not popular, but it was not, as Kendall has suggested, an exaction that had been moribund before Elizabeth revived it; Margaret of Anjou had attempted to collect queen's gold, but with mixed results.[33] The question of whether Elizabeth was entitled to claim it at all from Cook has been debated. Anne Crawford has stated that because the sum was imposed only on voluntary fines, Elizabeth had no claim at all, whereas Michael Hicks notes that by the late fifteenth century the prerogative was imposed upon fines offered at the courts of common law and in chancery, although convictions of misprision did not automatically result in the imposition of queen's gold. Fabyan, moreover, states that the 'statute made of old time' applied to fines for misprision. It seems unlikely that Elizabeth, who had successfully upheld her right to queen's gold in other cases, would have pursued it now if she thought that she had no colourable claim.[34] In the event, however, it appears that Elizabeth was either unsuccessful or settled her case – incidentally, undermining the argument that the queen and her family were able to manipulate the courts to do their bidding.[35]

Even if Cook's case cannot be attributed simply to the rapacity of the Woodvilles, it is possible that Cook was innocent and that his actions were misinterpreted by a panicky government nervous about Cook's influence, particularly at a time when it well suited the cash-strapped king to be able to impose a large fine.[36] Whether Cook was innocent or not, it was clear as the affair came to an end that trouble was afoot, and that the Woodvilles, as both royal relations and royal favourites, would be in the thick of it.

4

Murder at Coventry

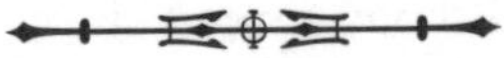

In 1469, a royal jester named Woodhouse, wearing high boots and clutching a staff, ambled into the king's chamber. Questioned by the curious king, he explained, 'I have passed through many countries of your realm, and in places that I have passed the Rivers have been so high that I could hardly escape through them, but was fain to search the depth with this long staff.' Lest the reader miss the point, the *Great Chronicle* explained helpfully, 'The king knew that he meant It is by the great rule which the lord Ryvers & his blood bare that time'.[1] The Woodvilles had come a long way since their 'rating' at Calais nine years before. Unfortunately, they had also made an implacable enemy – Richard Neville, Earl of Warwick.

Edward IV's own relationship with Warwick had been going downhill. As the Crowland Chronicler points out, the break between the men seems to have been precipitated not by Edward's marriage (although the marriage certainly served notice that Edward was his own man), but by foreign policy.[2] Warwick favoured an alliance with France, Edward IV (and the Woodvilles) with Burgundy. In September 1465, an opportunity presented itself when the Duke of Burgundy's heir, Charles, Count of Charlois, became a widower. Edward possessed a valuable bargaining tool: his youngest sister, Margaret, who was attractive and of marriageable age.

Keeping his options open, at the end of 1466 Edward IV employed Earl Rivers and his son Anthony to treat with Burgundy while Warwick negotiated with France.[3] During June 1467, when Warwick was in France, things at home were staying quite busy. The earl's younger brother George, the Archbishop of York, was dismissed from his post as chancellor; in a particularly tactless move, Edward IV had gone to the archbishop's sickbed at home to take away the Great Seal.[4] Anthony, Count of la Roche, a half-brother of Charles known as the Bastard of Burgundy, had come to England to take part in a tournament with Anthony Woodville.[5] The tournament, one of the great spectacles of the decade, had been in the making since April 1465, when Anthony, coming from Mass, was surrounded by the queen and her ladies, who tied a collar of gold around his right thigh and dropped a billet in Anthony's cap, which he had removed from his head while kneeling before Elizabeth. Perceiving that he was charged with undertaking a chivalric enterprise, Anthony quickly consulted the king, who authorised his brother-in-law to issue an invitation to the Bastard, in which Anthony assured his opponent that he offered the challenge not through arrogance, presumption or envy, but only to obey his fair lady.

Minutely described by contemporaries, the tournament shows Edward IV's court – and the Woodvilles – at their most glittering. On the first day of the tournament, 11 June, in the presence of King Edward and many nobles, Anthony made his entrance in a horse trapped with white cloth of gold, embroidered with a cross of St George of crimson velvet and bordered with a fringe of gold half a foot long. Eight other horses, also elaborately trapped, followed. The Duke of Clarence, the Duke of Buckingham, the Earl of Arundel, the Earl of Kent, Lord Herbert and Lord Stafford bore Anthony's two helms, two spears and two swords. Anthony also had his own pavillion of blue satin, embroidered with his (unrecorded) motto and topped with eight banners.

The fighting between Anthony and the Bastard was spread over two days and is marked by both controversy and confusion. On the first day, the men's horses slammed into each other, killing the Bastard's unfortunate steed. Chester Herald reported that after the Bastard's horse struck his saddle, Anthony rode to the king and removed his own horse's trapper to show that there was no steel spike that could have harmed his opponent's horse, while the Great Chronicle indicates that there was indeed a steel spike that pierced the horse's nostrils. Olivier de Marche, a Burgundian, wrote that the stroke and the fall happened by mischance. An anonymous Burgundian, on the other hand, wrote that when the horse was examined the following day, a large piece of metal was found in its throat. As Sydney Anglo, trying to make sense of the divergent accounts five hundred years later, remarked, '[T]he Smithfield tournament of 1467 is especially salutary in demonstrating the dubious nature of eyewitness evidence'.

If Anthony had indeed engaged in foul play, it seems unlikely that the Bastard would have agreed to fight him the next day. Fight again the men did, this time on foot with axes and daggers, King Edward having vetoed the use of casting spears. After Anthony's father made the sign of the cross three times over his son, and the two men exchanged taunts – Anthony is said to have yelled, 'Ha, sa, sa, sa, sa!' – the knights exchanged blows with their axes until the king at last called a halt to the proceedings. Chester Herald claimed that the men ignored the king's cry of 'Whoo!', while the anonymous Burgundian chronicler maintained that Anthony unilaterally disregarded the order to stop. Olivier de la Marche, who described the axe fighting as the fiercest he had seen, claimed that Anthony's armour was covered with gashes inflicted by the Bastard, and the other Burgundian chronicler noted that the third shoulder plate of the Bastard's armour had been hacked away. The exhausted men parted courteously and repaired to their lodgings. Over the next few days, other men fought, including Anthony's friend Louis de Bretaylle, a Gascon who was attended by both Anthony and his father.

The Smithfield tournament was not the Bastard's only mission in England, however. While lodging at the Bishop of Salisbury's house at Chelsea, he received a visit from Edward IV, Lord Hastings, Earl Rivers, and others. The king and the Bastard met privately in the garden for over half an hour, after which they were joined by Earl Rivers and treated to wine and spices. It seems likely that the visit was not merely a social occasion, but an occasion for some negotiations behind the scenes.[6] The issue of Charles's marriage assumed even more importance when, on 19 June, the festivities were cut short by the news that Philip, Duke of Burgundy, had died on 15 June, leaving Charles as the new Burgundian ruler. On 25 June, Anthony bade farewell at Dover to the Bastard.[7]

Warwick, who had been heaped with gifts of plate and luxurious fabrics during his stay at the French court, came back to find himself in eclipse. He had brought his own French embassy with him, who departed in August with no more than some modest gifts of hunting horns, leather bottles, and mastiffs and the king's promise to send a return embassy.[8] Lest anyone be in doubt as to how the wind had shifted, on the same day that the French embassy embarked for home, Edward announced that he had renewed a peace pact with Burgundy.[9] Warwick returned in high dudgeon to his estates in the north, while Margaret of York agreed on 30 September to marry the new Duke of Burgundy. Ten days earlier, Anthony Woodville and others had been commissioned to go to Burgundy and treat with the duke.[10]

Warwick made no secret of his displeasure with this turn of events. Sent to England by Louis XI to make contact with Warwick, the pleasantly named William Monypenny wrote that on 7 January 1467, Warwick had refused a summons to court on the grounds that he would not go to the king as long as Earl Rivers, his son Lord Scales, and William, Lord Herbert (another upstart, and a Welsh one at that) were with him. That same month, Earl Rivers's house at Maidstone was attacked by Warwick's tenants, probably at Warwick's instigation.[11] Despite this, Earl Rivers met at Nottingham with the Archbishop of York, who in turn persuaded Warwick, his brother, to attend a council meeting at Coventry. There, Warwick was reconciled with Herbert, as well as with some other men who had landed on Warwick's enemies list. No reconciliation with the Woodvilles, however, was forthcoming.[12]

Warwick was on sufficiently good terms with the king in July 1468 to join Edward and his brothers in escorting Margaret, the king's sister, to Margate, from where she was to embark to go to her new groom in Burgundy.[13] It was Anthony Woodville, however, who crossed the seas with Margaret, serving as her presenter and underscoring the role that the queen's relations had taken in promoting the Burgundian match. First among Margaret's ladies was Elizabeth Talbot, Duchess of Norfolk; the second was Lady Scales, Anthony's bride, making a rare appearance in the historical records. Anthony's younger brother John (he of the elderly bride) was on hand as well. They were in rarefied company: as John Paston III wrote to his mother from Bruges, 'And as for the duke's court, as of lords, ladies and gentlewomen, knights, squires and gentlemen, I have never of no like to it, save King Arthur's court. And by my troth, I have no wit nor remembrance to write to you, half the worship that is here'.[14]

Both Anthony and his brother took part in the splendid tournaments that followed the ducal wedding. Anthony did not joust against the Bastard of Burgundy this time, as, according to John Paston, the men had vowed at Smithfield not to meet again in arms. The Bastard, however, led Anthony onto the field.[15] As for John, he was beginning to come into his own as a jouster; in the spring of 1467, he and Lord Hastings, among others, had jousted against a team which included Edward IV and Anthony Woodville.[16] In Burgundy he was declared the prince of the tournament for three reasons: he was a foreigner; he was young and handsome; and he had acquitted himself honourably.[17]

Even at the glittering Burgundian court, however, reality had intruded itself upon the wedding celebrations. The Duke of Burgundy had been supporting several Lancastrian exiles, notably Edmund Beaufort, who thanks to the killing of his father at St Albans in 1455 and the execution of his brother at Hexham in 1465 was the latest Duke of Somerset, at least nominally.

To avoid the awkwardness of having a prominent Lancastrian present at the Duke of Burgundy's marriage to the sister of the Yorkist king, Somerset had been sent out of Bruges the day before Margaret's arrival.[18] His absence did not stop two members of the Duchess of Norfolk's train, John Poynings and William Alford, from being executed in November on suspicion of having had 'familiar communication' with Somerset during their trip abroad.[19]

Edward's reign was, in fact, running into problems. Edward had raised taxes, a move as unpopular as such moves generally are, with little to show for it, and he had failed to contain the lawlessness which had been a hallmark of the last disastrous years of Henry VI's reign.[20] It was a situation ripe for exploitation by Edward's enemies, at home and abroad. In June, in the midst of the wedding preparations, the suspected Lancastrian courier Cornelius had been arrested, leading to the arrest of Thomas Cook and others. Sir Richard Woodville, the queen's brother, himself captured Thomas Danvers, the recipient of a letter carried by Cornelius. More arrests, including those of Poynings and Alford, followed in November, including that of one Richard Steres, recalled fondly as one of 'the cunningist players at the tennis in England'.[21] Besides the sporting Richard Steres, the government netted three alarmingly high-profile individuals: Sir Thomas Hungerford, whose Lancastrian father had been executed at Hexham in 1464, after fighting for Henry Beaufort, Duke of Somerset, Henry Courtenay, the Earl of Devon's heir, and John de Vere, Earl of Oxford, Warwick's brother-in-law. Said to be kept in irons in his Tower cell, Oxford 'confessed much things' and was eventually released. The others were not so lucky: Poynings, Alford, and Steres were executed in November 1468, and Hungerford and Courtenay were tried and executed the following January.[22] Oxford was eventually released.

The Earl of Warwick then began brewing trouble of his own. His rebellion started at the altar. For some time, the earl had been hoping to marry his eldest daughter, Isabel, to Edward IV's brother George, Duke of Clarence, and when the king balked at the idea, Warwick and his prospective son-in-law, aided by the earl's younger brother, the Archbishop of York, secretly procured a papal dispensation in March 1469 for the couple to marry.[23]

That same spring, a pair of mysterious characters named Robin of Redesdale and Robin of Holderness stirred risings against the king in Yorkshire, which were put down handily by Warwick's younger brother, John Neville, Earl of Northumberland. When another rising broke out around 28 May 1469, ostensibly by Robin of Redesdale again, the king was not unduly alarmed. He went on pilgrimage to Walsingham, taking with him his father-in-law, Anthony and John Woodville, and his younger brother Richard, among others.[24] Elizabeth had borne her husband his third daughter, Cecily, on 20 March 1469;[25] as Walsingham was strongly associated with childbirth, perhaps the king was giving thanks for the latest arrival as well as making a heavenly request that his next child would be a son. As he made his way toward the shrine, he was making preparations to go to the north in person. The queen, who would have recently returned to public life after her churching, was staying at Fotheringay, where the king arrived on 25 June and spent a week.[26]

Warwick too was travelling – to Calais, with his brother the archbishop, his daughter Isabel, and Edward's brother George in tow. This was no innocent voyage, for this latest rebellion, far from being the product of spontaneous outrage, was almost certainly instigated by Warwick, with Robin de Redesdale being the *nom de guerre* of a member of the prominent Conyers family, who were Warwick's retainers.[27]

The earl arrived in Calais on 6 July, soon after which Edward's suspicions of his cousin and brother were awakened. On 9 July, he wrote to Warwick, Clarence, and the Archbishop of York, asking courteously that they come to him and refute the rumours that had been circulating about them. Instead, at Calais on 11 July in front of an assembled company which included five Knights of the Garter, the Archbishop of York officiated at the wedding of Clarence and Isabel.[28]

Clarence did not tarry in the marital bedchamber. The next day, he and his new father-in-law issued a manifesto, one of the sort that would make any medieval king's heart sink. Comparing Edward to Edward II, Richard II, and Henry VI, all of whom had been deposed (and two of whom had been murdered afterward), Warwick and Clarence accused Edward of having fallen prey to the 'covetous rule and guiding of certain seditious persons', namely, Earl Rivers and his wife Jacquetta, William Herbert, Earl of Pembroke, Humphrey Stafford, Earl of Devon, Anthony Woodville, Lord Scales, John, Lord Audley, Sir John Woodville and his brothers, John Fogge, and 'others of their mischievous rule, opinion, and assent'.[29]

All of these people were upstarts, at least in Warwick's eyes. William Herbert, a Welshman known as Edward IV's 'master-lock', had been made the Earl of Pembroke in September 1468; he was Edward's principal lieutenant in South Wales and the first full-blooded Welshman to enter the English peerage.[30] Humphrey Stafford was an even newer earl, having been granted his Devon title in May 1469 along with the forfeited lands of Henry Courtenay, executed in January.[31] John Fogge, a former treasurer of Edward IV's household, was a royal councillor and was also married to Alice Haute, whose mother, Joan Woodville, was Earl Rivers's sister.[32] John Tuchet, Lord Audley, had become a Yorkist after being taken prisoner at Calais in 1460.[33] None of these men were parasites; all gave the king valuable services in return for the royal favour they enjoyed. But Warwick wanted them gone. To accomplish this end, he summoned his supporters to meet him at Coventry on 16 July. Having crossed the Channel, he marched from Canterbury to London, then began a march toward Coventry.[34]

Meanwhile, as 'Robin of Redesdale' and his northern followers headed south, the earls of Devon and Herbert led troops to confront them. The details of the battle that followed are thoroughly murky. Even the date is in dispute; Barry Lewis has argued for 24 July 1469.[35] The outcome, at least, is clear: Herbert's men were defeated by the rebels, after a fierce battle to which Devon's men arrived late or even not at all. Herbert and his younger brother were captured.

Warwick and his son-in-law arrived at Northampton, where they began the congenial business of killing their enemies. Herbert and his brother were executed there – entirely illegally, as they had not been in rebellion against the king – on 27 July.

During this time, Queen Elizabeth, accompanied by her young daughters, had been enjoying the hospitality of the town of Norwich, following her husband's successful visit to the city during his recent pilgrimage.[36] The town had spared no effort in impressing the queen, even engaging the services of a John Parnell to assist it in staging pageants. When the big day arrived, sometime in the middle of July, a stage had been erected at the Westwick Gate. On stage were two giants made of wood and leather, stuffed with hay, as well as two patriarchs, twelve apostles, sixteen virgins, and Gabriel, played by a local friar. A Gilbert Spirling staged a pageant of the Salutation of Mary and Elizabeth, a theme evidently chosen as a nod to the queen. At Blackfriars, the queen, seated in a great chair brought over from Norwich Cathedral for her use, enjoyed a musical performance by a boys' choir. The occasion was literally dampened by a torrential rain, but the townspeople, well prepared for disaster, hustled the queen to dry lodgings inside the Blackfriars and quickly moved the props and performers out of harm's way.

As the citizens of Norwich relaxed after this latest royal visit, Edward IV, writing from Nottingham on 29 July, thanked the citizens of Coventry for sending men to his aid. He seems to have been unaware of the disaster at Edgecote.[37] Shortly thereafter he rode south, where at some point most of his entourage seems to have deserted him, perhaps spooked by the news of the battle. Learning of his whereabouts and his vulnerable position, George Neville, Archbishop of York, captured the king, acting on the advice of Warwick and Clarence. England was now in the bizarre position of having two captive kings.

Edward IV, no doubt reflecting on the fates of Edward II, Richard II, and Henry VI, as encouraged to do by Warwick's manifesto, was at Coventry on 2 August and at Warwick Castle from 8 to 13 August.[38] At Nottingham, he had sent his Woodville in-laws away for safety, Earl Rivers and his son John to Wales, Anthony Woodville to Norfolk. Waurin (not, however, an eyewitness) tells us that the king, believing that 'everything came from the envy that people had for the said Lord Rivers', spoke to Rivers, who responded, 'Sire, I am ready to do your will, because I do not wish that there should be discord between you and your blood on account of me'.[39] Nothing is heard of Earl Rivers again until 12 August, when, in the same lawless spirit that had prompted the executions of Herbert and his brother, father and son were executed at Gosford Green outside of Coventry, having been captured at Chepstow.[40] Another death soon followed: The Earl of Devon, who had escaped from Edgecote, was caught by a mob at Bridgwater in Somerset and murdered on 17 August.[41]

We know nothing about the last hours of the queen's father and brother. It was a sad end for Earl Rivers, whom fortune had flung so high, and for John, only about age 25. In June 1470, Jacquetta brought an action in King's Bench against those she held responsible for her husband's death, including Warwick, who by then had fled for France. Nothing seems to have come of it, probably due to the political upheavals of 1470–71 and the death of the main culprit at Barnet in May 1471.[42] Later, Walter Blount, Lord Mountjoy, would provide in his will for masses to be said for the souls of Earl Rivers and John, who must have been friends of his.[43] For his part, Anthony Woodville arranged for his younger brother's memory to be commemorated at Eton College, for which, he recalled, John had had 'zeal love and sing[u]ler devotion'. Anthony may have had his brother buried there. Waurin indicates that the king also mourned the deaths of Earl Rivers and John, 'because he loved them very much'.[44]

At what time Elizabeth Woodville learned of the deaths of her father and her brother and of the capture of her husband is unknown, but she appears to have returned to London by 31 July, when the mayor and aldermen voted to make her a gift of wine.[45] On 16 August, the Milanese ambassador reported from London, 'The Earl of Warwick, as astute a man as ever was Ulysses, is at the king's side, and from what they say the king is not at liberty to go where he wishes. The queen is here and keeps very scant state'.[46]

In the midst of their mourning, the queen and her family also had the fate of Edward IV to worry about. Would Henry VI be brought out of captivity to rule as Warwick's puppet? More likely, would Warwick's new son-in-law, the Duke of Clarence, take his brother Edward's place on the throne? Or would Edward be the subject of a protectorate, as the hapless Henry VI had been after the first Battle of St Albans? While Warwick pondered these possibilities, he appointed Sir John Langstrother as treasurer in place of Earl Rivers and himself as Chief Justice and Chamberlain of South Wales in Pembroke's place. He also summoned Parliament, presumably to give its stamp of approval to whatever course of action he had in mind.[47]

But events intervened. Far from settling into docility after the killing of the king's favourites, the mischief-makers of England took full advantage of this confused state of affairs. London rioted; the Burgundian ambassadors there, probably much to Warwick's chagrin, were able to help sooth matters.[48] The Duke of Norfolk, who claimed a right to the Paston family's prized Caister Castle, laid siege to it, crisply snubbing the Duke of Clarence's attempt to intervene – a failure which hardly boded well for a reign of King George.[49] The Berkeley and Talbot family feud reignited, as did the feud between the Stanleys and the Harringtons. More problematically, a cousin of Warwick's, Sir Humphrey Neville, staged a revolt on behalf of Henry VI. This rising proved impossible to put down without royal authority, and it seems that Warwick was compelled to back down. Edward raised troops in his own name, crushed the rebellion, beheaded Humphrey and his brother, summoned his lords, and returned to London in October, a free man.[50]

Warwick's rebellion had expired with a whimper, but not before costing two of the Woodvilles, and others, their lives. Oddly, a third Woodville, Anthony, had not shared their fate: around the time of his father's and brother's deaths, he had been captured and taken to Norwich, where he remained as a prisoner until 25 August, at which time he was removed to an unnamed location. Nothing indicates why Warwick spared his life; perhaps Edward IV's reaction when told of the death of his other followers had shaken the earl's nerve, or perhaps Warwick had decided for some reason that Anthony's execution would not be advisable.[51]

By the autumn of 1469, soon after Edward IV's own return to London, Anthony Woodville, now Earl Rivers, was back at court, where he was soon mingling uneasily with Warwick, who at least on the surface had reconciled with the king. Life was very far from returning to normal for the Woodvilles, however. The matriarch of the family, Jacquetta, Duchess of Bedford, was facing trial as an accused witch.

5

Witchcraft and Sorcery

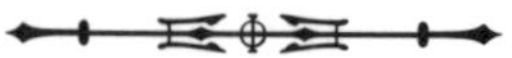

Jacquetta and her children were still reeling from the deaths of Earl Rivers and John when their enemies struck a second blow. This time, one Thomas Wake, Esquire, brought to Warwick Castle, where Edward IV was still being held prisoner, 'an image of lead made like a man of arms of the length of a man's finger broken in the middle and made fast with a wire, saying that it was made by [Jacquetta] to use with witchcraft and sorcery'. Wake also enlisted the aid of John Daunger, the parish clerk of Stoke Brewerne, to say that Jacquetta had made two other images, 'one for the king and one for the queen'.[1] The Duchess of Bedford was arrested and brought to Warwick Castle.[2]

This was not the first time a high-born lady in fifteenth-century England had been accused of dabbling in the supernatural. In 1419, Joan of Navarre, queen to the late Henry IV, was accused by her confessor, Friar Randolf, of 'compassing the death and destruction of [Henry V] in the most treasonable and horrible manner that could be devised'.[3] Friar Randolf himself fled abroad but was eventually captured and sent to the Tower, where he is alleged to have been murdered by a crazed priest in 1429. Joan, accused but never tried, was confined in various castles for three years. As A.R. Myers's studies of her household accounts for that period indicates, her confinement does not seem to have been overly rigorous; her expenses included outlays for rich fabrics, fine wines, and horses for her chaise, and she played hostess to distinguished visitors, including the Archbishop of Canterbury and Humphrey, Duke of Gloucester. One visitor, Thomas, Lord Camoys, stayed nine months! Joan was freed in 1422 by orders of the dying Henry V and lived a comfortable, uneventful life until her death in 1437, when Henry VI buried her next to her husband in a manner befitting a queen. Myers has suggested that the charges against her might have been prompted by mistrust of her Breton connections and by rumours of other plots to use witchcraft against Henry V. Once the initial scare passed, there were sound reasons for keeping the queen in captivity without further investigation: her imprisonment allowed the Crown to avoid having to pay her dowry of 10,000 marks per annum, while holding her without trial spared the crown from having to free her if she were found innocent and from having to punish her if she were found guilty.

A very different situation was that of Eleanor Cobham, Duchess of Gloucester, wife to Henry V's younger brother, Humphrey, Duke of Gloucester.[4] The death of Humphrey's brother John, Duke of Bedford (Jacquetta Woodville's first husband) in 1435 meant that Humphrey was next in line to the throne of the adolescent king, Henry VI. A beautiful, proud woman who had been Gloucester's mistress before she became his wife, Eleanor seems to have been unable to resist employing astrologers to find whether a crown might be in her husband's future. In 1441, two of her associates, Master Roger Bolingbroke and Master Thomas Southwell, were accused of using astrology to predict the king's death in his twentieth year. Soon Eleanor, who had fled into sanctuary, was forced to stand trial in an ecclesiastical court for heresy and witchcraft. By this time, Margery Jourdemayne, known as 'the witch of Eye', had been added to the list of suspects. Ultimately, Southwell died in prison, perhaps a suicide, Bolingbroke was hanged, drawn, and quartered, and Margery was burned alive at the stake. Found guilty of the charges against her, Eleanor was made to do public penance, forcibly divorced from Gloucester, and imprisoned for the rest of her life on an allowance of 100 marks a year. She died in 1452 at Beaumaris Castle, little noticed by the chroniclers.

Jacquetta, who certainly would have met the Duchess of Gloucester – her sister-in-law – during her own marriage to the Duke of Bedford, would have been well aware of the duchess's grim fate. She had every reason to fear for the future, especially if Edward IV remained in Warwick's control. But Jacquetta, though she must have been still labouring under the shock of the deaths of her husband and her son, did not panic. Instead, on 31 August 1469, she called in a favour by reminding the mayor and aldermen of London of the service she had done the city in 1461 by begging Margaret of Anjou to spare the city from Lancastrian destruction. The city officials readily agreed – it helped that the current mayor, Richard Lee, had held the same position in 1461 – and forwarded Jacquetta's letter to Warwick's ally, George, Duke of Clarence.[5]

Thomas Wake's son and heir had died fighting for Warwick at the Battle of Edgecote, and Wake himself was clearly a follower of Warwick, as he was one of the men Jacquetta would later seek to bring to justice for the murder of Lord Rivers.[6] It is hard, therefore, to avoid the suspicion that Warwick had something to do with the charges against Jacquetta. But what precisely was Jacquetta suspected of doing? The person represented by the 'image of lead made like a man of arms of the length of a man's finger broken in the middle and made fast with a wire' is unidentified, nor is it clear whether Jacquetta was trying to destroy the person in question (by breaking him in the middle) or healing him (by making him fast with the wire). Nor is there any inkling of what was being done with the figures of the queen and the king, although John Leland has suggested that the figures might have been used to bring about their marriage, which of course would indicate that they had served their purpose some time ago.[7] Another possibility might have been that Jacquetta was attempting to help the couple, who had thus far produced only daughters, to have a son. As Leland notes, there is certainly no reason to think that Jacquetta might have been cursing them.

All this, however, supposes that Wake's allegations about the figures were true. In the event, although the captive Edward IV dutifully appointed lords to examine the witnesses, the case against Jacquetta collapsed once the king shook off Warwick's control. On 19 or 20 January 1470, Jacquetta went before the king's great council, where she accused Thomas Wake of being of a 'malicious disposition' toward her 'of long time continued, intending not only to hurt and impair her good name and fame, but also purpos[ing] the final destruction of her person'.[8] When the council acquitted her, Jacquetta insisted that its exoneration of her be made part of the official record. On 10 February 1470, the king and his council, including the Earl of Warwick, agreed to Jacquetta's request. They set down what, in the wake of Edward IV's recovered power, had become an almost farcical series of backpedalling statements by the witnesses against Jacquetta:

> Thomas Wake says that this image was shown and left in Stoke with an honest person who delivered it to the clerk of the church and so showed it to divers neighbours after to the parson in the church openly to men both of Shetyllanger and Stoke and after it was shown in Sewrisley, a nunnery, and to many other persons, and of all this he heard or wist nothing till after it was sent him by Thomas Kymbell from the said clerk. John Daunger of Shetyllanger said that Thomas Wake sent to him one Thomas Kymbell, then his bailiff, and bad the said John send him the image of lead that he had and so he sent it, at which time he heard no witchcraft of the lady of Bedford, and

> that the image was delivered to him by one Harry Kyngeston of Stoke, who found it in his house after the departing of soldiers, and that the said Thomas Wake after he came from London from the king sent for him and said that he had excused himself and laid all the blame on John and bad him say that he durst not keep the image and for that cause sent it to Thomas and also bad him say that there were two other images, one for the king and one for the queen, but he refused to say so.[9]

Jacquetta also let it be known that she had always 'truly believed in God according to the faith of Holy Church, as a true Christian Woman ought to do'.[10]

The notion that Jacquetta practised witchcraft would be revived in 1484, when Richard III's only parliament declared Edward IV and Elizabeth Woodville's marriage invalid, partly on the ground that it had been made by sorcery and witchcraft committed by Elizabeth and Jacquetta 'as is the common opinion of the people and the public voice and fame throughout this land, and as can be adequately proved hereafter at a convenient time and place'.[11]

Were Jacquetta or Elizabeth witches, or at least dabblers in witchcraft? In recent years, popular fiction, especially the novels of Rosemary Hawley Jarman and Philippa Gregory, has portrayed them as practising the magical arts, and some writers of non-fiction, particularly those eager to vindicate Richard III, have followed suit.

Much has been made, to begin with, of Jacquetta's mythical descent from Melusine, a 'serpent woman' who was the supposed ancestor of the House of Luxembourg. Jonathan Hughes proposes, 'As the disastrous political consequences of the marriage became apparent and Edward's reputation as a voluptuary grew, the demonic aspects of the king's falling into the clutches of these two descendants of Melusine [i.e. Jacquetta and Elizabeth] would have preoccupied those prosecuting the charge of witchcraft'.[12] There is little evidence, however, that Jacquetta took a special interest in the Melusine legend, and none that Elizabeth did. Jacquetta owned a copy of the ancestral romance *Mélusine*, but only as part of a collection of treatises and histories of the crusades and the Holy Land.[13] *Mélusine* was, in fact, a popular fifteenth-century text, owned by other high-born ladies besides Jacquetta.[14] In any case, Melusine was not the only mythical figure from which a great family could claim descent; the Beauchamp family, of which the Earl of Warwick's own countess was a member, was supposed to have sprung from Eneas, transformed from a swan into human form when his golden chain was restored to him. His less fortunate brother, whose chain had been used to mend a cup, remained enchanted. Warwick did not have to look outside of his own household for ancestral magic; the mended cup associated in legend with the swan knight's brother was said to be in his own castle.[15] In 1474 at a pageant at Coventry, it was Elizabeth's supposed descent from the Magi, not that of Melusine, that was pointed out.[16]

Aside from Jacquetta's ancestor Melusine, those eager to find truth in the allegations that Elizabeth's marriage to Edward was procured through witchcraft have pointed to the date of the wedding – 1 May, the day after the witches' Grand Sabbath of Walpurgisnacht. We have seen in Chapter 2 that in the one detailed, but not quite contemporary, account of Elizabeth and Edward's wedding, the king rode early in the morning of 1 May to Grafton and wed his bride. 'After which spousals ended, he went to bed, and so tarried there three or four hours, and after departed and rode again to Stony Stratford, and came as though he had been hunting, and there went to bed again'. Fabyan, our source, added delicately, 'What obloquy ran after this marriage, how the king was enchanted by the Duchess of Bedford, and how after he would have refused her, with many other things concerning this matter, I here pass it over'.[17]

Modern writers have not shared Fabyan's inhibitions. Undaunted by the fact that no source actually places the king at Grafton (less than 6 miles from Stony Stratford) on the evening of 30 April, W.E. Hampton moved Edward's ride ahead a few hours to that date, just in time for Walpurgisnacht. After describing the rites of witches' sabbaths in some detail, without troubling to explain why Edward IV would be misguided enough to be in attendance at one, Hampton lets his imagination run wild:

> Remembering the description of Edward's night ride, and that of the King's irregular and profane, 'pretensed' marriage given [in 1484 by Richard III's Parliament], it is clearly apparent that the young king, one of our history's notable voluptuaries, on a date of obvious significance, and in circumstances and company which were, to put it mildly, dubious, entered into a form of marriage which may well have been precisely what [Parliament] claims, a marriage made by 'sorcerie and wichecrafte' [...] Even the fatigue of which Edward, a young man of exceptional physique, complained so sorely acquires an added significance when one considers the orgiastic nature of the rites to which he may have been introduced.[18]

Fabyan, as we saw in Chapter 2, listed the 'company' present at the wedding – the 'spouse, the spousess, the Duchess of Bedford her mother, the priest, two gentlewomen, and a young man to help the priest sing'. Assuming this account is correct, the company hardly merits Hampton's description as dubious. Moreover, Fabyan's account does not have Edward complaining 'sorely' of fatigue, but as simply going to bed upon his return to Stony Stratford in the pretence that he had been hunting. In any case, Edward might have had some cause to feel fatigued, after three or four hours in bed sandwiched by horseback rides to and from Grafton. (Fabyan does not state that the king spent those three or four hours in bed with his attractive new bride in slumber.) The most serious flaw in Hampton's argument, however, is that there is not a shred of evidence that any Grand Sabbath rites were held in the environs of Grafton on 30 April, much less that Edward or any of the Woodvilles attended them.

Annette Carson, while not matching Hampton in sheer creativity, nonetheless quotes his reconstruction of Edward IV's wedding night approvingly before positing her own rather operatic theory: that Edward was given a love potion by the queen and her mother. '[W]as he fed a potent cocktail of aphrodisiacs and love-charms and intoxicating potions to confound his senses and induce him to answer "Yes" when asked, "Do you intend to marry this woman?"'[19] While this scenario is not as far-fetched as Hampton's – one of the charges against Eleanor Cobham had been that she procured 'medicines and drynkis' in order to induce Humphrey, Duke of Gloucester 'to love her and wed her'[20] – it is still rather implausible. Unless the potion was exceptionally long-acting, it would have surely worn off well before Edward announced his marriage at Reading. Are we really to believe that a man who had fought his way to the throne at age 18 was incapable of disentangling himself from a marriage he had been tricked into making? Elizabeth might have been able to embarrass Edward had she raised a fuss over his refusal to acknowledge his marriage, but if the matter came down to the king's word versus that of a relatively impoverished widow with Lancastrian connections, it is not difficult to imagine which party would have prevailed.

The fact remains that there is simply no evidence, other than the unproven assertions of Jacquetta's and Elizabeth's enemies, that Elizabeth used anything other than conventional means – beauty and a winning personality – to lure Edward into marriage. (After all, no fewer than four commoners appealed sufficiently to Edward's grandson Henry VIII for him to marry them – all without benefit of witchcraft or sorcery.) Thomas Wake's 'evidence' –

which, it should be remembered, involved images, not Hampton's Grand Sabbaths or Carson's elixirs of love – crumbled in the face of Edward IV's recovered power, and Jacquetta vigorously denied his accusations. As for the 1484 accusations against mother and daughter, Richard III's parliament put forth no evidence at all to support the claim that Jacquetta and Elizabeth had practised witchcraft to bring about Elizabeth's royal marriage. By that time, Jacquetta was dead and could not defend herself. While Elizabeth never denied the allegations, she was hardly in a position to stand up to Richard III, who had executed her brother Anthony and her son Richard Grey and who had her royal sons in his power (if they had not already been disposed of). When Henry VII came to the throne and ordered the destruction of Titulus Regius, the Act of Parliament invalidating Elizabeth's marriage to Edward, there was no longer any need for Elizabeth to defend the validity of her marriage, especially when Henry tacitly affirmed the legitimacy of Elizabeth's children by marrying her eldest daughter.

It is not inconceivable, of course, that Jacquetta and Elizabeth employed supernatural means to lure Edward into marriage or against the unidentified knight whose image was supposedly in Jacquetta's possession. As Jessica Freeman notes, women like Margery Jourdemayne, the Duchess of Gloucester's associate, offered services to clients such as love potions and fertility charms; indeed, the duchess acknowledged employing Margery to help her bear a child by Humphrey. Authorities in fifteenth-century England were tolerant of such 'practical magic' if it was not employed to harm others.[21] The fact that a high-ranking lady such as the Duchess of Gloucester, whose husband was next in line for the throne at the time, could mingle with the likes of Margery shows that high status was no bar to one's dabbling in witchcraft. But because the allegations against Jacquetta and Elizabeth came solely from their enemies in times of turmoil, and were vigorously denied by one of the ladies in question, we should at the very least regard the accusations against them with the greatest of scepticism.

6

Exile and Sanctuary

In October 1469, John Paston II wrote a letter to his mother updating her on events:

> The King himself has good language of the lords of Clarence, of Warwick, and of my lords of York, of Oxford, saying that they be his best friends. But his household men have other language, so what shall hastily fall I cannot see.[1]

Paston was right to have his doubts about the situation between Edward and his erstwhile enemies following Warwick's short-lived hostile takeover, but in the autumn of 1469, a sullen peace had settled over the court after a series of largely behind-the-scenes negotiations between Edward and his rebellious lords.[2] It could not have been easy for the Woodvilles. The possibility of being tried for witchcraft still loomed for Jacquetta, and she and her children would have been mourning the loss of Earl Rivers and John as well. The one bright spot would have been Anthony's safe return to court, bearing his father's title of Earl Rivers. During the upheavals of the summer, John Knyvet, who had disputed Anthony's title to the manors of Babingley and Wolferton, had seized them as well as Middleton and Sandringham; by November, he was forced to return them to the new earl.[3]

By the spring of 1470, Warwick and his son-in-law Clarence had returned to their old tricks. Unable to take on the royal forces, the pair, along with their wives and Warwick's youngest daughter, Anne, took ship with the plan of landing at Calais. Meanwhile, Warwick sent Sir Geoffrey Gate to Southampton to retrieve his ship, the *Trinity*, from its dock at Southampton. Edward, however, was ready for him and had already ordered Anthony, Earl Rivers, to guard Southampton. Unlike the debacle at Sandwich years before, Rivers was ready for attack. He captured a number of their ships and many of those onboard, twenty of whom would later be hanged, drawn, and quartered at the order of John Tiptoft, Earl of Worcester, sent to Southampton to judge them.[4] As Gate had been involved in the murders of his father and brother, Anthony must have found his humiliation particularly gratifying, although Gate was not condemned to death by Worcester.[5]

Barred from Calais, Warwick did not lose his nerve even when his heavily pregnant daughter, the Duchess of Clarence, gave birth aboard ship to a child, who did not survive his ordeal. He turned to piracy and captured about forty vessels. By 1 May, Warwick was at Honfleur, while the French king, Louis XI, was pondering how to make the most of this visitor.[6]

On 11 June, Anthony was appointed Governor and Lieutenant of Calais and Guines. He set off from Southampton with a fleet, which combined with the Duke of Burgundy's ships to attack Warwick's ships. After a fight at sea where 500 to 600 men were killed, Anthony and Hans Voetken seized fourteen of the ships carried off by Warwick during his piratical adventures.[7]

Meanwhile, Jacquetta Woodville took the opportunity of Warwick's status as a rebel to bring an action in the King's Bench for the murder of her husband. Chief among those men ordered to be brought before the court in June 1470 was Warwick himself, along with such distinguished men as John Langstrother, prior of the hospital of St John of Jerusalem, Sir Geoffrey Gate (the same man who had been captured by Anthony Woodville at Southampton), and Sir Edward Grey, 'late of Groby in the county of Leicester'. Not surprisingly, Thomas Wake, who had accused Jacquetta of witchcraft, was on the list as well.[8] I have found no further documents regarding this action; probably it was brought to a standstill by the events that were soon to transpire.

In France, Louis XI soon succeeded in bringing together two unlikely allies: Warwick and his old enemy Margaret of Anjou, Henry VI's exiled queen. Henry VI had been shut up in the Tower since 1465, but his son, Edward, a small boy when he accompanied his mother into exile, was now nearly 17, old enough to join the fight for the English crown. For Louis XI, putting Henry VI back on the throne – a throne that would presumably be controlled by Warwick – would punish his old enemy Edward IV and gain him an ally against Burgundy.[9] He persuaded Warwick and Margaret to seal their alliance by marrying Edward to Warwick's younger daughter, Anne. On 25 July 1470 at Angers, the home of Margaret's father René of Anjou, the young couple were betrothed.[10]

Having sworn to recover Henry VI's throne for him, Warwick sailed for England in September – leaving his family and his new son-in-law behind, for a wary Margaret was not willing to send her son to England until Warwick had fulfilled his part of the bargain.[11]

Astonishingly, he succeeded. Lured away from London by more turmoil in the north, King Edward had lodged the heavily pregnant queen and his daughters in the Tower and left the city at the end of July. Apparently believing that his presence was more needed in the north than it was in London, he was still in Yorkshire in mid-September when news arrived that Warwick had landed in the West Country. Edward set out toward London but was greeted on the way by the news that John Neville, Marquis of Montagu – Warwick's younger brother, but hitherto faithful to Edward – had shifted his loyalties toward Warwick. Believing that flight was his best option, Edward, accompanied by Anthony Woodville and his other followers, hastened to Bishop's Lynn (now King's Lynn), near Anthony's manor of Middleton, where they arrived on 30 September. Having obtained the necessary ships, probably with the assistance of Anthony, on 2 October the king, accompanied by a band of loyalists that included Anthony and William, Lord Hastings, sailed into exile. The royal party, short of funds and of the furred gown Edward had to give the master of ships in reward for his passage, found shelter at the Hague with Louis de Bruges, who served as Governor of Holland for Edward IV's brother-in-law Charles, Duke of Burgundy.[12] Later, the exiles moved to Bruges. Since Louis was noted for his fine library, the bibliophilic Anthony's stay in exile could not have been without its compensations.

Back in London, Edward IV's supporters were hastening into sanctuary, Lancastrians were just as hastily scrambling out of it, and Geoffrey Gate was releasing adherents to the House of Lancaster from the King's Bench prison. A thirsty mob began to rob and plunder beerhouses outside the city, though the mayor and the Londoners managed to keep the crowd outside the city gates. Fearing that the Kentishmen – who had entered London with Jack Cade at their head two decades before – would 'despoil and kill' her, Elizabeth, joined by her daughters and by her mother, secretly fled into sanctuary on 1 October. She had previously fortified the Tower, which she now handed over to the mayor and the alderman, who in turn agreed with Geoffrey Gate that all those within would be conducted to sanctuary, either at Westminster Abbey or at St Martin's.[13] The queen's apartments in the Tower, which had been furnished comfortably for her lying-in, were given over on 3 October to the restored Henry VI, who had been in less spacious quarters elsewhere in the Tower.

Presumably the cradles that would have been made ready for Elizabeth's child were thoughtfully moved out of the king's way.

Although the fate of Elizabeth's father and brother, John, had given the queen good cause to worry about her prospects at the hands of a government controlled by Warwick, the earl was in fact considerate toward the Yorkist queen. This may have been because Warwick scorned to harm a woman, or perhaps he might have been influenced by the Earl of Oxford, who would be noted later on for his kind dealing with the widows of the vanquished, or by Henry VI himself. Only the Earl of Worcester, who had executed Warwick's men following Anthony Woodville's capture of them at Southampton, was sent to the block, perhaps at the behest of Oxford, whose father and elder brother had been executed by Worcester years before.

William Gould, a London butcher, kept the queen supplied with 'half a beef' and two muttons each week, for which he was later duly rewarded by the restored king.[14] On 30 October 1470, the king's council appointed Elizabeth, Lady Scrope, to attend the queen, for which she received £10. The appointment was a timely one, for on 2 November, the king's first royal son, Edward, made his arrival into the world.[15] Despite the awkwardness of having a Yorkist heir born in a Lancastrian England, the boy was christened in Westminster Abbey, with Lady Scrope serving as the godmother and the abbot and prior of Westminster, Thomas Milling and John Eastney, serving as his godfathers.[16]

Elizabeth Woodville's brother, Richard – the most obscure of the male Woodvilles – had not joined his brother Anthony in exile. He was evidently considered a low security risk, for he was issued a general pardon on 27 November 1470.[17] The rest of Elizabeth's siblings are unaccounted for during this period. Lionel Woodville, destined for the Church, was probably at his studies, while Edward may have accompanied his brother, Anthony, into exile.

Edward IV and his fellow exiles were not merely soaking up Burgundian culture during their stay abroad, but were laying plans to recover their kingdom. In his quest for ships, men, and money, he was aided by his brother-in-law Anthony, who as of 19 January 1471 was reported to be at Bruges bargaining for ships, although it was noted that he was unlikely to acquire very many due to Edward's lack of funds. According to evidence cited by Peter Hammond, Anthony was probably staying with Joos de Bul, a wealthy nobleman.[18]

In March, the exiles returned to England. On 14 March, Edward IV, accompanied by Hastings and 500 men, landed at Ravenspur; Richard, Duke of Gloucester, and his 300 men landed about 4 miles away; and Rivers, with 200 men, landed about 14 miles from the king at Powle, which Peter Hammond identifies as Paull or Paghill.[19] The next month, Anthony sent letters to Lynn ordering that three ships be fitted out for the king, to which the authorities agreed on the condition that they be held harmless against any act of war committed by the crews.[20]

Having made his way through England safely and reconciled with his brother, George, Duke of Clarence, Edward IV rode into London on 11 April. He first went to St Paul's and then to the Bishop's Palace, where he took Henry VI into custody. The next stop was Westminster, where he offered prayers of thanksgiving. Then he finally went to the queen, and comforted her:

> that had a long time abiden and sojourned at Westminster, assuring her person only by the great franchise of that holy place, in right great trouble, sorrow, and heaviness, which she sustained with all manner patience that belonged to any creature, and as constantly as hath been seen at any time any of so high estate to endure, in the which season nonetheless she had brought into this world, to the king's greatest joy, a fair son, a prince, where with she presented him at his coming, to his heart's singular comfort and gladness, and to all them that him truly loved and would serve.[21]

The family reunion was a brief one. On 13 April, leaving behind Elizabeth, her children, and his mother in the Tower for safekeeping, and taking with him the hapless Henry VI, Edward IV and his forces rode out of London.[22]

What follows is well known, but Anthony Woodville's role in it is sometimes given short shrift. On Easter Sunday, 14 April, Edward's forces met the Earl of Warwick and his men at Barnet, where Edward IV scored a victory and Warwick and his brother, John, Marquis of Montagu, were killed in battle. Anthony's role in achieving this Yorkist victory is unrecorded, but Hammond suggests that he might have commanded the reserve.[23] He certainly seems to have played an active part there, for in a newsletter, the merchant Gerhard von Wesel reported that 'the duke of Gloucester and Lord Scales were severely wounded, but they had no harm from it, God be praised'.[24]

Margaret of Anjou, meanwhile, had crossed from France with her son, Edward. Despite her initial misgivings after hearing of the death of Warwick, she rallied and began raising troops herself, forcing Edward, who had returned to London in triumph the afternoon after the Battle of Barnet was fought, to take to the field once more.[25] At Tewkesbury on 4 May, Edward again defeated a Lancastrian army, this time killing Edward of Lancaster and taking Margaret captive shortly thereafter.

Anthony Woodville had not accompanied the king to Tewkesbury, but remained in London, which soon came under attack by Thomas Neville, who as an illegitimate son of William Neville, Lord Fauconberg, was known reasonably enough as the Bastard of Fauconberg. As Hammond points out, if Fauconberg succeeded in entering London and gaining control of King Henry, who was once again in the Tower after his excursion to Barnet, Edward IV's position might have been seriously threatened.[26]

As it was, however, the Londoners, under the leadership of Anthony and of Henry Bourchier, Earl of Essex, were ready for Fauconberg when he attacked on 12 May.[27] He started off by burning a gate at the Southwark end of London Bridge, then set fire to some beerhouses – not the way to endear himself to the locals. Hammond suggests that this was merely a trial to test the city's resistance. The next day, Fauconberg marched to Kingston, but did not cross the river, possibly because Anthony had sent bargeloads of men to prevent him or possibly because of promises that Rivers made him. On 14 May, however, Fauconberg arrived at St George's Fields and began his attack in earnest.

Fauconberg targeted London Bridge (the only bridge there at the time), Aldgate, and Bishopgate. Encouraged by Essex and many knights, squires, gentleman, and yeoman, the citizens of London put up a fierce fight, which, the author of the *Arrival of King Edward IV*, the official account of the king's victory, tells us, they might not have done if left on their own. At this point, Anthony stepped into the fray:

> And so, after continuing of much shot of guns and arrows a great while, upon both parties, the Earl Rivers, that was with the Queen, in the Tower of London, gathered unto him a fellowship right well chosen, and habiled, of four or five hundred men, and issued out at a postern upon them, and, even upon a point, came upon the Kentish men being about the assaulting of Aldgate, and mightily laid upon them with arrows, and upon them with hands, and so killed and took many of them, driving them from the same gate to the water side.[28]

The Crowland Chronicler also singled out Anthony for praise:

> [I]t was not God's will that such a famous city, the capital indeed of the whole realm of England, should be given over to pillage by such great rogues. He gave stout hearts to the Londoners to enable them to stand firm on the day of battle. In this they were especially assisted by a sudden and unexpected sortie from the Tower of London by Anthony, Earl Rivers. As the enemy were making fierce assaults on the gate […] he fell upon their

> rear with his mounted troops and gave the Londoners the opportunity to open their gates and fight it out hand to hand with the enemy so that they manfully put each and every one of them to death or to flight.[29]

Anthony even rated a poetic tribute in 'On the Recovery of the Throne by Edward IV':

> The earl Rivers, that gentle knight,
> Blessed be the time that he borne was!
> By the power of God and his great might,
> Through his enemies that day did he pass.
> The mariners were killed, they cried 'Alas!'
>
> ✣ ✣ ✣
>
> God would the earl Rivers there should be;
> He purchased great love of the commons that season;
> Lovingly the citizens and he
> Pursued their enemies, it was but reason,
> And killed the people for their false treason ...[30]

Essex, meanwhile, had led an attack on the rebels at Bishopsgate, while guns placed at the north end of the bridge prevented Fauconberg's men from advancing further along the structure. At last, the rebels withdrew in defeat to Blackheath, leaving 700 dead according to the *Arrival*. Fauconberg remained at Blackheath until 18 May, when he rode to Sandwich. He eventually surrendered his ships to Richard, Duke of Gloucester, and received the king's pardon, but by September 1471 he had got into trouble again and was executed.[31]

Edward IV rode into London in triumph on 21 May, bringing a captive Margaret of Anjou in his train. Having lost her only child and her freedom, she was hours from becoming a widow as well. That night, the *Arrival* dutifully and unconvincingly reported, the imprisoned Henry VI was so downcast at the recent turn of events that he died 'of pure displeasure, and melancholy'.[32] More likely than not, however, the king was helped to his death on orders of Edward IV. With no viable Lancastrian claimant to the throne left, or so it seemed in 1471, the peace-loving King Henry had ushered in a dozen years of quiet within England, though not precisely in the way that he would have wanted it.

7

A Woodville Abroad

As Edward IV settled back onto his throne for a second time, Anthony Woodville made a request: he wanted to fight the Saracens, probably in fulfilment of a vow. The proposal dismayed Edward, who could not understand why his brother-in-law would choose this busy time to demonstrate his piety. According to John Paston III, who was hoping for Anthony's help in getting him a pardon, 'The King is not best pleased with him for that he desireth to depart, in so much as the King hath said of him that when so ever he has most to do, then the Lord Scales will soonest ask leave to depart, and [knows] that it is most because of cowardice'.[1]

Just two months before Paston wrote his letter in July 1471, Anthony had been instrumental in saving London from the Bastard of Fauconberg, so the king's accusation of cowardice seems misplaced. Perhaps it was pique at Anthony that led Edward on 18 July 1471 to appoint William, Lord Hastings, as Lieutenant of Calais instead of Anthony, who had held the position before the Lancastrian readeption.[2] It was certainly an appointment that would have disastrous consequences for Anthony a dozen years later. Nonetheless, Anthony remained determined to join the Portuguese in their fight. By 15 September, the king had relented and given Anthony royal permission to depart for Portugal, rather to the amusement of Paston, who commented sarcastically before Christmas, 'I ensure you he thinketh all the world goeth on their side [again]'. On 8 January, Paston II wrote that Rivers had taken ship on Christmas Eve for Portugal, but he was not certain of it.[3]

If Anthony did indeed go to Portugal, he did not stay long there, for in April 1472, he was off on yet another military adventure – aiding Francis, Duke of Brittany, against the French. Francis had asked Edward for 6,000 archers, but when Anthony landed in Brittany on 6 April, he had brought only thirty archers and a small entourage with him. By 20 June, however, Edward IV had given Anthony permission to bring 1,000 men at arms and archers with him to Brittany – at his own expense. This time there was no talk of cowardice. The French retreated in August. In the meantime, in July, Anthony entered into negotiations with Francis for an English attack on France. The result, the Treaty of Châteaugiron, was signed on 11 September 1472. Unfortunately, during their mission abroad, many of Anthony's men died of the flux and other sicknesses, as John Paston II reported in November. Fittingly, in light of his later career, it was on this expedition to Brittany that Anthony's younger brother, Edward, made his first recorded appearance as a member of Anthony's entourage.[4]

John Paston had said in November that Anthony and his men would be returning home shortly, but Anthony did not tarry long in England. By July 1473, Anthony Woodville took ship from Southampton. His destination was the shrine of St James at Santiago de Compostela in Spain, a popular pilgrimage destination. Anthony's journey may indicate that he had not succeeded in fulfilling his vow to fight the Saracens in 1471. Clearly, the tumultuous events of the last few years, perhaps especially the deaths of his father and his brother, were still weighing on his mind. He wrote later:

> Where it is so that every human creature by the sufferance of our Lord God is born and ordained to be subject and thrall unto the storms of fortune, and so in divers and many sundry wises man is perplexed with worldly adversities; of the which I Antoine Wydeuille Earl Ryuyeres, Lord Scales, &c. have largely and in many different manners had my part; and of them relieved by the infinite grace and goodness of our said Lord, through the mean of the Mediatrice of Mercy, which grace evidently to me known and understood compelled me to set apart all ingratitude, and drove me by reason and conscience as far as my wretchedness would suffice, to give therefore singular lovings and thanks to God; and exhorted me to dispose my recovered life to his service in following his laws and commandments; and in satisfaction and recompence of mine iniquities and faults before done, to seek and execute the works that might be most acceptable to him; and as far as my frailness would suffer me, I rested in that will and purpose.[5]

Anthony's journey, as we shall see later, would be notable more for what Anthony read aboard ship than for the pilgrimage itself.

A new loss, however, awaited Anthony at home: his wife, Elizabeth Scales, died on 2 September 1473.[6] Anthony and Elizabeth had married sometime in the tumultuous months before Towton, a period that for them was marked by the capture of Anthony at Sandwich and the murder of Elizabeth's father. Elizabeth was the daughter of Thomas, Lord Scales, and his wife Ismania, who in turn was a daughter of a Cornishman by the name of Whalesburgh.[7] Described in Anthony's inquisitions post-mortem as 24 or more at her father's death in 1460,[8] Elizabeth Scales was born around 1436. The couple had been married since at least 4 April 1461, when William Paston II reported mistakenly that Anthony, Lord Scales – the title that Anthony took in right of Elizabeth – had been killed at the Battle of Towton.[9]

Elizabeth had been married previously to Henry Bourchier, the second son of the Earl of Essex by the same name. A 27 August letter in the Paston collection announcing his sudden death at Ludlow from an unspecified cause probably dates to 1458.[10] If any children were born to the couple, they did not survive.

Whether Anthony and Elizabeth's parents helped bring the couple together, or whether the couple themselves initiated their marriage, is unknown. Elizabeth's inheritance as Scales's only surviving child gave her an obvious attraction for Anthony, and his own status as the eldest son gave him an obvious attraction for Elizabeth, but there is nothing to indicate whether personal attraction played a role in the marriage as well. It is not certain how great the age difference between the pair was, although Anthony, born anytime between late 1437 and about 1442, was the younger of the spouses.[11]

Elizabeth's father had strong ties with the Woodville family from early on. Created a Knight of the Garter in 1425, Lord Scales successfully nominated Anthony's father as a Garter knight in 1450.[12] That same year, Lord Scales and Lord Rivers were among the men appointed by the king to put down Jack Cade's rebellion.[13] Interestingly, when Richard, Duke of York placed his grievances before the king that autumn, Lord Scales and Lord Rivers were said to have accompanied him.[14]

Lord Scales, however, remained loyal to Henry VI during the upheavals of the 1450s. In the summer of 1460, when the exiled Earls of March, Warwick, and Salisbury returned to England with the intention of seizing power, Lord Scales and Robert, Lord Hungerford, held the Tower for the king. Besieged by the Yorkists, the forces inside the Tower shot guns and cast wild fire into the city, to the injury of 'men and women and children in the streets', as reported by the *English Chronicle*.[15] When the Yorkists, having defeated the Lancastrians at Northampton, returned to London with Henry VI in their power, Scales and Hungerford surrendered on 19 July.[16]

Uncertain how he would fare at the hands of the Londoners, Scales, accompanied by three others, found a boat late that evening and rowed toward Westminster with the intention of taking sanctuary there. Tipped off by a woman who recognised Lord Scales, a group of boatmen surrounded him, murdered him, and dumped his naked body at St Mary Overy at Southwark, where he lay for several hours before his godson, the Earl of March (later Edward IV), came upon the scene and arranged a proper burial for him. It was, as the *English Chronicle* noted, a 'great pity' that 'so noble and worshipful a knight', who had served so valiantly in France, should meet such an ignominious death.[17]

Chroniclers seldom bothered to record the reactions of the wives and daughters of those slain during the Wars of the Roses, and they made no exception in the case of Elizabeth Scales. We know only that her father's death left her with lands in Norfolk, Cambridgeshire, Hertfordshire, Essex, and Suffolk.[18] The heart of the Scales's estate was Middleton, near Bishop's Lynn (later King's Lynn).

Glimpses of Anthony's and Elizabeth's married life can be found in contemporary records. The town of Lynn often sent gifts of wine or fish to the couple, whose minstrels also appear in the records.[19] Elizabeth herself features in the household books of John Howard, who later became the Duke of Norfolk. In September 1464, Howard rewarded her messenger with the amount of 6*s* 8*d* for bringing him a letter from Elizabeth. When, with the king at Reading in November, Howard lent Elizabeth, who was also there with her husband, 8*s* and 4*d* to play at cards. The party moved on to spend Christmas at Eltham with the king; there, on 1 January 1465, Howard gave 12*d* to 'my lord Scales child'. Anne Crawford has pointed out that the 'child' was probably a page who was bringing a New Year's gift to Howard from Anthony and Elizabeth, as opposed to the offspring of either spouse.[20]

After Anthony's sister married Edward IV, Elizabeth Scales was prominent among the attendants of her sister-in-law the queen. In 1466–67, like the queen's sister, Anne, Elizabeth Scales received £40 per annum for her services (the same rate that her mother had received when serving Margaret of Anjou). She and Anne were the highest paid of the queen's attendants; the next tier of ladies received only £20 a year.[21]

In 1466, Anthony and Elizabeth engaged in a series of complex legal manoeuvres, detailed in his inquisitions post-mortem, to ensure that if Elizabeth predeceased Anthony without having borne him a child, the Scales's estates would stay in Anthony's hands instead of going to Elizabeth's heirs. While this did have the effect of subverting the normal laws of inheritance, there is no reason to assume that Elizabeth was forced into the transaction by her husband or that she would have preferred that the land go to her rather distant cousins instead of to Anthony.[22]

What none of this tells us is the quality of Anthony and Elizabeth's relationship. As Anthony's wife she certainly enjoyed high status at court, accompanying Margaret of York to her wedding in Bruges, serving in the highest rank of the queen's ladies, and sitting with Louis de Bruges during his 1472 visit. Clearly, she was not relegated to her estates in the country. When Anthony's father was murdered in 1469, Elizabeth, whose father had been murdered nine years before, would have been well-placed to offer him comfort.

Anthony's marriage with Elizabeth was childless, but Anthony himself was a father: he had an illegitimate daughter, Margaret. Margaret's mother has been identified as Gwenllian, the daughter of William Stradling of Glamorgan and his wife Isabel.[23] Nothing more is known about Gwenllian or her relationship with Anthony, nor is it known whether their liaison predated Anthony's marriage to Elizabeth Scales or occurred during it. Margaret's name raises the possibility that the child might have been named for Margaret of Anjou, in which case she would have most likely been born at some point before the Battle of Towton in 1461, after which Anthony changed his allegiance from the Lancastrian cause to the Yorkist one.

Nothing else is heard of Margaret until her marriage to Robert Poyntz of Iron Acton in Gloucestershire. According to E.L. Barnwell, on 12 September 1479, Anthony settled 800 marks on Margaret, with 200 to be paid on the sealing of the deed; he also settled on her lands worth 100 marks a year.[24] Poyntz was born in the late 1440s and thus was about 30 or so. The first of five sons, Anthony, was born around 1480; Margaret also bore her husband four daughters.[25]

Facing execution ten years after the death of Elizabeth Scales, Anthony remembered his wife's soul in his will, written at Sheriff Hutton two days before his death on 25 August 1483. Having left the Scales' lands to his brother Edward, Anthony asked that 500 marks be used for prayers for the souls of Elizabeth, her deceased brother Thomas, and the souls of all of the

Scales family.[26] For Lynda Pidgeon, the author of a recent assessment of Anthony, these last requests did not go far enough. Pidgeon writes that Anthony 'makes no affectionate mention of [Elizabeth] or desire to be buried beside her' and that he appeared to do only the bare minimum to provide for her soul and those of others. As for Margaret, Pidgeon finds Anthony lacking as a father as well: she states that Anthony 'forgot' his daughter in his will, and that he 'seems to have had little feeling' for her. She concludes, 'The will was business like: it met the requirements of his soul and those of his family and little else. [...] Perhaps he simply did not have feelings for anyone else.'[27]

This harsh assessment, based on a single document, is unwarranted. Lacking more complete records of Anthony's, we have no way of knowing whether he was generous to his daughter in other ways or whether he held her in his affection. The fact that he failed to name her in his will – especially in a will executed under such unfavourable circumstances – need not indicate lack of feeling. Having settled estates upon Margaret and arranged her marriage to a prosperous man, Anthony may have simply felt that his daughter was well provided for. Notably, Margaret's husband was named one of Anthony's executors, suggesting good relations between Anthony and his son-in-law.[28]

As for Anthony's failure to speak affectionately of his wife in his will, Pidgeon overlooks the fact that many wills of the period are businesslike documents, without sentimental effusions; it also fails to consider that Anthony, unlike testators expecting to meet a natural death or preparing for the eventuality of dying honourably in battle, was under the enormous stress of facing execution for a crime he most likely did not commit. Moreover, as one who was about to be executed, he could expect his lands to be forfeit to the Crown and would have to hope that arrangements would be made to pay his debts and to honour his bequests; he was hardly in a position to make more than the requisite provisions for the dead.

Anthony's failure to request burial by his first wife is equally unreliable as a gauge of his affection, or lack thereof, toward her. Possibly anticipating that he would be brought to London for the trial before his peers that was his right as an earl, Anthony initially asked in his will that if he died beyond the River Trent, he be buried in the chapel of St Mary the Virgin besides St Stephen's College at Westminster, known familiarly as the Lady of Pewe. The Pope himself had recognised Anthony's 'singular devotion' to this chapel in 1476.[29] Contrary to Pidgeon's surmise, Anthony's failure to request burial beside Elizabeth Scales (whose burial place is not known) need not show lack of affection for her; his request to be buried at the Lady of Pewe may simply indicate a strong devotion to the Virgin or to the chapel that took precedence over earthly attachments. Moreover, as a condemned man Anthony could not expect that the Crown would go to the expense and trouble of bringing his body to lie beside that of his deceased wife, unless she happened to have been buried at a place that was convenient for her husband's burial, or that his survivors would be allowed to bury him in accordance with his wishes. Anthony had, in fact, little choice in where he would be buried, as he implicitly acknowledged at the end of his will, when, having learned that he would be executed at Pontefract, Anthony asked that he be buried there with his nephew Richard Grey, who was also facing execution, before an image of the Virgin Mary.[30]

Whatever the nature of his feelings for his deceased wife, Anthony would soon have a new responsibility to divert his thoughts: the care of his nephew, Prince Edward, the king's oldest son.[31]

Anthony had played an important role in his young nephew's life from the very beginning. Edward made his son Prince of Wales on 26 June 1471.[32] That same year, the king appointed a fifteen-member council for his son, of which both the queen and Anthony were members. In February 1473, Edward IV added ten more members, a number with ties to the Woodville family, to the council.[33] The king took an even more important step later that spring. Unrest in Wales led him to determine to establish a household for his son at Ludlow, where the king himself had spent time as a child. He sent his wife, by now showing the signs of another pregnancy, to get young Edward settled in his new lodgings. By 2 April 1473, Elizabeth and her son were established in Wales but were expected to join the king at Leicester for Easter.[34] It was in this household at Ludlow that Anthony would spend much of the rest of his life.

Edward IV issued ordinances committing his heir to Anthony's care on 27 September 1473.[35] The ordinances governed the daily life of the prince from when he rose in the morning 'at a convenient hour according to his age' to when he went to bed at eight o'clock, at which time his attendants were to make him 'joyous and merry towards his bed'. No one was to enter the prince's chamber except for Anthony, the prince's chamberlain, and his chaplains, or such other persons as Anthony thought proper. Anthony also had control over who was to sit at the prince's board at mealtimes. When the prince's revenues were brought to Ludlow, they were to be locked in a chest to which only three people had keys: the queen, Anthony, and John Alcock, Bishop of Rochester. Anthony and the bishop also had the authority to move the prince from place to place as was convenient for the season.

On 10 November 1473, the king appointed Anthony as 'governor' and 'ruler' of the prince and Alcock as his 'teacher' and president of his council. Nicholas Orme notes that the titles 'governor' and 'ruler' were new, although the function was not; the older term was 'master', which by this time was becoming associated with schoolmasters, who were lower down on the social scale. Likewise, Orme notes, the term 'teacher' was also new, although Alcock's true function was likely to rule the prince's household rather than to attend personally to his lessons, a task he delegated to others.

Anthony, as D.E. Lowe has pointed out, was well suited to his role as governor. Described by Mancini as one who had been 'always considered a kind, serious, and just man, and one tested by every vicissitude of life', he was also as adept at looking out for his own interests as any other fifteenth-century nobleman and was not overly fussed with legal niceties.[36] His letters to his agent show him looking around for weaknesses in others' title to land that could be exploited, and in his will, he felt the need to ask that the widowed Lady Willoughby be recompensed for his servants' seizure of her goods. In 1465, in exchange for a pardon to her husband, the Lancastrian Gervase Clifton, this lady had been required to grant him lands to the value of 400 marks per year amounting to a whopping 80 per cent of her inheritance. Not surprisingly, Clifton had supported Henry VI in 1470–71 and had been executed after the Battle of Tewkesbury.[37] But we can admit Anthony's occasional capacity for ruthlessless without going so far as to say, with Michael Hicks, that 'far from doing harm to no-one [...] there was nobody he hesitated to harm'.[38] D.E. Lowe's assessment is far more balanced:

> a powerful personality – a predatory magnate rather than a mere courtier or dilettante patron of the arts – exercising a personal authoritative supervision over the conduct of his officials and the management of his affairs, with a keen grasp of detail and jealous to maintain his rights, real or imagined, against others, and resolved to exploit his assets to their fullest advantage.[39]

Anthony's new responsibilities did not mean that he would spend the rest of the prince's youth at Ludlow. In 1474, King Edward had made a pact with his brother-in-law, Charles, Duke of Burgundy, to invade France before 1 July 1475 – an essential undertaking for an English king. In April 1475,

Anthony and Richard Martyn were sent on an embassy to Charles, who despite having agreed to aid in the invasion was preoccupied with the siege of Neuss as part of his attempt to gain control of Cologne. Their mission, to persuade Charles to give up his siege and turn his attention to the invasion, was unsuccessful. Having assembled a large force at enormous cost, Edward had no choice but to carry out his plan, Charles or no Charles.[40]

The English nobility was very well represented on the expedition, and Anthony was no exception. He raised a force of two knights, forty men at arms, and two hundred archers. Henry Percy, Earl of Northumberland, brought ten knights and the same number of men at arms and archers. William Herbert, Earl of Pembroke, likewise brought forty men at arms and two hundred archers, but no knights. The king's brothers, the Dukes of Clarence and Gloucester, each raised a force of ten knights, one hundred men at arms, and a thousand archers. Also joining the expedition was Elizabeth's eldest son by her first marriage, Thomas Grey, who had been made the Marquis of Dorset on 18 April 1475.[41] Back on the home front, the young Prince of Wales was appointed 'keeper of the realm' and was brought to London to join the queen.

Though Edward had prepared for the eventuality of being crowned King of France by having a suitable robe made, the expedition, which set off for Calais on 4 July 1475, ended anticlimactically, if profitably. Charles of Burgundy, having been forced to abandon Neuss by a French invasion of his own dominions, turned up to meet the English king. He was full of advice for Edward, but came without the expected army. Another would-be ally, Louis, Count of St Pol, Jacquetta Woodville's brother, failed to keep his promise to deliver St Quentin to the English. Disgusted, Edward entered into negotiations with King Louis XI of France. On 29 August 1475, in what was known as the Treaty of Picquigny, the two nations made their peace. Among the treaty's provisions was that Edward's eldest daughter, Elizabeth, or, in case of her death, her sister Mary, was to marry the Dauphin Charles of France. Louis was to pay 75,000 crowns to Edward, followed by a pension of 50,000 crowns per annum. William, Lord Hastings and other royal confidants were to receive pensions as well. Commyns claimed that the Marquis of Dorset was among the pensioners, but historians have not found corroboration of this in the records. Though the peace was unpopular with some hawkish Englishmen, notably Richard, Duke of Gloucester, it benefitted English trade and relieved Edward's subjects of parliamentary taxation.[42]

Anthony is not named among those receiving pensions, and what he thought of the treaty is unrecorded. His trip to France, however, seems to have reawakened his taste for foreign travel, for on 1 October 1475, Edward IV wrote a letter to Galeazzo Maria Sforza, Duke of Milan, informing him that Rivers, 'one of his chief confidants and the brother of his dear consort', would be travelling to Rome and would like to visit Milan and other places belonging to the duke, as well as the duke himself if it were convenient.[43]

Sadly, we do not have a detailed description of Anthony's travels, or an account of whom he visited, but several years later, William Caxton, whose printing press Rivers patronised, recalled in his epilogue to *The Cordyale* (translated by Rivers) that Anthony had been on pilgrimage to Rome, to shrines in Naples, and to St Nicholas at Bari.[44] In April 1476, Anthony obtained a papal indulgence for the Chapel of Our Lady of Pewe at Westminster, where Anthony hoped to be buried.[45]

All did not go smoothly for the English traveller, however. On 7 March 1476, Francesco Pietrasancta, Milanese Ambassador to the Court of Savoy, reported to the Duke of Milan that all of Rivers's money and valuables had been stolen at the Torre di Baccano and that Queen Elizabeth was sending a royal servant to Rome with letters of exchange for 4,000 ducats.[46]

Anthony's misadventures had also come to the attention of John Paston III, who wrote on 21 March 1476, that Lord Rivers 'was at Rome right well and honorably' and had travelled 12 miles outside the city when he was robbed of all of his jewels and plate, which were worth at least 1,000 marks.[47]

The saga of Anthony's jewels did not end there, however. On 10 May 1476, the Venetian Senate issued this sinister-sounding decree:

> That for the purpose of ascertaining the truth as to this theft, in the neighbourhood of Borne, of the precious jewels and plate belonging to Lord Anthony Angre Lord Scales, brother of the Queen of England, and for the discovery of the perpetrators and of the distribution made of the property, – Be the arrest of Nicholas Cerdo and Vitus Cerdo, Germans, Nicholas Cerdo, and Anthony, a German of Schleswick, dealer in ultramarine, (arrested by permission from the Signory,) ratified at the suit of the State attorneys; and as they would not tell the whole truth by fair means, be a committee formed, the majority of which to have liberty to examine and rack them all or each; and the committee shall, with the deposition thus obtained, come to this Council and do justice.[48]

Three days later, the Senate issued another decree, showing that when travelling abroad, it was extremely helpful to have royal connections:

> Lord Scales, the brother-in-law of the King of England, has come to Venice on account of certain jewels of which he was robbed at Torre di Baccano, near Borne. Part of them having been brought hither and sold to certain citizens, he has earnestly requested the Signory to have said jewels restored to him, alleging in his favour civil statutes, enacting that stolen goods should be freely restored to their owner. As it is for the interest of the Signory to make every demonstration of love and good will towards his lordship on his own account, and especially out of regard for the King, his brother-in-law, – Put to the ballot, that the said jewels purchased in this city by Venetian subjects be restored gratuitously to the said lord; he being told that this is done out of deference for the King of England and for his lordship, without his incurring any cost.
>
> As the affair is committed to the State attorneys. – Be it carried that they be bound, together with the ordinary councils, to dispatch it within two months, and ascertain whether or not the purchasers of the jewels purchased them honestly. Should they have been bought unfairly, the purchasers to lose their money. While, if the contrary were the case, Toma Mocenigo, Nicolo de Ca de Besaro, and Marin Contarini shall be bound as they themselves volunteered to pay what was expended for the jewels, together with the costs, namely, 400 ducats. These moneys to be drawn for through a bill of exchange by these three noblemen on the consul in London, there to be paid by the consul and passed by him to the debit of the factory on account of goods loaded by Venetians in England on board the Flanders galleys (Ser Antonio Contarini, captain,) on their return to this city; and in like manner to the debit of the London factory here, on account of goods loaded on board the present Flanders galleys (Ser Andrea de Mosto, captain), bound to England, on their arrival in those parts. If the attorneys and the appointed councils fail to dispatch the matter as above, they shall be fined two ducats each; yet, on the expiration of the said term, the said three noblemen shall be bound to pay the moneys above mentioned.[49]

Having recovered part of his jewels, Anthony resumed his travels. (As his stay had been an expensive one, it may be that the Venetians were not entirely sorry to see him on his way.) In June, he arrived at the camp of Charles, Duke of Burgundy, who was preparing to fight the Swiss. Giovanni Pietro

Panigarola, the Milanese ambassador, reported on 9 June that Anthony planned to stay two or three days before returning to England. On 11 June however, he wrote:

> M. de Scales, brother of the Queen of England, has been to see the duke and offered to take his place in the line of battle. But hearing the day before yesterday that the enemy were near at hand and they expected to meet them he asked leave to depart, saying he was sorry he could not stay, and so he took leave and went. This is esteemed great cowardice in him, and lack of spirit and honour. The duke laughed about it to me, saying, he has gone because he is afraid.[50]

This was the only time Anthony shirked battle. Perhaps, recalling the Duke of Burgundy's betrayal of the English of the year before, he had decided he owed the duke no favours; perhaps he had simply realised that this was not his fight. Whatever Anthony's motives, his decision was a fortunate one, for at the Battle of Morat that ensued on 22 June, the duke lost thousands of men, and would lose his own life at the Battle of Nancy six months later. Anthony's decision to avoid this one battle meant that he would return to England with his life, if not all of his goods, intact.

8

Pomp and Printing

While Anthony and his younger brother, Edward, were in Brittany, the Woodville family lost its matriarch. Jacquetta, Duchess of Bedford, wife to a duke and to a knight, mother of a queen, and an accused witch, died on 30 May 1472, bringing her full life to a quiet close.[1] Neither the place of her death nor her burial spot is known, and her will has not survived. Her son Richard, along with one William Kerver, 'citizen and mercer of London', were still acting as the administrators of her goods and chattels in 1480.[2] Jacquetta's last years had been saddened by the murders of the husband she had married for love and of her son, John, but the restoration of her son-in-law to the throne and the birth of his heir must have cheered her in her final months. She had lived long enough to welcome yet another royal grandchild: Margaret, born at Windsor on 10 April 1472.[3]

While the Woodvilles mourned the loss of the great lady who had brought them into the world, life went on at Edward's court. During his exile, Edward IV had enjoyed the hospitality of Louis de Bruges, and in the autumn of 1472, the king repaid his host in high style.[4] Two days after arriving at Westminster in late September or early October, Louis rode to Windsor, where the king and his family were in residence. Having greeted his guest, Edward IV led him to the queen's chamber. Unlike the stately, silent post-churching feast that had overawed the Bohemian visitors in 1466, Louis saw the 'full pleasant' sight of Elizabeth and her ladies at play. The queen herself was playing at 'morteaulx', a game similar to bowls, while other ladies were amusing themselves with 'closheys of ivory' (ninepins) or dancing. Edward improved the occasion by dancing with his 7-year-old daughter, Elizabeth. The next morning, the infant prince, borne by his chamberlain, Thomas Vaughan, personally (if not very articulately) welcomed Louis. After a day of hunting, the queen hosted a banquet in her own chamber. There, the queen, the king, young Elizabeth, the king's sister, Anne, Duchess of Exeter, Countess Rivers, and Louis shared the same mess. The other company at the table included the queen's sister, Katherine, Duchess of Buckingham, her husband, the duke, and Lord Hastings.[5] After supper, Elizabeth of York again showed off her dancing ability, this time with the 17-year-old Duke of Buckingham.

At about nine o'clock, the king, the queen, and the queen's attendants ushered Louis to his three chambers, which were carpeted and hung with white silk and linen. Louis was to sleep on a bed 'as good down as could be thought', with a counterpane of cloth of gold furred with ermine and with the testers and canopy of cloth of gold as well. The sheets and pillows were of the 'queen's own ordinance'. Another bed awaited in the next chamber, along with a couch with featherbeds, underneath a 'tent knit like a net'. A bath, or perhaps two, were in the next chamber, also covered with tents of white cloth. The king and the women departed, leaving Louis with Lord Hastings, who shared a leisurely bath with him, after which the sparklingly clean pair dined on green ginger, syrups, comfits, and hippocras before retiring. Edward and Elizabeth had shown their Burgundian guest that they could entertain in high style. We can get an idea of the splendour of Edward's court from an inventory of clothing purchased for his toddler son at around this time: two velvet doublets, three satin doublets, three satin gowns and two black velvet gowns, a bonnet of purple velvet and another of black velvet, each lined with satin, and a long gown of cloth of gold on damask.[6]

At about ten o'clock on 13 October 1472, the king, clad in his Parliament robes, entered the Parliament chamber and listened to the Speaker of the Commons, William Allington, heap praise upon those who had been loyal to the king the previous year. Allington singled out the king's brothers, the Dukes of Clarence and Gloucester, for their 'knightly demeaning' and commended Earl Rivers and Lord Hastings for their 'constant faith'. Edward's queen was praised for her 'womanly behavior' and 'great constancy' while the king was in exile, as well as for 'the great joy and surety' occasioned by the birth of the king's son. Last, Allington praised the 'great humanity and kindness' of Louis de Bruges, upon which the king returned to his chambers to preside over the ceremony in which Louis de Bruges was created Earl of Winchester. It was the first time in nearly a hundred years that a foreigner had been granted an English earldom.[7]

The year 1472 ended on a sad note for the king and queen. The latest addition to the family, Margaret, died on 11 December 1472 and was buried in Westminster Abbey.[8] It was the first time Edward and Elizabeth had suffered the death of a child. Fortunately, it soon became apparent that there was another child on the way. Richard, Duke of York, was born at Shrewsbury on 17 August 1473.[9]

For the Woodvilles, the next few years would be largely a series of ceremonies, most of them of the cheerful sort. In August 1472, the queen's older son from her first marriage, Thomas Grey, was created Earl of Huntingdon.[10] More honours followed on 18 April 1475, when, at St Edward's Chamber at Westminster, Edward IV made his sons and others Knights of the Bath. Sharing in the honour with two princes were their half-brothers, Thomas and Richard Grey, and their uncle Edward Woodville. That same day after dinner, Thomas Grey exchanged his earldom for a higher rank: Marquis of Dorset.[11]

As Edward IV headed off that summer for France, he made his will. It is a document that plainly shows his esteem for his queen. Edward appointed William Grey, Bishop of Ely, Thomas Rotherham, Bishop of Lincoln, John Alcock, Bishop of Rochester, William, Lord Hastings, Master John Russell, Sir Thomas Montgomery, Richard Fowler, Richard Pygot, and William Husee as his executors – after his queen, 'our dearest Wife in whom we most singularly put our trust', who headed the list. Elizabeth was to choose which of the king's household goods she thought were 'necessary and convenient' for her and have the use of them for her life; she was also to enjoy her revenues from the duchy of Lancaster. Edward provided for prayers to be said for himself, the queen, their fathers, and other of their ancestors.[12]

Interestingly, the king left no instructions in his will as to how his kingdom was to be run during his heir's minority. Fortunately, on this occasion, his kingdom was not put to the test, for Edward returned both intact and richer, thanks to Louis XI's pension. At the time of his departure, the queen had been expecting another child, who was born at Westminster on 2 November 1475.[13] The latest arrival, Anne, shared her day of birth with her oldest brother, Edward, five years her senior.

The following year, King Edward decided to honour the memory of his father, Richard, Duke of York, killed at the Battle of Wakefield on 30 December 1460, by moving his body and that of his son Edmund from Pontefract to Fotheringhay. The ceremonies began on 21 July 1476, when the bodies were exhumed, and ended with the reburial on 30 July 1476.

The Woodvilles, who had supported the Lancastrian cause at the time of York's death, dutifully played their part in the reburial. Anthony Woodville's pursuivant was among the officers of arms who accompanied the bodies south. When the funeral cortege arrived at Fotheringhay on 29 July, the king, dressed in the blue mourning peculiar to royalty, was there to meet it. With him were his brothers and a number of other noblemen, including Anthony Woodville and the Marquis of Dorset, along with the queen and two of her daughters, presumably the oldest two. At the requiem mass the next day, the queen and her daughters offered mass pennies – the queen 'dressed all in blue without a high headdress' and making 'a great obeisance and reverence to the said body'. On both 29 and 30 July, the queen, through her chamberlain, offered to the body cloth of gold, which was arranged along with the other cloth offerings in the shape of a cross. Anthony himself, along with other earls, offered cloth of gold on 30 July.[14]

It was probably sometime in 1477, as noted by Ralph Griffiths, when the king and queen's third son, George, was born. He could have been named after Edward IV's younger brother, George, Duke of Clarence, though any such tribute to Clarence would have taken place before George's arrest in June 1477 (see Chapter 9); it may be that George's naming, which might have been accompanied by asking Clarence to serve as his godfather, was the king's last attempt to reconcile with his mercurial brother. Griffiths also suggests that George might have been named for Saint George, prompted by Edward IV's rebuilding of St George's Chapel at Windsor.[15]

Meanwhile, around late 1475 or early 1476, a birth of a rather different sort had taken place: William Caxton, an English merchant who had been living abroad, returned to England with a precious object in tow: his printing press, the first to be introduced to England.[16] Caxton set up shop at the Almonry at Westminster, in a house known as the Red Pale.[17] By 1476, he had printed his first major project: Chaucer's *Canterbury Tales*.

Anthony Woodville was quick to see the possibilities of this new technology. Caxton's next major publication, *The History of Jason*, was dedicated to the Prince of Wales, and perhaps, as Lotte Hellinga suggests, the prince's governor, Anthony, backed the project.[18] There is no doubt about Anthony's involvement in Caxton's next publication, *The Dicts and Sayings of the Philosophers*: Anthony was the translator.

Translation was an important activity in the fifteenth century, and a highly valued one. As John Trevisa wrote in his 'Dialogue between a Lord and a Clerk upon Translation', it allowed men access to 'cunning, information and lore' that they might have otherwise been denied.[19] In Anthony's case, as he explained in the preface to his translation, he happened upon the book, while travelling to Santiago in 1473. After Anthony expressed his wish to read some 'good history' for 'a recreation and passing of time', his travelling companion, Louis de Bretaylle, handed him the *Dicts*, itself a translation from Latin to French by Guillaume de Tignonville. Having not been able to read the book carefully during his pilgrimage due to his obligations as a pilgrim and the 'great acquaintance' he found on his journey, Anthony explained, in the time-honoured manner of a reader who has not been able to get around to a certain book, that it was not until he entered the service of Prince Edward that at his leisure 'he looked upon the said book, and at last concluded [...] to translate it into the English tongue [...] Thinking also full necessary to [Prince Edward] the understanding thereof'. Anthony concluded with a charming apology for any errors that he, as an amateur, might have fallen into.[20]

A collection of maxims and improving moral stories, 'often arbitrarily ascribed to ancient philosophers', as Anne Sutton and Livia Visser-Fuchs put it, *Dicts*, unlike the enduringly popular *Canterbury Tales* that was Caxton's first production, contains little appeal for modern audiences.[21] Its charm comes chiefly in Caxton's epilogue, where, noting that Earl Rivers had asked him to correct any faults he might find, he wrote that he could not find any except that Anthony had left out certain unflattering observations of Socrates concerning women, which Caxton undertook to include in the text. Why, Caxton pondered, did Anthony omit this material?

> But I suppose that some fair lady hath desired him to leave it out of his book. Or else he was amorous on some noble lady, for whose love he would not set it in his book. Or else for the very affection, love and good will that hath unto all ladies and gentlewomen ...[22]

Entertaining as this is, Caxton was taking liberties here with a social superior, and it has been suggested that Anthony took offence at this 'rather cavalier treatment of his translation, his editorial decisions, and his private life'. Certainly in his next production for Rivers, a translation of Christine de Pisan's *Moral Proverbs* published on 20 February 1478, Caxton was careful to note that he had followed every word of the manuscript Rivers supplied to him, as Rivers's secretary could record. Nonetheless, any authorial pique does not seem to have harmed the men's relationship, for the *Dicts* went through several editions, and Rivers went on to translate yet another manuscript for Caxton, the *Cordiale*, which Caxton printed on 24 March 1479.[23] The fact that Caxton felt free to take such liberties to begin with suggests that Anthony may not have been the cold and chilly creature his detractors depict him as.

In itself, Anthony's interest in this new technology is telling, for Caxton's press attracted only a few noble patrons in England: from 1476 to 1491, only two other peers, John de Vere, Earl of Oxford, and William Fitzalan, Earl of Arundel, patronised Caxton by asking him to translate and print works (and neither patronised Caxton until after Anthony's death in 1483). In doing his own translations, moreover, Anthony was unique among the three.[24] In patronising Caxton, therefore, he was not following fashion.

Anthony followed his first printed edition of the *Dicts* with a presentation copy, in manuscript form, intended for the king and completed on 24 December 1477. In a leaf inserted at the beginning of the manuscript, Anthony kneels besides a tonsured figure, probably Guillaume de Tignonville, the original author, or the scribe who prepared the manuscript. Edward IV, flanked by his queen and Prince Edward, is shown in the act of accepting the book. Among the onlookers, one figure is uncrowned but clad in ermine like the king, queen, and prince: probably this represents Richard, Duke of Gloucester. (The Duke of Clarence, as we shall see, would not have been pictured at court at this time.)[25]

If the 1470s was a watershed for printing in England, the social highlight of the decade was the wedding, on 15 January 1478, between the king's second son, Richard, Duke of York, and Anne Mowbray, the heiress to John Mowbray, Duke of Norfolk. The groom was 4 years old; the bride – a great-granddaughter of John Woodville's elderly bride – a year older.[26] Earl Rivers and John de la Pole, Earl of Lincoln, led the little girl into the chapel at Westminster, Rivers on the left hand, Lincoln on the right hand. Under a canopy waited the king, the queen, Prince Edward, the Ladies Elizabeth, Mary, and Cecily, and the king's mother, Cecily, Duchess of York. Following the wedding ceremony, Richard, Duke of Gloucester and Henry Stafford, Duke of Buckingham led the bride to dinner, where the Duchess of Buckingham – Elizabeth Woodville's youngest sister, Katherine – sat with the groom's mother. The Marquis of Dorset sat at a side table.

The wedding festivities concluded on 22 January with the royal jousts. The first to enter was the Marquis of Dorset, his helm carried by the Duke of Buckingham. Following Dorset were five coursers, their rich trappers 'enramplished with A's of gold curiously embroidered' and a void courser for the accomplishment of his arms. His younger brother, Richard, clothed in blue and tawny, followed with three coursers, with trappers of crimson cloth of gold and tissue. Edward Woodville was accompanied by servants clad in blue and tawny velvet, embroidered with gold 'E's'. The showstopper, however, was Earl Rivers, who made his entrance arrayed in the habit of a white hermit, inside a black-velvet-walled hermitage. Dorset and Richard Grey competed in Jousts Royal, Edward Woodville in 'Ostinge Harnesse' (hosting harness, or field armour), and Earl Rivers in Tourneying.

Dorset, Richard Grey, and Edward Woodville each managed to break their opponent's spears, though the day was marred for Edward by the injury of one of his horses. As for Earl Rivers, he and Thomas Hansard 'charged together so furiously to the Tourney, that all the field gave laud to both parties', but Thomas 'rudely let fly a spring between the shoulder and the helm' of Rivers after 'Ho!' had been cried. 'This the Earl furiously returned upon him, and so accomplished six strokes between them'. None of the Woodville men, however, carried away the prizes, in the form of golden letters set with precious gems, that were distributed by Elizabeth, the king's oldest daughter. Nonetheless, Earl Rivers rewarded the kings of arms and heralds with 20 marks.

Dazzling as the wedding festivities were, however, there must have been a sense on the part of the wedding guests that some grim business lay around the corner, because there was one member of the family who was conspicuously absent from the celebrations: George, Duke of Clarence. He was a prisoner in the Tower.

9

The Downfall of a Duke

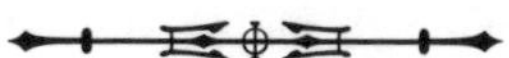

George, Duke of Clarence, had allied with the Earl of Warwick against Edward IV, the duke's brother, in 1469. Before the Battle of Barnet, Edward IV had won his brother back to his side, but their relationship had been an uneasy one since then.

Clarence had married Warwick's daughter, Isabel, whose sister, Anne, married Henry VI's son, Edward of Lancaster. The death of Warwick at Barnet, and the death of Edward at Tewkesbury, plunged Clarence and his brother Richard, Duke of Gloucester, into a nasty dispute regarding the lands of Warwick and those of his widowed countess, who had fled into sanctuary at Beaulieu.[1] As Isabel's husband, Clarence naturally wanted the lands for himself, while the unmarried Gloucester just as naturally wanted to take the widowed Anne for his bride and thereby lay claim to her share of his inheritance. The feelings of Anne, who was just a few weeks away from her 15th birthday when she was widowed, are not recorded, but after the debacle at Tewkesbury, marriage to the king's loyal brother, Gloucester, offered her security, wealth, and a powerful protector, advantages of which she could have hardly been unconscious. No one seemed at all interested in protecting the rights of the Countess of Warwick, an heiress in her own right, to her own inheritance and to her dower and jointure lands.

While the countess remained immured at Beaulieu, frantically writing petitions to the queen and other great ladies in hopes of gaining their sympathy,[2] Clarence went so far as to hide Anne from Gloucester in order to avoid sharing the Warwick inheritance. He was no match for Gloucester, however; the Crowland Chronicler, tells us, so bizarrely the story could well be true, that he discovered the earl's daughter 'dressed as a kitchen-maid in London', whereupon he took her to sanctuary at St Martin's, no doubt having provided her with a change of clothing first.[3] No later than 6 June 1474, when records first refer to them as a married couple, and probably soon after the pair received a papal dispensation on 22 April 1472, Gloucester and Anne had married.[4] The dispute about the sisters' inheritance dragged on, however, and was finally settled by Parliament in successive acts in 1474 and 1475, in a division that satisfied neither brother entirely. The Countess of Warwick, stripped of her rights by a provision that declared her to be as if one naturally dead, left sanctuary and went to live with Gloucester. With his share of the Warwick inheritance, Gloucester set off to establish himself in the north, where much of his share of the spoils were concentrated.

The Woodvilles took little part in this quarrel, which did not concern them. On 17 February 1472, John Paston II wrote that the king, the queen, Clarence, and Gloucester had gone to the manor of Sheen, 'not all in charity', and that when the king spoke to Clarence in favour of Gloucester's marriage to Anne, Clarence replied that 'he may well have my lady his sister-in-law, but they shall part no livelihood' – in other words, Clarence was quite happy to concede Anne's person, but not her property.[5] What role, if any, the queen took during this conference is not stated, but Michael Hicks has pointed out that a few days later, she renewed a grant to Gloucester of a stewardship carrying a fee of £100. This may mean that she sided with Gloucester in his quarrel with Clarence, as Hicks suggests;[6] alternatively, Elizabeth may have simply been following her husband's wishes or continuing the status quo. Hicks also posits that the Woodvilles supported Gloucester's bid to remove the Countess of Warwick from sanctuary in June 1473, a move that John Paston II noted met with Clarence's disapproval. The evidence that the Woodvilles got involved in this fraternal dispute at this point rests mainly on their physical proximity to the king at the time, however, and seems rather tenuous.[7]

With the matter of his estates wrapped up, Clarence dutifully joined the expedition to France in 1475, but otherwise was at the margins of political life, especially compared to his younger brother Gloucester, who was becoming a powerful and popular figure in the north. Yet that was soon to be the least of his problems, for on 22 December 1476, Clarence's wife, Isabel, died. Her infant son, Richard, followed her to the grave on 1 January 1477. Four days later, yet another death occurred, but this one had political, not personal consequences: Charles, Duke of Burgundy, was killed in battle at Nancy, leaving his unmarried daughter, Mary, as his heir.[8]

With the death of her father, the question of a marital alliance for Mary suddenly became a question of the greatest importance. For the widowed

Duchess of Burgundy, there was an obvious solution: to wed Mary to her favourite brother George, Duke of Clarence. Unfortunately, this solution did not appeal to Edward, who had not forgotten his brother's rebellion a few years earlier. Twenty-year-old Mary herself preferred Maximilian of Austria, while Louis XI of France offered her the 6-year-old Dauphin of France. The prospect of the latter match was equally distasteful to Edward, who sent an embassy to his sister's court. The ambassadors, Dr John Coke and Louis de Bretaylle, Anthony Woodville's friend, put forth Edward's own offer of a husband: Anthony Woodville. That it was a serious offer is indicated by the fact that Edward offered military support if Mary agreed to make a Woodville marriage. Anthony had indeed come a long way since Edward had 'rated' him at Calais years before! Mary, however, was unlikely to have been enthusiastic about such a match, for, as Philippe de Commynes pointed out, 'he was only an earl, and she the greatest heiress of her time'. In any case, she had already decided upon Maxmilian by the time the English proposal arrived.[9]

None of this could have been gratifying to Clarence, especially when, during the same year, Edward refused yet another potential match for his brother: this time between Clarence and a sister of James III of Scotland. He explained piously that Clarence and the Duchess of Burgundy, who had been offered the hand of James's brother, the Duke of Albany, could not consider any offers during their year of mourning for their spouses.[10]

Edward's reservations about allowing Clarence to marry outside England would prove to be well justified, for Clarence began to act erratically – and murderously. On 12 April 1477, his men seized Ankarette Tywnho, who had served the Duchess of Clarence, on the grounds that she had given her mistress poisoned ale at Warwick on 10 October 1476 – more than two months before the duchess actually died. John Thursby, in turn, was accused of poisoning Clarence's young son, Richard, with ale administered on 21 December 1476, while Sir Roger Tocotes was accused of aiding, abetting, and harbouring the other two defendants. Ankarette Twynho and John Thursby were hauled to Warwick Castle, where a jury, thoroughly intimidated by the Duke of Clarence, found them guilty. They were executed that same day. Roger Tocotes was indicted but evaded capture; later, when it was safe for him to do so, he surrendered himself and was later acquitted. The charges seem unlikely at best: the *Tewkesbury Chronicle*, which attributed Isabel's death at age 25 to complications from her recent childbirth, places Isabel at Tewkesbury at the time she was supposedly being poisoned at Warwick, and there seems little point in murdering Clarence's younger son while leaving his older son, Edward, unharmed.[11]

Meanwhile, an astronomer at Oxford named John Stacy, accused of using sorcery to procure the death of a cuckolded husband, implicated Thomas Burdett, who was a member of Clarence's household. As the details emerged, the allegations became even more serious: the men, along with a Thomas Blake, were accused of using astronomy to predict the deaths of the king and his eldest son – the most frightening charge that could be levelled against an astronomer of the day. The men were tried on 19 May 1477. Blake was pardoned due to the intervention of the Bishop of Norwich, but Burdett and Stacy were hanged the next day at Tyburn.

A day or so after the hangings, the Duke of Clarence, with Dr William Goddard, a Franciscan friar, in tow, barged into a council meeting at Westminster. There, Goddard read Burdett's and Stacy's declarations to the council, after which he and Clarence abruptly departed. The king, who was at Windsor, missed this show, but when he returned to Westminster, he summoned Clarence, who appeared before him around 10 June 1477, when Edward charged him with having violated the laws of England and threatening the security of judges and jurors – the latter, as Charles Ross points out, probably a reference to the Ankarette Twynho incident. Clarence was sent to the Tower, where he would remain a prisoner for months.[12]

On 19 January 1478, after the wedding of Edward's young son, Parliament opened with Bishop Rotherham setting the tone with St Paul's words, 'For he beareth not the sword in vain'. The chief business of the Parliament was to try Clarence. His attainder, introduced by the king himself, read:

> The king is mindful of the many conspiracies against him which he has repressed in the past, and although many of the rebels and traitors have been punished as an example to others yet, as a merciful prince, he spared not only the rank and file but also some of the movers and stirrers of such treasons. Notwithstanding, a conspiracy against him, the queen, their son and heir and a great part of the nobility of the land has recently come to his knowledge, which treason is more heinous and unnatural than any previous one because it originates from the king's brother the duke of Clarence, whom the king had always loved and generously rewarded. In spite of this, the duke grievously offended the king in the past, procuring his exile from the realm and labouring parliament to exclude him and his heirs from the crown. All of which the king forgave, but the duke continued to conspire against him, intending his

> destruction by both internal and external forces. He sought to turn his subjects against him by saying that Thomas Burdet was falsely put to death and that the king resorted to necromancy. He also said that the king was a bastard, not fit to reign, and made men take oaths of allegiance to him without excepting their loyalty to the king. He accused the king of taking his livelihood from him, and intending his destruction. He secured an exemplification under the great seal of an agreement made between him and Queen Margaret promising him the crown if Henry VI's line failed. He planned to send his son and heir abroad to win support, bringing a false child to Warwick castle in his place. He planned to raise war against the king within England and made men promise to be ready at an hour's notice. The duke has thus shown himself incorrigible and to pardon him would threaten the common weal, which the king is bound to maintain.[13]

For the Crowland Chronicler, this brotherly strife was almost too painful to write about:

> The mind recoils from describing what followed in the next Parliament – so sad was the dispute between two brothers of such noble character. No-one argued against the duke except the king; no-one answered the king except the duke. Some persons, however, were introduced concerning whom many people wondered whether they performed the offices of accuses or witnesses. [...] The duke swept aside all charges with a disclaimer offering, if it were acceptable, to uphold his case by personal combat. Why make a long story of it?[14]

Parliament condemned the Duke of Clarence to death on 7 February 1478. Edward, however, delayed carrying out the sentence until the Speaker of the Commons asked that it be carried out. On 18 February 1478, the Duke of Clarence was executed privately, quite possibly through drowning in a vat of Malmsey wine or in a bath made from a Malmsey barrel – a curious method of death indeed, but the only one specified by the English and foreign chronicles. Before his death, Clarence asked that certain land be given to Anthony Woodville 'in consideration of the injuries perpetrated on him and his parents' by the duke. Edward IV carried out this wish.[15]

Where do the Woodvilles fit into all this? In 1483, Dominic Mancini, an Italian observer who had been visiting in England earlier that year, wrote:

> The queen then remembered the insults to her family and the calumnies with which she was reproached, namely that according to established usage

> she was not the legitimate wife of the king. Thus she concluded that her offspring to the throne would never come to the throne, unless the duke of Clarence was removed; and of this she easily persuaded the king. [...] At that time [of Clarence's execution] Richard duke of Gloucester was so overcome with grief for his brother, that he could not dissimulate so well, but that he was overheard to say that he would one day avenge his brother's death. Thenceforth he came very rarely to court [...] After the execution of the duke of Clarence, and while Richard, as we have said, kept himself to his own lands, the queen ennobled many of her family. Besides, she attracted to her party many strangers and introduced them to court, so that they alone should manage the public and private businesses of the crown, surround the king, and have bands of retainers, give or sell offices, and finally rule the very king himself.[16]

As a contemporary observer of the events leading up to Richard III's taking the crown, Mancini is an invaluable source, whose account is often consistent with English accounts. When Mancini speaks of events occurring several years before his visit to England, however, he is less reliable, and there are several reasons why his claim that Elizabeth procured the death of Clarence should be regarded with scepticism. Mancini's statements about Elizabeth ennobling her family *after* Clarence's demise are demonstrably wrong, nor is there evidence of 'strangers' being introduced to court by the queen. As for Gloucester's brooding Hamlet-like in the north, there is nothing to suggest that he avoided court because of the Woodvilles; rather, he stayed in the north because of his enormous responsibilities there, which demanded his full attention. He came to court when family ties demanded it, as when his sister Margaret visited in 1480, or when his responsibilities as a great lord required it, as when Parliament met early in 1483. As A.J. Pollard points out, these slurs by Mancini likely have their origins in the propaganda being put forth by Richard, Duke of Gloucester in the spring and summer of 1483, when he was in the process of seizing the crown and was intent on destroying the Woodvilles.[17]

But what of Mancini's claims that Elizabeth feared Clarence because she believed that her children would never come to the throne if he survived? Mancini's explanation is that in 1483, Richard claimed that Edward's marriage to Elizabeth was invalid because before Edward married Elizabeth, Edward had been married by proxy to a continental bride, the betrothal having been arranged by the Earl of Warwick.[18] In fact, Gloucester's official claim, as enshrined in the 1484 Act of Parliament spelling out Richard's claim to the throne, was not that Edward IV had been betrothed to a foreign princess, but that he had been precontracted to an Eleanor Butler, a widowed daughter of the Earl of Shrewsbury.[19] One source, the Burgundian Chronicler, Philippe de Commynes, would claim that Robert Stillington, Bishop of Bath and Wells, who had been appointed keeper of Edward IV's privy seal in 1460, actually married Edward to Eleanor, although he adds that Edward's promise was made to the lady only to delude her so that he could enjoy her body.[20] From this, and from the arrest of Stillington for obscure reasons in 1478, it has been suggested, chiefly by Paul Murray Kendall, that Clarence had learned about Edward's previous marriage from Stillington and was killed at the instigation of the Woodvilles because they could not risk the truth being known.[21]

Kendall's theory has attracted a great deal of support, yet there are sound reasons to doubt it. Prior to 1483, no trace of any rumour that Edward IV's marriage was invalid can be found, though such an allegation would have been of immeasurable value to the king's and queen's enemies. Kendall's suggestion that Clarence knew of the precontract but dared not to reveal it makes little sense, as Mortimer Levine points out, since he apparently had no fear of making the even more explosive accusation that Edward IV himself was illegitimate.[22] Moreover, if Clarence or anyone else had been raising uncomfortable questions about the validity of Edward's marriage, the solution lay in Edward's hands via an application to the pope to smooth out any irregularities: Eleanor Butler, having died in 1468, was in no position to complain.

As for Stillington, his arrest, which was noted in passing by Elizabeth Stonor on 6 March 1478, may or may not have some connection with Clarence; he was pardoned in June 1478 for the offence of uttering words prejudicial to the king and his state. No more specific information is given to us.[23] Even before his pardon, however, he was appointed to a commission of the peace on 14 April 1478, suggesting a short imprisonment and perhaps an equally short royal displeasure.[24] Moreover, having released Stillington, Edward IV did not treat him as a person with dangerous knowledge; indeed, on 21 January 1479, he was appointed (along with the Earl of Essex, the Bishop of Ely, and Anthony Woodville) to treat with the Bishop of Elne, Louis XI's ambassador in England.[25] Surely a man ruthless enough to murder his own brother in order to keep his marital escapades from coming to light would have not risked the possibility that a disgruntled

Stillington might gossip to the French. Following this assignment, life went on smoothly enough for Stillington, who continued to be named to commissions of the peace by Edward IV.[26] As for Kendall's claim that Stillington 'was held in intense enmity by the Woodvilles' after Clarence's death, there is simply no evidence to support this; whatever the Woodvilles' thoughts about Stillington were, no one took the trouble to record them.

In the end, attempts to deflect responsibility for Clarence's death off the shoulders of Edward IV and onto those of the Woodvilles are unconvincing. Regardless of his motives for proceeding against his brother, Edward IV was no one's puppet, as Warwick had found out in the 1460s. He took the leading role in the prosecution of Clarence: as Crowland puts it with stark simplicity, 'No-one argued against the duke except the king'.

There is no reason to assume that the Woodvilles did anything to dissuade Edward from his purpose; indeed, given the deaths of the queen's father and of John Woodville at Warwick's and Clarence's hands, they might well have approved and applauded the king's actions. They might well have done their part in making certain that Parliament was complaisant. But the evidence does not point to more than this. The simple fact is that Clarence's record of disloyalty, his coldblooded destruction of his wife's old servants, and his association with men who had committed the treasonous act of forecasting the king's death in itself made him a volatile and dangerous subject. In a ruthless age, such a man was courting death, and no help in the wooing would have been required from the Woodvilles or from anyone else.

10

Before the Storm

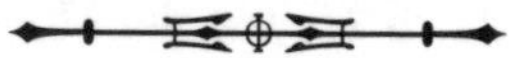

Having disposed of Clarence, Edward IV was free to turn his attention to foreign affairs, specifically, Scotland. Edward IV's daughter, Cecily, had already been betrothed to James III's heir. Now James III of Scotland proposed that his sister, Margaret, marry Anthony Woodville. Earl Rivers might not have had the rank or wealth to appeal to the Burgundian heiress, but he clearly was considered suitable for a king's sister.[1]

Edward was amenable to the match. On 14 December 1478, he appointed the Bishop of Rochester and Edward Woodville – the latter making his first recorded appearance on the diplomatic front – to enter into negotiations, which quickly bore fruit. Margaret was to have a dowry of 4,000 marks, which because of James's straitened finances would be deducted from the payments Edward was making toward the dowry of his daughter, Cecily. Margaret was to come to England by 16 May 1479, for which purpose Edward issued her and a retinue of 300 as safe conduct. On 6 March 1479, the Scottish parliament granted James 20,000 marks toward the expenses of the marriage.[2] The bride's arrival was delayed, however, apparently by James's difficulties with his own troublesome brother, the Duke of Albany. Edward IV nonetheless made plans for the wedding, which was to be held at Nottingham. On 21 August 1479, he instructed the magistrates of York that when Margaret arrived there on 9 October 1479, they should give her 'loving and hearty cheer'.[3]

While Anthony awaited his bride, Queen Elizabeth awaited the arrival of yet another child. Katherine was probably born in early 1479 at Eltham; her name suggests that the queen's youngest sister, Katherine, Duchess of Buckingham, acted as one of her godmothers.[4]

Sadly, at about the same time Katherine came into the world, the king and queen's little-known third son, George, departed from it.[5]

Edward IV named George as his Lieutenant of Ireland on 6 July 1478 and appointed Henry, Lord Grey of Codnor, as the infant's deputy. Young George never got a look at the emerald isle before he died in March 1479, probably a victim of the plague or another epidemic disease. Ralph Griffiths believes that the boy was staying at Sheen at the time of his death.

George's half-brother, Thomas, Marquess of Dorset, attended George's funeral at Windsor on 22 March 1479, as did his uncle Anthony, Earl Rivers; John, Lord Strange, the husband of Elizabeth's sister Jacquetta; John Blount, Lord Mountjoy; Richard Hastings, Lord Welles; and Lord Ferrers of Chartley. No narrative of the funeral is extant; we know of the mourners and their attire only through wardrobe accounts. Edward IV himself was issued a robe of blue, the colour of royal mourning, suggesting that he might have observed the ceremony from a private chamber, screened from public view. The queen's accounts, which would have listed her own expenses, do not survive.

For Lionel Woodville, one of the queen's younger brothers, 1479 was more auspicious. In a typical moment in his biography of Richard III, Paul Murray Kendall praises Anthony Woodville (meagerly, which is as far as Kendall could bring himself to praise a Woodville) by first cataloguing his family's supposed vices. He writes, 'Anthony Woodville's father was a rapacious adventurer [...] His brother Lionel was a type of their father in the gown of a bishop'. Elsewhere in the book, Kendall describes Lionel as 'haughty'.[6] As is far too often the case when Kendall writes about the Woodvilles, he offers no evidence to support his assessment of Lionel's character, and indeed there seems to be none.

Described in 1482 as being 29 years of age,[7] Lionel was intended for the Church from a young age. John Thomson notes that he received a canonry at Lincoln in 1466 as his first benefice, when he would have been around 13.[8] Lionel was educated at Oxford, where appears to have been studying as late as 1479: on 22 May 1479 Walter Paston, a fellow student, wrote that the queen's brother should have 'proceeded' at midsummer but would 'tarry now till Michaelmas'.[9]

The newly graduated Lionel did not have to wait long for honours. That same year, William Waynflete, Bishop of Winchester, appointed him Archdeacon of Surrey,[10] and he was also Dean of Exeter by then.[11] Most important, Lionel's alma mater elected him as its chancellor in 1479. University officials then offered him, in fulsome terms, an honorary degree:

> Our predecessors always seem to us to have acted wisely, O most eminent lord, in showing especial respect for learning in men of high social rank; for this is demanded by the degree of their nobility and the greatness of their merits. So great was the nobility of many and so great were their merits, that the one redounded to the glory of the University and the other to the advancement of its work. Therefore since we know that you are powerful in a nobility to which none of your forbears could have aspired, it is right that we should not be behindhand in conferring upon you a corresponding degree of advancement in the academic disciplines long practised in Oxford. [...] It has pleased us to agree by unanimous consent, that you should first be admitted to the extraordinary reading of decretals; your excellency is to understand that you are not compelled to begin lecturing at any time. [...] This gift is certainly not unworthy of your dignity. Therefore there is, O most distinguished man, a great expectation of your uprightness in protecting our community, for you have already aroused expectations by your many merits, and so we hope the more readily that you will long be the special patron of our University.[12]

By the following year, Anglo-Scottish relations had deteriorated, putting paid to Anthony's Scottish marriage. Sometime in 1480,[13] Anthony remarried. His bride was not a foreign princess but a young Englishwoman. She was Mary FitzLewis, the daughter of Henry FitzLewis, who had died in May 1480, and Elizabeth Beaufort. Elizabeth Beaufort was a daughter of Edmund, Duke of Somerset, killed at the first Battle of St Albans in 1455, and Elizabeth Beauchamp. Through her father, Mary inherited the manor of Bromfields in Newington; the moiety of 862 acres in that parish and Wickford, along with the advowson of the church of Newington; the parcels of Oakfield and Shortcroft; and 130 acres of land in Vange. She was said to have been 15 at the time of her father's death; a calendar in a book of hours made for Jacquetta Woodville, however, gives the birth date of 'maria fitz loys' as 30 May 1467, making Mary around 13 at the time of the marriage.[14]

For Anthony to turn his sights from a princess to a minor heiress seems odd. Both Michael Hicks and Lynda Pidgeon suggest that Anthony might have sought to claim some of the Beaufort inheritance through Mary's mother, whose brothers had all died fighting for the House of Lancaster.[15] Pidgeon goes on to speculate that Anthony chose such a young bride 'because he was not really interested in having a wife and providing an heir' – though this seems to lose sight of the fact that even if Mary was only 13 in 1480, she would be at an age suitable to safely begin childbearing in only a couple of years.[16] Indeed, the very opposite could be true: with no legitimate offspring of his own, Anthony, having married his first wife when she was in her twenties, might have found the fact that Mary was just at the cusp of her childbearing years to be appealing. Moreover, Mary was well connected: she was a first cousin of Henry Stafford, Duke of Buckingham, married to Anthony's sister; Margaret Beaufort, Countess of Richmond, was her aunt. Her Beaufort blood meant that, like the king, she was a descendant of John of Gaunt and Katherine Swynford.

Sadly, we know even less about Anthony's second marriage than we do his first. In his will, made three years later, Anthony asked that prayers be said for the soul of his father-in-law. He left Mary the plate – items of precious metal such as cups, bowls, and salt cellars that were among the most valuable items in a medieval household – that had belonged to her father and enough of his own plate to make up any deficiency. Mary was also to receive the plate that had been given her at their marriage, a sparver of white silk with four pairs of sheets, two pairs of fustians, a featherbed, and a chambering of Griselda – presumably a tapestry illustrating the famous tale. She would also, of course, be entitled to a jointure interest in her husband's land. But we have scarcely a glimpse of Mary during the couple's marriage, though this is hardly unusual for women of her time.

Around the time that Anthony entered into his second marriage, Edward IV's court prepared for a visit from the king's sister, Margaret, Duchess of Burgundy. Edward Woodville and Sir James Radcliffe, described as knights of the king's body, were appointed to travel to Calais to meet the duchess, who was travelling from Bruges. Edward and Radcliffe were splendidly attired for the occasion in jackets of purple velvet and blue velvet, supplied to them by the king especially for this purpose. Edward's ten servants received jackets of murrey and blue cloth. Even grander were Anthony and his nephew the Marquis of Dorset, who were allowed purple cloth of gold upon satin.[17]

Edward Woodville left England in the *Falcon*, a royal ship, and brought Margaret from Calais to Dover in late June of 1480. It was the first and the last time she was to return to England since her marriage to Duke Charles, and she would spend more than three months there. For the first time, she met her nephews, Prince Edward and Richard, Duke of York, both of whom had been born during her absence. It was a meeting that would prove to be of significance some years later.

In mid-September, the king rode with Margaret to Rochester, where Margaret wrote a letter home stating that she and the king would be staying at Anthony's estate in Kent, before she embarked for the coast.[18] Margaret had met William Caxton, the printer, while he was resident in Bruges, and had become his patron. Seeing a translation from French into English on which he was working, *The Recuyell of the Historyes of Troye*, she had corrected his English but ordered him to complete his translation, which he did, and duly dedicated to her. It was printed abroad, probably in late 1473 or early 1474, several years before Caxton brought his press to England.[19] As Anthony had translated three books for Caxton's press, the most recent, *The Cordiale*, being published the year before Margaret's visit, the duchess and the earl would have likely found common ground in applauding the success of the man, and the industry, they had each supported.

Queen Elizabeth, meanwhile, was preparing for the birth of what would prove to be her last child, who was born on 10 November 1480. The baby's name, Bridget – unusual for a royal child, and a welcome respite from the Elizabeths, Katherines, and Annes of the day – was probably inspired by St Bridget of Sweden and may have been the choice of the king's pious mother, Cecily, Duchess of York, making a rare appearance at court as one of the infant's godmothers.[20] Margaret, one of the queen's sisters, and her husband, Thomas, Lord Maltravers, were prominent in the ceremony, as was the queen's son, the Marquis of Dorset. The next day, the morning of St Martin's Day, the infant was christened in the Chapel of Eltham by the Bishop of Chichester. A detailed description has survived:

> First a hundred torches borne by knights, esquires, and other honest persons.
> The Lord Maltravers, bearing the basin, having a towel about his neck.
> The Earl of Northumberland bearing a taper not lit.
> The Earl of Lincoln the salt.
> The canopy borne by three knights and a baron.
> My lady Maltravers did bear a rich crysom pinned over her left breast.
> The Countess of Richmond did bear the princess.
> My lord Marquess Dorset assisted her.
> My lady the king's mother, and my lady Elizabeth, were godmothers at the font.
> The Bishop of Winchester godfather.

And in the time of the christening, the officers of arms cast on their coats.
And then were lit all the foresaid torches.
Present, these noble men ensuing:
The Duke of York.
The Lord Hastings, the king's chamberlain.
The Lord Stanley, Stewards of the King's house.
The Lord Dacre, the queen's chamberlain, and many other estates.
And when the said princess was christened, a squire held the basins to the gossips [the godmothers], and even by the font my Lady Maltravers was godmother to the confirmation.

And from thence she was borne before the high altar. and that solemnity done she was borne eftsoons into her parclosse, accompanied with the estates aforesaid.
And the lord of Saint Joans [probably John St John, according to Pauline Routh] brought thither a spice plate.
And at the said parclose the godfather and the godmother gave great gifts to the said princess.
Which gifts were borne by knights and esquires before the said princess turning to the queen's chamber again, well accompanied as appertaineth, and after the custom of this realm.[21]

Nobody could have guessed that the next royal christening would be that of the Countess of Richmond's grandson, Prince Arthur.

On 22 September 1481, William Waynflete, Bishop of Winchester, visited the king, at Woodstock and invited him to Oxford. The king promptly accepted the invitations and arrived at St Giles' parish that night after sunset 'with a multitude of lights', where he was greeted by the chancellor, Lionel Woodville, who had added to the Woodville presence at Oxford by appointing his brother Richard as understeward. The next day, the chancellor, who apparently was now at ease in his new role, delivered a divinity lecture to the king, who went on to visit other parts of the university, before departing 'with great content'.[22]

Sadly, on 19 November 1481, little Anne Mowbray died at Greenwich, leaving Richard, Duke of York a widower at the age of 8. Edward IV honoured the little duchess with a funeral costing over £215. Three barges escorted the body to Westminster Abbey, where Anne was buried in the chapel of St Erasmus, founded by her mother-in-law the queen. During construction of

Henry VII's chapel in the next century, the coffin was moved to the convent of the Minoresses of St Clare, where it was found in 1964 by workers excavating the site. Anne was reburied in the Henry VII chapel in 1965.[23]

A month before Anne Mowbray's demise, Richard Beauchamp, Bishop of Salisbury, died, leaving a vacancy to be filled.[24] On 7 January 1482, Pope Sixtus IV provided Lionel Woodville to the bishopric.[25] Lionel had undoubtedly achieved his position through the influence of his brother-in-law the king, but nothing indicates that he was incompetent or unworthy to hold it. His case was not an isolated one: While some bishops were from humble families, Lionel's own predecessor had family ties to Richard Beauchamp, Earl of Warwick, while George Neville, Archbishop of York, was a son of Richard Neville, Earl of Salisbury, and a younger brother of Richard Neville, Earl of Warwick.

One aspect of Lionel's life has proven controversial: did he forget his vows of chastity and father Stephen Gardiner, later Bishop of Winchester? In the sixteenth century, a tradition arose to this effect. It can still be found in older books and, of course, on the Internet, but James Arthur Muller, a biographer of Gardiner, weighed the evidence and rejected it in 1926. He noted that Gardiner's enemies never accused him of illegitimate birth and that Gardiner was probably not born until the 1490s, eliminating Lionel, who died in 1484, as a father. More recently, C.D.C. Armstrong has estimated Gardiner's birth date as being between 1495 and 1498.[26] It seems safe to say, then, that the Bishop of Salisbury was not the sire of the Bishop of Winchester.

The year took a tragic turn, however, when Mary, the king and queen's second daughter, died in May at Greenwich, a few months short of her 15th birthday. Mary's burial at Windsor, also her birthplace, took place on 27–28 May 1482. Among the ladies present were Jane (or Joan), Lady Grey of Ruthin (Elizabeth Woodville's sister), the widow of Sir Anthony Grey of Ruthin; Joan, Lady Strange, a niece of Elizabeth Woodville who was married to George Stanley; and Katherine Grey, probably the daughter of Lady Grey. The chief mourner is not identified but may have been Lady Grey, the first woman named by the herald who recorded the funeral ceremonies. Had Mary lived, she might have become the Queen of Denmark, for her father had proposed her as a bride for its king, Frederick.[27]

The king and queen did not have long to mourn their daughter, for there was a distraction: Scotland. Relations had been tense for some time, with raiding by both sides, but in June 1482, events took a new turn when Edward and James III's brother, Alexander, Duke of Albany, entered into a treaty under which the English would support Albany's claim to the throne in exchange for certain conditions, among them the return of Berwick, ceded to the Scots in 1461 by Margaret of Anjou during a period when she was in particularly desperate straits. After signing the treaty, Edward commissioned his youngest brother, Richard, Duke of Gloucester, as lieutenant general. In July, Gloucester began assembling an army against the Scots. The Earl of Northumberland, the Marquis of Dorset, Lord Stanley, and Edward Woodville were among his lieutenants.[28]

Edward Woodville took a force of 500 men with him, raised under the name of the Prince of Wales. On his way to the border, he stopped at Coventry, which offered £20 instead of men.[29]

The campaign, though successful in part, was somewhat anticlimactic. Richard and his men, numbering between 15–20,000, captured the town of Berwick without resistance and marched on to Edinburgh, leaving behind a force to besiege Berwick Castle, which had resisted. The hapless James III, meanwhile, was arrested by his own nobles and was imprisoned at Edinburgh when Richard's army entered the unresisting capital. At that point, Albany abruptly dropped his claim to the throne, and Richard entered into a treaty with a Scottish delegation, which agreed to return the sums that had been paid toward the abortive marriage of Edward IV's daughter Cecily to James III's heir. Richard then headed back to Berwick, leaving Edinburgh unscathed. At Berwick, he disbanded most of his army, leaving only a small force to besiege Berwick Castle, which did surrender on 24 August. The Crowland Chronicler, albeit with a touch of the armchair warrior, grumbled that Richard had let the 'very wealthy town' of Edinburgh escape unharmed while gaining only Berwick, which counted more as a loss since it cost the crown 10,000 marks a year.[30] Coincidentally, Margaret of Anjou, who had been responsible for the loss of Berwick in the first place, was near death in France when the castle surrendered on 24 August; had she not died the next day, she might have been amused at the bother to which she had put her old enemy, Edward IV.

In light of future developments, one looks for friction between Gloucester and his Woodville lieutenants, Edward and Dorset, but nothing indicates any. Indeed, Gloucester created Edward, along with other men, a knight banneret on 24 July. It is possible that he acted simply to please his brother the king, of course, but his later actions as Richard III indicate that he had a sufficiently high opinion of Edward's military capacity to be worried about him mounting an invasion.

The Crowland Chronicler closes his account of the year 1482 with an account of Edward IV's Christmas court at Westminster: 'In those days you might have seen a royal Court such as befitted a mighty kingdom, filled with riches and men from almost every nation and (surpassing all else) with the handsome and most delightful children born of the marriage [...] to Queen Elizabeth'. His account is an elegiac one, and for good reason: he knew, unlike the Woodvilles, that their world was about to vanish.

11

Welcome Fortune!

On 8 March 1483, Anthony Woodville wrote a letter to his man of business, Andrew Dymmock. Anthony and his nephew, Dorset, had agreed that Dorset would take over Anthony's position as deputy constable of the Tower, and that Anthony and his sureties would be discharged from the bond they had entered into with the constable of the Tower, John, Lord Dudley. In a postscript, he asked for 'the patent of mine authority about my lord prince' and a patent given to him by the king regarding his power to raise forces in the march of Wales. The patents were to be delivered to him by 'some sure man'.[1]

The patent about Prince Edward concerns the ordinances issued in 1473 that governed the upbringing of the prince, Anthony's charge.[2] What was suitable for a 3-year-old no longer quite worked for a 12-year-old, and one provision gave Anthony, along with his nephew Richard Grey and John Alcock, Bishop of Worcester (formerly the Bishop of Rochester) instructions on what to do if Edward exhibited 'any unprincely demeaning'. (They were to confront the prince with his misbehaviour and, if the prince would not amend his conduct, raise the matter with the king or the queen or incur the king's 'grievous displeasure'.) More important, the prince was not to

> give, write, send or command anything without the advice of the said Bishop, Lord Richard, and Earl Rivers, and that none of his servants presume nor be so bold to move, steer, or cause him to do to the contrary of these ordinances upon pain of grievous punishment and losing his service.

He was always to be accompanied by at least two people – this not being an age that put a high premium on privacy. The prince's bedtime was raised from eight to nine, and some restrictions about who could come to meals and where they could eat were added – the latter a reaction, perhaps, to the problem of outsiders finding their way to the dinner table. There were also some accounting changes. None of these revisions could be termed drastic, but they did reflect the fact that Richard Grey, Elizabeth Woodville's younger son from her first marriage, had acquired considerable importance in his half-brother's household and was now a member of his council. Richard Haute, the queen's cousin, was the controller of the household. The other officers included the Bishop of Worcester, who was president of the council; Sir Thomas Vaughan, the chamberlain; Sir William Stanley, steward; Sir Richard Crofte, treasurer; and Richard Martyn, Bishop of St David's, a councillor.

The late Eric Ives, who studied Anthony's correspondence with Dymmock some years ago, attached particular significance to the 8 March letter in the context of the power struggle that was to erupt after Edward IV's death a month later. For him, the letter suggested that Anthony and Dorset were 'making sure that their centres of power were under control in case of trouble', and perhaps justified the concerns about Woodville power that were to manifest themselves after the king's death, although Ives added a caveat: '[T]oo much can easily be built on the slim evidence of one letter'.[3]

There may indeed be less to this letter than meets the eye. In asking Dymmock to send him copies of the patents, Anthony may have simply been making sure his papers were in order. Furthermore, the ordinances concerning Edward V had been revised on 25 February 1483 by, it should be remembered, the king himself. The revised ordinances, instructing that the prince do nothing contrary to the advice of Alcock, Anthony, or Richard Grey, adressed the situation within the prince's household and would not have suffered to protect Anthony against a threat from outside it. Despite a theory by certain partisans of Richard III that Anthony's letter is evidence of a Woodville plot to poison Edward IV and seize power[4], the ordinances most certainly did not address who was to govern if Prince Edward became king; they covered the upbringing of a young prince, not a royal minority.

As for the patent allowing Anthony to raise troops, the date of its issuance by the king is unknown: Ives notes that such a patent was not enrolled in the royal records, and nothing in Anthony's letter indicates the date of the patent. There were a couple of reasons, however, why Anthony might have wanted a copy of it. In December 1482, France and Burgundy had entered into the Treaty of Arras, which meant that Edward IV had lost his French pension and that his daughter Elizabeth had lost her promised marriage to the Dauphin of France. The news had infuriated the king, who in the parliament of 1483 obtained a subsidy for 'the hasty and necessary defence of the realm'.[5] While the king may not have intended a full-scale invasion of France, Anthony might have wished to be prepared for such a possibility. It is also noteworthy that the 1483 parliament confirmed an exchange of land made in 1479 between the Prince of Wales and William Herbert, Earl of Huntingdon, then the Earl of Pembroke. The transaction, which had conferred the Pembroke lands upon Prince Edward in exchange for manors in Somerset and Dorset, was initiated by the crown and was to Huntingdon's disadvantage. Perhaps Anthony was anticipating trouble following Parliament's confirmation of the exchange. The request that the documents be delivered by 'some sure man' – assuming this is not merely a catchphrase – need not be sinister.[6] Given the tension between France and England, there were no doubt spies about who would have been interested in any preparation for war.

This brings us to Anthony's transfer of his deputy constableship to Dorset. While the king is not mentioned by Anthony, there is no reason to suppose that he was unaware of this arrangement or disapproved of it; clearly, Lord Dudley knew what was going on. Perhaps Anthony's intent was to allow his nephew, who had a large family that included a number of daughters to be married off, to enjoy the fees pertaining to the office. There are certainly no indications that Dorset made military use of his possession of the Tower in the days before or after the king's death; the story that he seized the royal treasure stored there, as we shall see, cannot be substantiated.

Dorset had something else on his mind during the early part of 1483: the marriage of his eldest son to Anne St Leger, the king's niece.[7] Anne was the daughter of Edward IV's sister Anne, Duchess of Exeter, and her second husband, Thomas St Leger. The duchess's Lancastrian first husband, Henry Holland, Duke of Exeter, had been imprisoned in the Tower after the Battle of Tewkesbury but had been released to join the 1475 expedition to France; on the way home, he drowned in what were considered suspicious circumstances. The duchess, however, had already been allowed to divorce Exeter, who had spent years in exile before the defeat at Tewkesbury, and marry St Leger. She had died in 1476, probably of complications from childbirth, soon after the birth of their daughter. Although the duke's estates had been forfeited due to his support for the Lancastrian cause, most of them had been granted to the duchess in 1461, and St Leger had enjoyed them after the duchess's death.

With the bethrothal of Anne St Leger and Dorset's heir in view, the parliament of 1483 settled the Holland estates upon Anne St Leger, save for lands totalling 500 marks per year, which were set aside for Richard Grey. This arrangement, for which the queen paid the king 5,000 marks, was at the expense of Ralph Neville, the heir to the Holland estates. Neville was technically barred from inheriting because of Exeter's attainder but could have petitioned for the reversal of the attainder, as heirs often did. Whether he would have succeeded in the absence of any Woodville interest in Anne St Leger's estates is far from certain, though, as Anne St Leger was the king's niece and the daughter of a favoured servant.

Anthony's care about obtaining his patents, and Dorset's wedding plans, were all for naught. On 9 April 1483, Edward IV died, of causes that remain uncertain. The Crowland Chronicler wrote that he had not been 'affected by old age nor by any known type of disease which would not have seemed easy to cure in a lesser person', while Dominic Mancini, an Italian observer who happened to be in England at the time, reported that the king had died after a boating trip in which he allowed a 'damp cold to strike his vitals'. The Burgundian chronicler, Commynes, variously named apoplexy, grief occasioned by the Treaty of Arras, and a catarrh, while Thomas Basin attributed the king's death to an overindulgence of fruit and vegetables on Good Friday. Polydor Vergil, writing his history of England in the sixteenth century, suggested poison, while Edmund Hall proposed an ague, contracted in France in 1475, that 'turned to an incurable quarten'.[8] Given the state of fifteenth-century medicine, Mancini's explanation seems as plausible as any.

Whatever the cause of death, the demise of Edward, just a few weeks shy of his 41st birthday, must have been a shock. At Christmas, the king had been resplendent in costly robes of a novel design which displayed the king 'like a new and incomparable spectacle set before the onlookers';[9] nothing indicates that that he was suffering from ill health at the time his parliament convened in January.

His illness allowed him time either to make a new will or to add codicils to his 1475 one, although only the 1475 will itself has survived. According to Mancini, it was said that the king had named his only surviving brother, Gloucester, as protector of the realm during the minority of Prince Edward, now Edward V.[10]

Neither Edward V nor Gloucester was at Edward's deathbed. Edward V was at Ludlow with Anthony Woodville; Gloucester was at his estates in the north, where he may have learned of the premature report of the king's death that reached the city of York on 6 April.[11]

It is at this point where the first of several myths surrounding the Woodvilles and the death of Edward IV creeps in: the story that the Woodvilles concealed Edward IV's death from Gloucester. The myth originates in Paul Murray Kendall's florid biography of Richard III, which informs us that Gloucester received no formal notification of the king's death until William, Lord Hastings, took it upon himself to break the news and to inform Gloucester that he had appointed a protector.[12] In fact, neither Mancini nor Crowland, the chief primary sources for this period, indicates that there was anything irregular in the way in which Gloucester was informed of the king's death or any unusual delay. Neither, in fact, has anything to say about when or how Gloucester was first told of his brother's death: Crowland is silent on the subject, other than to note that Gloucester was sending 'pleasant letters' to the widowed queen, while Mancini simply reports that Hastings kept Gloucester informed of the council's deliberations.[13] While Polydor Vergil, writing in the sixteenth century, does state that it was Hastings who informed Gloucester of Edward IV's death, he does not indicate that anything was amiss about the way in which Gloucester was informed. Indeed, if anyone had to complain of delay, it was Edward V, the new king, who did not receive the news until 14 April – four days after it was current in Calais.[14]

Meanwhile, the king's council, as Hastings informed Gloucester, was deliberating. As Charles Ross points out, contrary to Kendall's claim, there was nothing illegal about the council sitting without having been convened by Gloucester: in keeping the government running until a new council could be appointed, they were following the examples set during the royal minorities of Richard II in 1377 and Henry VI in 1422.[15] The council's main concern was how much power the king's Woodville relations would wield in the new government. At this stage, the Woodvilles' leading opponent was not Gloucester but Hastings.

Hastings, who was about 43 in 1483, had been on close terms with the king from the very beginning of his reign; the measure of their friendship can be found in Hastings's will, in which he stated, proudly and poignantly, that the king, 'for the true service that I have done and at the least intended to have done to his grace hath willed and offered me to be buried in the college or chapel of St George at Windsor in a place by his grace assigned, in the which college his highness is disposed to be buried'.[16] But his friendship with the king did not extend to the Woodvilles. Crowland reports that 'much ill-will' had long existed between them and Hastings, while Mancini claimed that Dorset and Hastings had a 'deadly feud' based on the mistresses they had attempted to steal from each other.[17] Thomas More, on the other hand, writing in the sixteenth century (but perhaps basing his account on information gained from people who were in a position to remember the events of 1483), claimed that Anthony bore a grudge against Hastings for the latter having been made Lieutenant of Calais and that Anthony had once made an accusation against Hastings that got the latter into temporary disgrace with the king.[18] Eric Ives has suggested that the rivalry between Anthony and Hastings might be behind a confession by a John Edwards that he had slandered Dorset, Rivers, and Robert Ratcliffe before the king's council at Calais 'for fear of his life and putting him in the brake at Calais'.[19]

Whatever the reason for the bad blood between Hastings and the Woodvilles, Hastings (as reported by the Crowland Chronicler) insisted that the escort accompanying the young king to London for his coronation be of a modest size, so as to prevent the king's Woodville brothers and uncles from seizing control of him. He threatened to withdraw to Calais if the matter of the escort could not be settled to his satisfaction. 'The benevolent queen, desirous of extinguishing every spark of murmurring and unrest', bowed to Hastings's argument and wrote to Ludlow to tell her son that his escort should be limited to no more than 2,000 men, a number that was satisfactory to Hastings. Meanwhile, Gloucester wrote the 'pleasant letters' mentioned above, swearing allegiance to Edward V, and staged a memorial service for the deceased king at York.[20]

While Gloucester, Anthony Woodville, and the new king remained in their respective locations, the council was also debating the shape the minority government would take – without, according to Mancini, waiting for the arrival of Gloucester, who would surely have an opinion on the matter. Dorset is said to have brushed off his fellow councillors' concerns with the contemptuous reply of, 'We are so important, that even without the king's uncle we can make and enforce these decisions'. After the council debated whether Gloucester would govern alone during Edward V's minority, or be the chief among his fellow councillors, the latter opinion carried the day.[21] A coronation date, 4 May, was set.[22]

The implications of when Edward V was to be crowned, and how the realm was to be governed, have been widely discussed. Under the precedent of 1429, when the 7-year-old Henry VI was crowned, the protectorate would end upon Edward V's coronation, leaving the council to govern until the king came of age.[23] Under the assumption that any such council would be dominated by the Woodvilles, Michael Hicks has argued that the plans for an early coronation, combined with the cavalier dismissal of the need to consult Gloucester, are evidence of an attempted Woodville *coup d'état*.[24] This is possible, but the ease with which Hastings prevailed on the matter of the king's escort suggests considerably less organisation on the Woodvilles' part – and also casts doubt on whether the Woodvilles could have taken their domination of a council for granted. In any case, if there was a concerted grasp for power on the Woodvilles' part, events would soon prove them to have been singularly inept about it.

According to Mancini, Hastings had been writing to Gloucester, keeping him informed of the council's deliberations and, more important, urging him to 'hasten to the capital with a strong force, and avenge the insult done him by his enemies'. To accomplish this, Hastings advised Gloucester to take Edward V under his protection and to seize his followers before the king's entourage reached London. Gloucester, meanwhile, was writing to Henry Stafford, Duke of Buckingham, 'complaining to the latter of the insult done him by the ignoble family of the queen', whom Buckingham himself had supposedly detested since being made as a child to marry her youngest sister, Katherine Woodville.[25]

Buckingham had enjoyed little more than a ceremonial role at Edward IV's court, where he played his part at the grand events of Edward IV's reign, such as the welcoming of Louis de Bruges to England in 1472 and the marriage of Edward IV's younger son, the Duke of York, to little Anne Mowbray in 1478. He accompanied Edward to France in 1475, when the Treaty of Picquigny was signed, but is recorded as having gone home prematurely, for unknown reasons.[26] Michael Jones has speculated that he may have shared Gloucester's distaste for the treaty and that he remonstrated with Edward IV about it, thereby consigning himself to oblivion for the rest of that king's reign.[27]

Other explanations for Edward IV's apparently aloof behaviour toward Buckingham abound. Some argue that Buckingham was squeezed out by the Woodvilles, while others suggest that Edward IV disliked him personally, regarded him as unstable or untrustworthy or incompetent, or distrusted him because of his Lancastrian connections or because of his royal ancestry. For his own part, Buckingham must have bitterly resented Edward IV's refusal to hand over his share of the Bohun inheritance, to which Buckingham had a claim after the deaths of Henry VI and Edward of Lancaster in 1471. As Carole Rawcliffe points out, doing so would have not only cost Edward IV over £1,000 per year in lost income but would have emphasised Buckingham's claim to the throne through the House of Lancaster.[28] In this respect, it probably did not help that Buckingham in 1474 had sought and received permission to use the arms of his ancestor Thomas of Woodstock.[29]

Whatever the reason the Crown had kept Buckingham at a distance, he must have seen a chance for a fresh start with Gloucester. The men would have had chances to encounter each other over the years; one of the occasions when they can be found together at court is when they, along with Rivers, Dorset, and other noblemen, had paid homage to young Prince Edward on 9 November 1477.[30] Whether they were previously close, or whether their newfound alliance was born of opportunism, is unknown.

Meanwhile, England was laying its Yorkist king to rest. On 17 April, the body was taken to Westminster Abbey. Lionel, Bishop of Salisbury was one of the ecclesiastics present. Among the lords following the coffin were Dorset, Edward Woodville, and Richard Woodville, the latter making one of his rare recorded public appearances. Early the next day, the mourners left for Windsor, where Edward IV was laid to rest on 19 April.[31]

Finally, Edward V and his entourage, including Rivers, Richard Grey, and Thomas Vaughan, left Ludlow on 24 April, having observed St George's Day the day before.[32] By 29 April, the king was at Stony Stratford, 52 miles from London. Buckingham and Gloucester arrived at Northampton, 11 miles south of Stony Stratford.[33] Rivers, accompanied by Richard Grey, either rode from Stony Stratford to Northampton to meet Gloucester or remained at Northampton to meet him while the king moved on to Stony Stratford. In any case, he paid his respects to Gloucester and Buckingham, and the men enjoyed a convivial evening before going to bed.

Then Gloucester struck. On the morning of 30 April, either before the company had left Northampton or as they were riding together toward Stony Stratford, he and Buckingham arrested Rivers and Richard Grey. At Stony Stratford, they seized Thomas Vaughan, who had been by Edward's side since the king's infancy, and informed the shocked young king that the they had acted out of necessity. According to Mancini, the king made a spirited reply to the two dukes, telling them that he had seen 'nothing evil' in the three men 'and wished to keep them unless otherwise proved to be evil'. His protests were to no avail, however, and Gloucester soon dispatched the men toward his castles in the north: Rivers to Sheriff Hutton, Richard Grey to Middleham, and Thomas Vaughan possibly to Pontefract.[34]

It would be a few hours before the news hit London. In the meantime, Edward Woodville set off to sea to deal with the French, on whose behalf Philippe de Crèvecoeur, also known as Lord Cordes, had been staging raids on English ships since the death of Edward IV. The council had appointed Edward to deal with this situation and put 2,000 men under his command. As he probably embarked from Porchester, and possibly had left on 29 April rather than 30 April, he likely had no idea, as he sailed out of the harbour, of the storm he was leaving behind.[35]

By the evening of 30 April, the queen heard the horrifying news that her brother Anthony and her son Richard Grey had been arrested and that the king was in the power of Gloucester, an uncle he hardly knew. Taking her remaining royal children with her, she fled into sanctuary at Westminster Abbey. Mancini reports that the queen and Dorset tried first to raise troops, whereas Crowland tells us that unnamed supporters of the queen stood by the queen at Westminster while supporters of Hastings collected in London.[36] Lionel Woodville, who had been at Oxford on 26 April, had joined his sister in sanctuary by 9 June, as reported by a private letter from Simon Stallworth to Sir William Stonor. Mancini thought Dorset to have accompanied his mother into sanctuary, although Gloucester himself appeared to have believed he was at large.[37]

This is a good time to pause to ask, was there a Woodville plot against Gloucester? We have only Gloucester's word for it, and on balance, it seems unlikely. Mancini, a foreigner with no reason to cover up evidence of such a plot if he believed in one, clearly was sceptical, and Crowland explicitly described Rivers and the rest as innocent.[38] Furthermore, Anthony's unguarded actions belie such a plot. Had he been planning to destroy Gloucester, it hardly seems logical that he would have taken no precautions when he met the duke at Northampton – indeed, there was no reason why he should have gone to Northampton at all when he could have been making his way with his charge to London, and to the rest of the Woodvilles, instead. His men at Stony Stratford were equally unprepared for trouble, and surrendered Edward V to Gloucester with no resistance. As for the queen, while her flight into sanctuary has been taken by some as consciousness of guilt, flight can be indicative of fear as well. Having lived through the events of 1469 to 1471, which included her husband's exile and the murders of her father and her brother, Elizabeth had every reason to fear for her future once she heard of the events in Northampton and Stony Stratford.

Why, then, did Gloucester move against the Woodvilles on the night of 30 April? He and the Woodvilles were not natural enemies, for there is no evidence predating April 1483 of ill-will between them and Richard. If Richard held them responsible for the death of Clarence, as claimed by Mancini, there are no signs of it at the time of Clarence's death, nor are there signs that Gloucester, who had been squabbling over the Warwick inheritance with Clarence in the 1470s, was particularly close to his brother. If Gloucester had any opinions about his brother's marriage to Elizabeth – as he was a youngster in 1464, his opinion hardly counted at the time – he kept them to himself, and he sided with his brother throughout the period of 1469 to 1471. Kendall's musings that the queen 'would have known how to show her haughtiness to the undersized lad from Yorkshire' and that she viewed him and his brother 'only as rivals of her family for the favors of her lord' are pure fantasy; no source suggests that the queen or her relatives treated the young Gloucester with disrespect.[39] The Woodvilles were no threat to his power and influence in the north, nor is there any evidence that they drove a wedge between Gloucester and the king. Two members of the family, Edward Woodville and the Marquis of Dorset, served under him in Scotland, and the former was made a knight banneret at Gloucester's hands. Just a few weeks before his arrest, Anthony Woodville named Richard as arbitrator of a dispute. In 1469, the queen had appointed Gloucester steward of certain of her estates at £100 per year.[40] None of Edward IV's deathbed worries centred around Gloucester's getting on with the Woodvilles. Though it is common for Richard's modern-day admirers to claim that Gloucester would have been eliminated by the Woodvilles if they had been given the chance, there is in reality no reason to believe that had Rivers and his entourage been allowed to bring Edward V to London undisturbed, they and Gloucester could not have cooperated during a royal minority. That there might have been some friction is inevitable, but it need not have been fatal.

With the dearth of any convincing evidence that the Woodvilles were plotting against Gloucester – and the fact that Rivers and the others were never given a proper trial, where such evidence could have been presented, is suggestive in itself – we are left with several alternatives. One is that

Gloucester genuinely believed that there was a plot against him, which is not impossible given the hysterical tone of his later propaganda. Another is that Gloucester was determined to have no rivals for power in his role as protector and was prepared to take whatever drastic measures were required to achieve this goal. Yet another is that Gloucester had already decided to seize the throne.[41]

But for the time being, the 12-year-old Edward V seemed destined to reign, and to someday rule. On 4 May – what would have been his coronation – Edward V rode into town, escorted with all due respect by Gloucester and Buckingham. Before the king arrived in the city, Gloucester and Buckingham sent cartloads of goods bearing the arms of the queen's brothers and sons, which criers claimed had been stored up at various spots outside the capital in readiness for the Woodvilles to ambush and kill Gloucester as he passed through the countryside. Mancini reported, however, that 'many knew these charges to be false, because the arms in question had been placed there [...] when war was being waged against the Scots'. Gloucester was equally unsuccessful at persuading the council to condemn the prisoners on grounds of preparing ambushes and of being guilty of treason. The councillors found that there was 'no certain case as regards the ambushes'; even if there had been, they pointed out, it could not be treason because Gloucester did not hold the regency or any other public office.[42] While Mancini was incorrect in his assumption that the council could itself condemn (or not condemn) Rivers and the others to death, and in his statement that Gloucester held no public office, there is no reason to doubt the gist of his statement – that the council was not willing to countenance bringing treason charges against the men.

His coronation now postponed to 22 June, Edward V lodged at the Bishop's Palace at St Paul's, where he remained a few days until the council decided to move him to more spacious lodgings. Buckingham suggested the Tower, to which the rest of the council (now presided over by Gloucester as protector), agreed. Nonetheless, Crowland reports, some were troubled about the detention of Rivers and the rest in prison, while others believed that Gloucester was not showing sufficient respect for the queen's 'dignity and peace of mind'.[423]

Far from reassuring the queen, Gloucester had turned his attentions to her brother Edward Woodville. On 9 May, he ordered that Porchester Castle, which had been put into Edward's keeping on 1 March 1480, be delivered to William Ovedale; he gave a similar order with respect to Carisbrooke Castle, of which Anthony had been constable. The next day, he ordered men to 'go to the Downs among Sir Edward and his company'. On 14 May, Gloucester issued a more explicit instruction: Edward Brampton, John Welles, Thomas Grey, and others were to go to the sea ('with ships', the order specified) to arrest Edward. The men were authorised to receive all who would come except for Dorset, Edward Woodville, and Robert Ratcliffe, an associate of Anthony's.[44] Most likely, Gloucester intended for Dorset and Edward Woodville to share the fate of Anthony and Richard Grey.

Edward, meanwhile, had been busy harassing French ships, evidently capturing some, as a later agreement between Gloucester and Lord Cordes referred to French ships being held at Sandwich and Plymouth as well as 'other prizes and takings'.[45] On 14 May, the very day that Gloucester ordered his arrest, Edward seized £10,250 in English gold coins from a vessel at Southampton as forfeit to the Crown. There is no reason to doubt that Edward, apparently unaware of events on shore, was acting in good faith. Edward gave an indenture in which he bound himself to repay the sum in English merchandise should the gold not be found to be forfeit; if the gold was found to be forfeit, he bound himself to answer to the king for this sum.[46]

Once word got out that Edward was a wanted man, according to Mancini, the Genoese captains of two of his ships, fearing reprisals against their countrymen in England if they disobeyed Gloucester's orders, encouraged the English soldiers on board to drink heavily ('for the tedium of navigation should be banished by joyous potations'), then bound the befuddled men with ropes and chains. With the Englishmen immobilised, the Genoese announced their intent to return to England, and all but two of the ships, those under the command of Edward Woodville himself, followed suit. Horrox, however, suggests more prosaically that this vinous tale aside, the majority of Edward's captains simply recognised Gloucester's authority as protector and obeyed his orders accordingly.[47]

Edward Woodville – perhaps with his gold coins seized at Southampton, unless he had been so unlucky as to have placed them on one of the deserting ships – sailed on to Brittany, where he joined the exiled Henry Tudor. There, he received a pension of 100 livres a month from Duke Francis of Brittany.[48]

Having failed to capture Edward Woodville, Gloucester contented himself with seizing Woodville possessions. Although nothing indicates that Richard Woodville, obscure as ever, had been accused of anything, the fact that he was a Woodville sufficed for Gloucester to seize his manor of Wymington in Bedfordshire on 19 May. Two days later, Gloucester's ally Francis, Viscount Lovell, received Richard Grey's manor of Thorpe Waterville in Northamptonshire. Even young Anne St Leger, who had been slated to marry Dorset's son, was handed over to the Duke of Buckingham, in preference to her own father, Thomas St Leger. Richard Haute, the queen's cousin, who had been arrested along with Rivers, Grey, and Vaughen, was relieved of his manor of Ightham Mote on 14 May on Gloucester's orders.[49] As Rosemary Horrox points out, these moves were of dubious legality, which contrasts poorly with the reputation for fair dealing that Richard III has acquired in the eyes of his admirers.

The question of the Woodvilles' goods and property leads to another question in a time period that brims with them: Had the Woodvilles – or at least three of them – made off with the royal treasury? This story, often reported as an established fact, comes from a single contemporary source: Mancini, who tells us that at about the time Edward Woodville put off to sea, 'it was commonly believed that the late king's treasure, which had taken such years and such pains to gather, was divided between the queen, the marquess, and Edward'.[50]

In looking at this statement, it should first be noted that Mancini is not giving an eyewitness account, but merely reporting that the story of the treasury raid was 'commonly believed'. Thus, Mancini's statement may merely reflect the current gossip – or propaganda – about the Woodvilles' doings. Mancini himself gives no indication of whether he shared the common belief or whether he thought it to be well founded.

Even more important, Rosemary Horrox in her examination of the financial memoranda of Edward V's reign has concluded that there was very little treasure to be divided. She writes that the measures against the French, costing £3,670, had depleted the cash reserves left by Edward IV and that these expenditures likely were the source of Mancini's tale of a Woodville treasury raid.[51] Moreover, as Horrox notes, Edward IV's cash reserves were low to begin with, thanks to two years of war with Scotland.[52]

If there was any treasure to be divided up, there is no evidence that Elizabeth Woodville had any share of it. Certainly, Gloucester took no steps, either as Edward V's protector or after he became King Richard III, to recover any treasure from Elizabeth. Had there been any in her possession, he would have certainly required her to disgorge it either on 7 May 1483, when the Archbishop of Canterbury ordered the sequestration of Edward IV's goods, jewels, and seals,[53] on 16 June 1483, when Gloucester sent numerous armed men to Westminster Abbey to help persuade Elizabeth to surrender her youngest son to Gloucester's custody,[54] or no later than 1 March 1484, when Elizabeth agreed to leave sanctuary and was given a pension by Richard III.[55] It is hardly comprehensible that Richard III, who as we have seen was actively seizing Woodville lands as early as mid-May of 1483, would have sat back passively and allowed Elizabeth to keep treasure to which she had no legal right.

There is no evidence that Edward Woodville took stolen royal treasure with him, although royal funds would have certainly been expended in fitting him and his ships out for his mission against the French. Notably, at around the time of his coronation in July, Richard instructed Doctor Thomas Huton to inform the Duke of Brittany that debts owed to his subjects by Edward IV would be paid once his goods had been administered. In the same letter, he charged Huton to inquire about the duke's intentions toward Edward Woodville; had Edward been in possession of royal treasure, Richard would surely have said so, as it would have given the duke an incentive to hand him over to Richard so that his subjects could more speedily collect their debts.[56]

As for Dorset, Simon Stallworth wrote a letter on 9 June 1483, stating, 'Where so ever can be found any goods of my lord Marquis it is taken. The Prior of Westminster was and yet is in a great trouble for certain goods delivered to him by my Lord Marquis'. Armstrong has interpreted this letter to mean that Gloucester, as protector, was attempting to recover Dorset's share of the treasure, but it is noteworthy that the reference is to 'goods of my lord marquis', i.e. to the marquis's own goods, not to goods in his possession belonging to the Crown. It seems more likely, then, that Gloucester's agents were simply rounding up property belonging to the marquis, as part of the seizure of Woodville property in which Gloucester then was engaged. The 'certain goods' delivered to the Prior of Westminster could refer to stolen treasure, but it could also simply mean that Dorset was attempting to conceal or safeguard his own property by leaving it with the prior. Thus, all Stallworth's letter tells us is that there was official interest in Dorset's goods, but it furnishes no clue as to their nature.

On 7 May, the king's executors met to discuss the king's funeral, and the supervisor of the king's will, the Archbishop of Canterbury, ordered the sequestration of the king's goods. Elizabeth was not among those at the meeting. Although some writers, such as Kendall, have asserted that her absence meant that the king had stricken her from the list of executors before his death, there is no evidence of this, given that only the king's 1475 will, not a subsequent will or codicils, has survived. As Anne Sutton and Livia Visser-Fuchs note, the list of executors meeting on 7 May does not purport to be a list of all those named as executors, and Elizabeth, being in sanctuary, had an obvious reason for not attending.[57]

Elizabeth's continuance in sanctuary, however, remained a concern. On 23 May, two oaths were read before the Common Council of London: the first being the oath that Gloucester, Buckingham, and others had sworn to Edward V; the second being the oath these same people were prepared to swear to Elizabeth if she wished to come out of sanctuary.[58] Whether Elizabeth herself was approached is unclear; if she was, she apparently was not reassured for her safety or that of her children. Perhaps she was waiting to see what would become of her brother and her son, still languishing in northern strongholds with no formal charges or indictments having been brought against them.

It may be that Elizabeth was also waiting for her son's coronation to determine her next move. In the first days of June, preparations were moving along briskly, leading Simon Stallworth to report to Sir William Stonor on 9 June that there was 'great business against [i.e. in preparation for] the coronation', which was to take place in a fortnight. Stallworth added, however, that although Gloucester, Buckingham, and other lords had met in council from ten to two, no one had spoken to the queen.[59]

Behind the scenes, something else entirely was going on. The next day, Gloucester wrote a letter to the mayor of York demanding that the city send forces:

> to aid and assist us against the queen, her blood adherents and affinity, which have intended and daily doth intend, to murder and utterly destroy us and our cousin, the duke of Buckingham, and the old royal blood of this realm, and it is now openly known, by their subtle and damnable ways forecasted the same, and also the final destruction and [disinheritance] of you and all other the inheritors and men of honour, as well of the north parts as other counties, that belong unto us.

On 11 June, Gloucester wrote to Lord Neville, a northern lord, asking that he send men defensibly arrayed 'in all the haste that was possible'.[60]

Was this a real crisis, or one manufactured by Gloucester? Because Elizabeth, her sons, and her brothers at this point were either in prison, in sanctuary, in hiding, or out of the country, they were hardly in a position to do Gloucester physical harm, much less his entire affinity. Gloucester did, however, lay a second charge against the Woodvilles, that they 'by their subtle and damnable ways forecasted the same' – a reference to making astrological predictions. At first glance, this charge is not implausible. There is no evidence that any of the Woodvilles possessed astrological skills, but as John Leland points out, there were astrologers with connections to the queen or to other opponents of Gloucester who could have been employed. Even if the Woodvilles were not using astrology against Gloucester, they might well have found a pressing need to determine what the future held.[61] The problem with this argument, however, is that none of the men suggested as candidates by Leland – Thomas Nandyke, Lewis Caerleon, and John Argentine – were accused by Gloucester of aiding the queen, nor did they suffer imprisonment or other penalties at the time. Argentine, Edward V's physician, remained with his charge until being dismissed sometime after the young king was deposed. Nandyken, who was associated with the Duke of Buckingham, and Lewis Caerleon, who was associated with Margaret Beaufort, Countess of Richmond, were at large to plot against Gloucester after he became king.[62] No one else is known to have been accused of practising astrology against Gloucester at this time. It defies reason that if Gloucester genuinely believed that astrology was being employed against him in his capacity as protector – which could be regarded as treason – he would do nothing to investigate or punish the astrologers responsible.

Whatever the plausibility of Gloucester's accusations against the Woodvilles in his requests for troops, the request themselves were certainly genuine. Was Gloucester simply taking precautions to make sure the coronation, and his continuance as protector, would go smoothly? Was he genuinely worried about a Woodville threat to destroy him and all of his followers? Or had he determined on another course of action? We can only guess at what might have been in Gloucester's mind, but the next two weeks would change the course of English history and ultimately lead to the destruction of an entire dynasty.

Since the coup at Stony Stratford, Crowland tells us, William, Lord Hastings, had been in the best of moods: 'bursting with joy over this new world' and 'asserting that nothing had so far been done except to transfer the government of the kingdom from two blood-relatives of the queen to two nobles of the blood royal [...] with only so much bloodshed in the affair as might have come from a cut finger'. Then, on Friday 13 June, he arrived for a council meeting at the Tower.

There are numerous versions of what happened next, some more embroidered than others, but all agree in substance: Gloucester accused Hastings of treason, then ordered his beheading without giving him anything faintly resembling a trial. Thomas Rotherham, Archbishop of York, and John Morton, Bishop of Ely were also arrested, as were several others, including Oliver King, secretary to Edward V. The next day, John Forster, who had been an official of the queen, was arrested at his home in Hertfordshire, while in the coming days, Mancini, who believed the charges against Hastings were fabricated, nonetheless noted that Gloucester had used Buckingham to sound the loyalty of him, Rotherham, and York and that he had learned that they foregathered in each other's houses.

There are broadly two schools of thought as to Hastings's arrest and murder – under the circumstances, 'execution' hardly seems adequate. One is that Gloucester killed Hastings purely as a preemptive strike, having determined at that point to seize the crown and knowing that Edward IV's close friend would stand in the way of his ambitions to supplant the late king's heir. The other, naturally, is that Hastings had begun to plot against Gloucester, either out of suspicion as to his intentions toward Edward V or for nefarious reasons of his own.[63]

Members of the second school of thought generally implicate Elizabeth Woodville in Hastings's supposed plotting, although the link between her and Hastings at this point is tenuous at best. Neither Crowland nor Mancini, both of whom view Hastings as innocent, mention the Woodvilles in connection with Hastings. It is only in the Tudor era that Elizabeth Woodville comes into the picture, most famously in the account of Thomas More, who claims that in the moments before accusing Hastings, Gloucester displayed his withered arm and accused the queen and Hastings's mistress, 'Shore's wife', of having used sorcery to waste his body.[64] Polydor Vergil tells us that Gloucester, having twice declared in front of his council that he was being destroyed by Elizabeth's sorcery, then accused Hastings himself of working to destroy him before ordering his summary execution.[65] From this scant evidence, it has been posited that Hastings, having thought better of his support of Gloucester, made common cause with Elizabeth Woodville in his scheming.

This scenario seems unlikely. While it could be argued that Gloucester's letters of 10 and 11 June could refer to a Hastings–Woodville plot, they do not mention Hastings. Furthermore, if Gloucester did have suspicions of Hastings at that point that were serious enough to justify calling for troops, it follows that these same suspicions would have justified the arrest

Above: Church of St Mary the Virgin in Grafton Regis. John Woodville, grandfather to Richard Woodville, 1st Earl Rivers, is buried here. The inscription of his slab indicates that he erected the church's bell tower.

Right: Artist Mark Satchwill's impression of how Jacquetta, Duchess of Bedford might have looked around the time of her second marriage (Mark Satchwill, 2013)

Signature of Jacquetta on receipt relating to Rockingham Forest, 4 November 1455 (Permission of National Archives)

Garter stall plate of Richard Woodville, 1st Earl Rivers. (*Stall Plates of the Knights of the Order of the Garter,* 1348–1485, edited by Sir William Henry St John Hope)

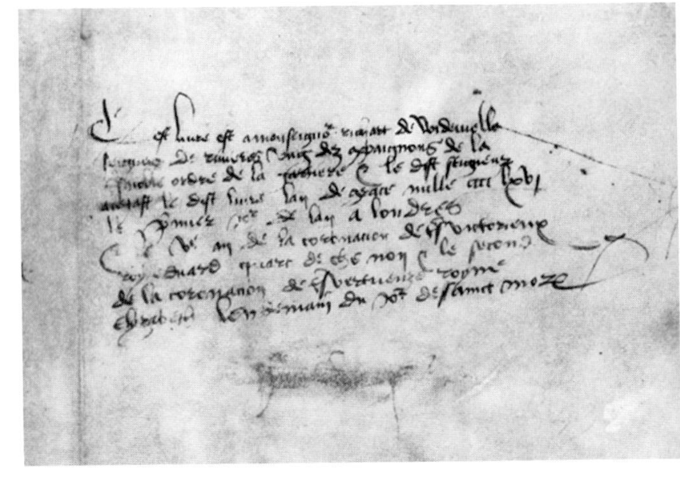

Inscription by Richard Woodville, 1st Earl Rivers, on a manuscript of the romance Alexander (MS Bodl. 264), purchased on the second aniversary of his daughter's coronation. (Permission of Bodleian Libraries)

Right: Portrait of Elizabeth Woodville, bearing the probably incorrect date of 1463. This, like other portraits of Elizabeth, is a copy of a lost original. (Heritage Images)

Right: Portrait of Edward IV. (Heritage Images)

Above: Manuscript illustration of Elizabeth Woodville commemorating her membership in the Fraternity of the Assumption of the Virgin Mary of the Skinner's Company of London. (Private Collection / The Bridgeman Art Library)

Opposite top: Stained glass at Canterbury Cathedral depicting Edward IV and his edlest son, the future Edward V. (Canterbury Cathedral, Kent, UK / The Bridgeman Art Library)

Opposite bottom: Stained glass at Canterbury Cathedral depicting Elizabeth Woodville and her daughters Elizabeth, Cecily and Anne. (Canterbury Cathedral, Kent, UK / The Bridgeman Art Library)

Elizabetha consors
gracia
dña Elizabeth
prima filia
Edwardi quarti
dña Cecilia
filia
Edwardi quarti
tertia filia
Edwardi quarti

Left: Stained glass at Little Malvern Priory depicting the future Edward V, dated 1480–82. (Adrian Fletcher, www.paradoxplace.com)

Right: Stained glass at Little Malvern Priory depicting four of Edward IV and Elizabeth Woodville's daughters, dated 1480–82. (Adrian Fletcher, www.paradoxplace.com)

Above: Presentation portrait showing a kneeling Anthony Woodville, Earl Rivers giving his translation of *The Dicts and Sayings of the Philosophers* to Edward IV. (Lambeth Palace Library, London, UK / The Bridgeman Art Library)

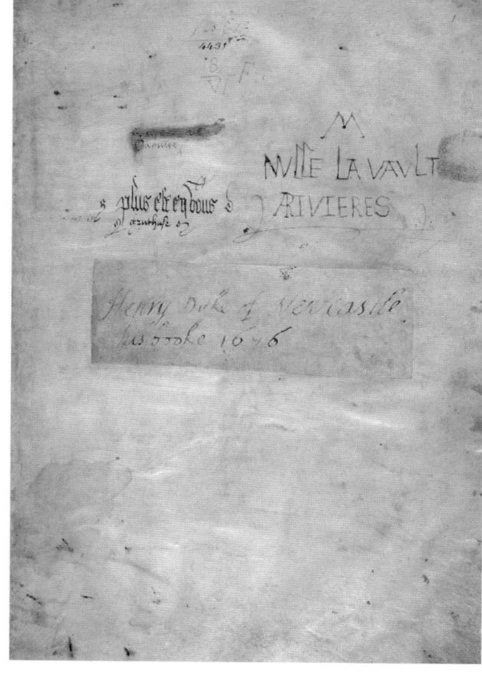

Right: Flyleaf from Harleian MS 4431, a manuscript of the works of Christine de Pizan signed by Jacquetta, Duchess of Bedford, her son Anthony, Earl Rivers, and Louis de Bruges. Anthony's motto *Nulle la Vaut* survives only here. Livia Visser-Fuchs has suggested it menas 'nobody is as worthy as she'. (British Library)

Left: Gatehouse of Carisbrooke Castle. Anthony, Earl Rivers was its constable. Edward Woodville was later granted the castle by Henry VII. (Chris Moncrieff / Dreamstime.com)

Below: Victorian stained glass at Cardiff Castle representing Katherine Woodville, Duchess of Bedford and Buckingham, and her second husband, Jasper Tudor, Duke of Bedford. (Wendy Marshall)

of Hastings then, instead of two or three days later.[66] As for the Vergil and More claims: while they may be correct in reporting that Gloucester linked the queen and Hastings in his accusations – his claim about the queen's sorcery echoes his 10 June letter – neither of them gave them credence. More scoffed, 'well they wist that the queen was too wise to go about any such folly', while Vergil spoke of Gloucester setting a trap for Hastings with his accusations.[67]

The notion of a Hastings–Woodville conspiracy has been further embroidered by modern conjecture that Mistress Shore – supposedly a former mistress of Edward IV, and in some accounts that of Hastings as well – was the go-between for Hastings and the queen.[68] This, though a beguiling theory, seems unlikely. Gloucester himself never linked Mistress Shore to Hastings, only to Dorset, whom he later accused of holding 'the unshameable and mischievous woman called Shore's wife' in adultery.[69] While Mistress Shore was indeed in prison as of 21 June, the cause of her incarceration is not recorded.[70] It seems likely that her crime was not in helping the queen and Hastings plot treason, but was connected with Dorset, whose goods, as we recall, were of great interest to the protector earlier in June. Notably, it is around this time that, according to Mancini, Dorset left sanctuary and was subject to a royal manhunt, which makes it all the more likely that Mistress Shore's arrest was connected with him.[71] Nor was Mistress Shore ideally placed to be a liaison between Hastings and the queen: visitors to Elizabeth in sanctuary would have doubtlessly been closely monitored by royal authorities, and as Dorset's mistress, Mistress Shore's visits to the queen would have aroused suspicion from the very beginning.

Hastings's killing was a turning point for Gloucester, after which, as Crowland puts it, he and Buckingham 'did whatever they wanted'. What they wanted to do next became apparent on 16 June, when, accompanied by a 'great crowd, with swords and clubs', they came by boat to Westminster and dragooned the old Archbishop of Canterbury to lead a delegation to persuade the queen to allow her younger son, the Duke of York, to leave sanctuary and join his brother Edward V in the Tower. Faced with the authority of the Church and the power of a group of armed men, Elizabeth, who may not have even known of Hastings's death the previous Friday, agreed. As Mancini put it, 'When the queen saw herself besieged and preparation for violence, she surrendered her son, trusting in the word of the cardinal of Canterbury that the boy should be restored after the coronation'.[72] In hindsight, it was the worst mistake of Elizabeth Woodville's life, but the queen could have hardly guessed what would happen next. She would never see her sons by Edward IV again.

With both Edward V and his younger brother lodged in the Tower, Gloucester postponed the coronation yet again, this time to 9 November. The mood in London was growing increasingly jittery: on 21 June, Simon Stallworth, reporting the departure of the Duke of York from sanctuary and the arrest of Mistress Shore, among other titbits, wrote to Sir William Stonor in the country, 'For tidings I hold you happy that you are out of the press, for with us is much trouble, and every man doubts other'. He added that 20,000 men belonging to Gloucester and Buckingham were expected: 'to what intent I know not but to keep the peace'.[73]

Gloucester, according to Mancini, by this time had cast off his mourning and was swanning about London clad in purple, surrounded by 1,000 men. On Sunday 22 June, he treated the Londoners to sermons claiming that Edward IV had been conceived in adultery and looked nothing like his alleged father, unlike Gloucester, the spitting image of the man. This line of argument, which is also mentioned by Thomas More, does not seem to have gone far. Either Gloucester belatedly remembered his filial duty to the old Duchess of York, who was very much alive, or the Londoners found it impossible to believe that the proud old lady had made a cuckold of her husband in her youth. It was the other thread of Gloucester's argument – that Edward IV's children were illegitimate – that ultimately carried the day.[74]

As embodied in the 1484 Act of Parliament confirming Richard III's title as king (known as Titulus Regius), there were four grounds for declaring Edward IV's marriage to Elizabeth invalid and his children thus illegitimate: that the marriage was made without the knowledge or assent of the lords of the land; that it was procured by sorcery and witchcraft on the part of Elizabeth Woodville and her mother; that it was made privately and secretly; and that before Edward had married Elizabeth, he had been married to Eleanor Butler, a daughter of the deceased Earl of Shrewsbury.[75] The first three grounds need not concern us much. It was certainly not necessarily to the validity of his marriage that Edward gain the consent of his lords, although doing so would have been politic. Secrecy did not in itself render a marriage invalid at the time, although as R.H. Helmholz points out, it could prevent a couple from arguing that a marriage was conducted in good faith and therefore could prevent the children of that match from being deemed legitimate.[76] As for witchcraft, as noted in Chapter 5, Parliament offered no proof of its allegations.

It is the fourth allegation – the alleged marriage to Eleanor Butler – that has excited the most debate. It is noteworthy that other than the lady's name and that of her father, Titulus Regius gives no details about the supposed marriage – a fact that is in itself suspicious, since surely on a matter as important as the entitlement to the crown, a draftsman would want to give as much credence to the claim as possible by including the pertinent facts.

Eleanor Butler, née Talbot, whose birth John Ashdown-Hill estimates as taking place around February 1436,[77] was married to Thomas Butler around 1449 to 1450 and widowed in 1459, having not borne any surviving children. Her uncle was the Earl of Warwick, and her sister, Elizabeth, was married to John Mowbray, Duke of Norfolk. Through these connections, and others, she certainly could have come into contact with the new Yorkist king, and the fact that she was a few years his senior would probably not have troubled him, as the case of Elizabeth Woodville shows. It is not implausible that Edward IV might have married her secretly – but it is entirely unproven, despite attempts by Richard III's modern-day defenders to build a case for the marriage based on the shakiest of evidence.

As noted in Chapter 9, only one source, Philip de Commynes, indicates that Robert Stillington, later Bishop of Bath and Wales, actually joined Edward and Eleanor in wedlock. (Admirers of Richard III have been less eager to support Commynes's claim in the preceding paragraph that Richard 'barbarously murdered his two nephews'.)[78] Other sources, however, suggest that rather than providing evidence, Stillington helped Gloucester frame his allegations. Eustace Chapuys, imperial ambassador and loyal partisan of Catherine of Aragon in Henry VIII's reign, wrote on 3 November 1534 that 'Richard III declared by definitive sentence of the Bishop of Bath that the daughters of king Edward [...] were bastards'. The previous year, on 16 December, he stated that Elizabeth of York 'was declared by sentence of the Bishop of Bath a bastard'.[79] More importantly, at Henry VII's first parliament in 1485, Stillington was spoken of as the man believed to have drawn up Titulus Regius; the peers asked whether he should be made to answer for it before Parliament. The king, having already pardoned Stillington, declined.[80] Stillington may indeed be the anonymous person referred to by Crowland, who writes that it was put about that the petition urging Gloucester to take the throne originated in the north, 'although there was no-one who did not know the identity of the author (who was in London all the time) of such sedition and infamy'.[81]

If Stillington was more than a draftsman, Henry VII's later treatment of him does not suggest this, for like Edward IV before him, as we have seen, he does not seem to have regarded Stillington as a person who had to be silenced. After having received his initial pardon, he was imprisoned in 1487, probably due to his involvement in the rebellions of that period, but seems to have been at his own episcopal manors in 1489 and 1491, albeit perhaps under house arrest.[82]

The circumstantial evidence given in support of the marriage is equally unconvincing. Ashdown-Hill notes that the source of certain lands in Wiltshire owned by Eleanor cannot be traced; he suggests that these were a gift from the king, either to support her or to keep her quiet, but is unable to provide evidence of the lands' royal origins.[83] Even if the lands were royal gifts, however, this need not mean that a marriage took place; the lands could equally be a parting gift from a lover. Another possibility is that they were a gift from Edward's predecessor, Henry VI, to Eleanor and her late husband. As further evidence, Ashdown-Hill offers the fact that Eleanor chose to deed certain land to her sister during her lifetime rather than to leave it to her in her will. She did this, he argues, because Eleanor considered herself to be married to the king and as a married woman could not bequeath real property by will without her husband's permission.[84] This argument, however, has a fatal flaw: a married woman also could not deed property without the permission of her husband. This was no arcane point of medieval law; it was a fact of everyday life of which anyone in the landowning classes would have been acutely aware. If Eleanor believed that she had a valid marriage to Edward IV that prevented her from making a will, she would have been equally unable to make a valid deed without her 'husband' joining in.

If Eleanor had any relationship with Edward before his marriage to Elizabeth Woodville, it could have as easily been as a mistress as a wife, which may have been what led to her name being linked to Edward's nineteen years after Edward had married Elizabeth Woodville. Eleanor's piety, well documented by Ashdown-Hill, need not have stopped her from falling for the handsome king's charms. It is true, as Ashdown-Hill states, that no contemporary source names Eleanor as his mistress,[85] but Eleanor's high social status may have led the pair to be discreet about their liaison. It is also noteworthy that the one person best placed to give evidence about Edward IV's sex life – his friend William, Lord Hastings, described by Mancini as 'the accomplice and partner of his privy pleasures'[86] – had been murdered just days before Gloucester began to circulate the story of the precontract. Did Gloucester know that Hastings was in a position to contradict him?

To clinch their argument that Eleanor Butler was indeed Edward IV's wife, Richard III's defenders have pointed to Elizabeth Woodville's failure to challenge Gloucester's claims, while excusing Eleanor Butler's own quite understandable failure to defy Edward IV by challenging the validity of the Woodville marriage. Annette Carson, for instance, writes in mitigation of Eleanor, 'One does not lightly attempt to enforce one's rights against a resistant king. Indeed, such an idea became fraught with difficulty, if not danger, once [...] the Woodville family entered the fray'. Aside from the gratuitous slur against the Woodvilles, this is a reasonable enough argument for Eleanor's failure to raise the issue, but all such considerations vanish when Carson contemplates Elizabeth Woodville's similar silence. Likewise, while Ashdown-Hill suggests that Eleanor 'may well have been putting her life in jeopardy' by taking her case to an ecclesiastical court, he sees no such obstacles in Elizabeth Woodville's case.[87] Such highly selective reasoning disingenuously ignores the position in which Elizabeth found herself. Gloucester had already murdered Hastings in cold blood, which could have hardly been reassuring. Even if Elizabeth herself was safe in sanctuary, three of her sons and one of her brothers were completely within Gloucester's power – and on 23 June, as we shall see, the situation would become even more grim. These circumstances were not conducive to taking a stand, either during the protectorate or thereafter. Nor was any canon lawyer inside England likely to dare to take such a claim on Elizabeth's behalf to the ecclesiastical courts, where, as Crowland points out, the matter of the validity of the king's marriage should have been decided in the first place.[88]

Part of the difficulty in proving (or disproving) the alleged precontract is that it took very little to enter into a valid marriage in medieval England.[89] A couple who exchanged vows of marriage in the present tense were (provided that they were legally able to consent) validly married, regardless of whether any witnesses were present. A couple who exchanged vows of marriage in the future tense were married once they consummated their relationship. Such informal marriages were frowned upon, but, in the eyes of the church they were as binding as a marriage preceded by banns and performed by a priest in front of a crowd of witnesses. Nonetheless, clandestine marriages presented obvious problems of proof when one spouse wanted to wriggle free; here, of course, the putative spouses were dead.

While the possibility that Edward IV did indeed marry Eleanor Butler cannot be ruled out entirely, in the end we are left with nothing to go on but Gloucester's self-serving, and conveniently vague, allegations. Certainly contemporaries were not universally convinced, as the later attempts to restore Edward V to the throne indicate.

On 24 or 25 June, Buckingham addressed a group of lords on the subject of the supposed illegitimacy of Edward IV's children and on the myriad advantages of having Gloucester as king instead. Unnerved by the prospect of 'armed men in frightening and unheard-of numbers' coming from the north and from Wales, and thoroughly rattled by the fate of Lord Hastings, the lords agreed. On 26 June, a bill setting out Gloucester's title to the throne was presented to Gloucester, who duly accepted and, as Crowland put it, 'thrust himself in the marble chair' at Westminster as King Richard III.[90]

Gloucester had taken care of one last bit of business before becoming king: ordering the execution of Rivers, Grey, and Vaughan. Rivers made his will at Sheriff Hutton on 23 June, indicating that the execution order had been sent from London at least a couple of days before that.

Rivers's will is a conventional one, in which Anthony is concerned with paying his debts, righting any wrongs he might have done, such as to Lady Willoughby, providing for the poor, and attending to the welfare of his soul. Perhaps anticipating that he would be brought south and given the trial in front of his peers that was his right as an earl, he asked that if he died beyond the River Trent, he be buried before Our Lady of Pewe at Westminster. During his stay up north, he had borrowed a sum of money from his fellow prisoner, Thomas Vaughen – an indication, perhaps that he and Vaughan had been imprisoned at the same castle. We learn the name of his barber, Tybold, who received 5 marks. Anthony appointed ten executors, one of which was his son-in-law, Robert Poyntz, and asked – fruitlessly, it appears – that Gloucester allow his executors to carry out the terms of his last testament.

After the seven witnesses signed the will, Rivers learned that he was to die at Pontefract. Dutifully, he changed his burial plans: 'My will is now to be buried before an image of our blessed Lady Mary, with my Lord Richard [Grey], in Pontefract'. Grey himself had been staying at Gloucester's stronghold of Middleton, along with his servants and horses, but was transported to Pontefract, where he and his uncle met for the last time on earth.[91] Thomas Vaughan, who had been serving the House of York when Gloucester was still a youngster, was also there at Pontefract to pay the price of his devoted service to his young charge, Edward V.

Crowland is adamant that Rivers, Grey, and Vaughan were beheaded 'without any form of trial' under the supervision of Sir Richard Ratcliffe, who was leading Gloucester's army south to London. John Rous, on the other hand, claims that Henry Percy, Earl of Northumberland, was their chief judge.[92] No records of their indictments or trial, if there were any, have survived, nor is there any indication of who besides Northumberland sat in judgement of the trio. One is inclined to suspect that any process must have been summary even by contemporary standards; certainly nothing indicates that a jury of peers was summoned to try Rivers, as was his right under Magna Carta.

Richard III laid out 46 shillings and fourpence (£2 *6s 4d*) for Richard Grey's burial; probably he paid for the other men's as well.[93] As Anthony's headless body was stripped, his executioners found next to his bare skin a hairshirt, a garment which, Rous tells us, he had long been in the habit of wearing. It came into the possession of the Carmelite friars at Doncaster, where for years after the earl's death, it hung before the image of the Blessed Mary the Virgin.

Before donning his hairshirt for the last time, Rivers had sought consolation in a time-honoured secular manner: writing poetry. Caxton tells us that Anthony had once made 'divers ballads against the seven deadly sins', but the last verses he wrote, printed in part by John Rous and later in full by Thomas Percy, are the only ones of his known to have survived:[94]

Somewhat musing
And more mourning
In remembering
The unsteadfastness;
This world being
Of such wheeling
Me contrarying
What may I guess?

I fear doubtless
Remediless
Is now to seize
My woeful chance;

For unkindness
Without the less,
And no redress
Me doth advance.

With displeasure
To my grievance
And no 'surance
Of remedy;
Lo! In this trance
Now in substance
Such is my dance
Willing to die.

Methinks truly
Bounden am I
And that greatly
To be content;
Seeing plainly
That fortune doth wry
All contrary
From mine intent.

My life was lent
Me to one intent
It is nigh spent;
Welcome Fortune!
But I ne'er went
Thus to be shent
But so it meant
Such is her won[t].

12

Under the Hog

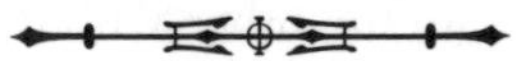

Because Richard III was a married man when he became king, his wife, Anne, would be crowned queen consort alongside him. She was not a well-known figure in London, so the crowd would have been especially interested to catch a glimpse of her on 6 July 1483 as she proceeded from Westminster Hall into Westminster Abbey. Few of those jostling for the best view would have wasted much time looking at the lady who was bearing the queen's train: Margaret, Countess of Richmond. Undersized and well past her youth at age 40, the stern-looking countess would have caught the eye not because of her person but because of her attire: a long gown of crimson velvet bordered with white cloth of gold.[1]

Eighteen years before, Jacquetta, Duchess of Bedford, had followed her daughter Elizabeth Woodville as she prepared to be crowned queen in this same abbey. Much had changed since then.

The nobility, many of whom were playing their parts in the coronation, either in the king's train or the queen's, might well have thought of that day in 1465. Others might have thought of the coronation that had never taken place, that of Edward V. That boy's mother, still in sanctuary elsewhere in the abbey, would have certainly heard the sounds of the coronation – the music and the cheers of the crowd – as she and her five daughters wondered what would become of them now that Elizabeth had been branded Edward IV's concubine and her children his bastards.

There were some conspicuous absences at the coronation. The king's mother, Cecily, Duchess of York, was not present. She had not attended Elizabeth Woodville's coronation either, so perhaps she simply preferred to avoid such events, or perhaps at her age she preferred not to travel beyond her castle of Berkhamsted. Then again, if her son had indeed impugned her honour, she might have chosen to stay away. The queen's mother, Anne, Countess of Warwick, was also absent. Perhaps she too chose not to make the long trip from the north, or perhaps, as one who had been declared by Parliament for the benefit of her sons-in-law to have the status of one naturally dead, her presence was considered rather awkward. And although Henry Stafford, Duke of Buckingham, was very much at the coronation – as the king's great chamberlain, he carried the king's train in one hand and his white staff of office in the other – his duchess was nowhere to be seen. As she was a Woodville, there is no need to wonder at her absence; the only question is whether she was ordered to stay away or chose of her own volition not to attend. Lionel, Bishop of Salisbury, was also missing, as were all of Queen Elizabeth's other surviving siblings.

The new king was a few months short of his 31st birthday and was, it seems, in excellent health. For Elizabeth Woodville, her siblings, and her children – some in hiding, some in sanctuary, some in exile, some sitting on their estates far from court, some locked in the Tower – it must have seemed that Richard would be on the throne for many years.

They reckoned without the lady carrying Queen Anne's train.

✣ ✣ ✣

Born in 1443, Margaret Beaufort was the daughter of John Beaufort, Duke of Somerset, who had returned to England in disgrace after an ill-managed campaign in France.[2] A possible suicide, he had hardly known his only daughter, who had been an infant when he died in 1444. After a brief, unconsummated child marriage to John de la Pole, Duke of Suffolk, Margaret had married Edmund Tudor, Earl of Richmond, Henry VI's half-brother, in 1455. Probably anxious to father a child on Margaret so that he could have her estates in the event of her death, Richmond had wasted no time in consummating his marriage to Margaret, but it was he who died in 1456, leaving a pregnant young widow behind. Margaret bore her only child, Henry Tudor, in January 1457, when she was not yet 14.

Taken under the protection of her brother-in-law, Jasper Tudor, Earl of Pembroke, Margaret married Henry Stafford, a younger son of Humphrey Stafford, Duke of Buckingham, in 1458. Despite the couple's Lancastrian ties – Buckingham, a supporter of Henry VI, died at Northampton, while Margaret's male Beaufort cousins all were either beheaded or killed in battle for their support of that king – Stafford supported Edward IV at Barnet, but was wounded and died later that year. Margaret had then married Thomas Stanley, the king's steward.

Her son, Henry, had had a precarious youth. He had been made the ward of William, Lord Herbert, in 1462. Like Richard, Earl Rivers, Herbert, made Earl of Pembroke by Edward IV in 1469, had been targeted by the Earl of Warwick as a royal favourite to be eliminated. When Warwick rebelled in 1469, Herbert was accompanied to the Battle of Edgecote by his young ward, whose first experience of war ended disastrously when his guardian was captured and led off to execution. Sir Richard Corbet took Henry from the battlefield to the home of Herbert's brother-in-law, Lord Ferrers.[3] Margaret's negotiations to recover her son's wardship were interrupted by the turmoil over the next few months, but when Henry VI's restoration to the throne brought the exiled Jasper Tudor back to England, Henry Tudor was reunited with his uncle and then his mother in October 1470. It was a brief reunion between mother and son: after a meeting with Henry VI, who supposedly prophesied that the boy would become king, Henry, in Jasper's care, departed for Wales in November. Holed up at Pembroke Castle after Edward IV's victories at Barnet and Tewkesbury, Jasper and Henry escaped to Brittany in September 1471 and had remained there in exile ever since.

Margaret had come near to restoring her son to his country and to his inheritance. In 1482, she and Edward IV agreed that Henry Tudor would return from exile and receive a portion of the estates of Margaret's recently deceased mother. A pardon was drafted, and there was even talk of Henry's marrying Edward's oldest daughter. Before the scheme could reach fruition, however, Edward IV died, leaving Margaret having to start over with a new king. Undaunted, she opened negotiations with Richard, using her kinsman Buckingham as an intermediary, to allow Henry to return to England and marry one of Richard's newly bastardised nieces. Soon, however, Margaret's plans changed radically.

Shortly after his coronation, Richard left on a royal progress, allowing his new subjects, many of whom in the hinterlands must have been bewildered at having had three kings in three months, to get a look at the latest wearer of the crown. One of his stops, on 26 July, was at Oxford. The chancellor who greeted him was likely not Lionel, Bishop of Salisbury, but Master William Harford, described as chancellor in a commission of the peace for Oxford dated 26 August.[4] For the bishop to have to exchange pleasantries with the man who had ordered his brother's and nephew's execution would have been an awkward business indeed.

Meanwhile, the Londoners were bestirring themselves at last. On 29 July at Minster Lovell, Richard III wrote a letter to his chancellor, John Russell, Bishop of Lincoln, in which he ordered him to take action against 'certain persons' who had been engaged in what is described only as an 'enterprise'.[5] As Rosemary Horrox has suggested, this probably refers to a plot, described by John Stow, to set fires around the city and to rescue Edward V and his brother from the Tower under cover of the resulting confusion. Robert Russe, a sergeant of London, William Davy, a pardoner, John Smith, Edward IV's groom of the stirrup, and Stephen Ireland, a wardrober in the Tower, were sentenced to death at Westminster and beheaded on Tower Hill, after which their heads were placed on London Bridge. The French chronicler, Basin, believed that fifty Londoners joined the conspiracy. The men were also accused of having written to Jasper Tudor and to Henry Tudor, as well as to other lords – the first hint of trouble from this quarter for Richard. The names of Jasper and Henry also suggest, as pointed out by Horrox, that Margaret Beaufort might have been involved, probably with the hope that Edward V would restore her son to his inheritance.

The executions of Russe and the others, however, did nothing to silence the growing unrest. Crowland reports that the people of the south and the west began to plot to release Edward IV's sons from the Tower and that those who had taken refuge in sanctuaries were advising that Edward IV's daughters be smuggled overseas in case 'any human fate, inside the Tower, were to befall the male children'. Hearing of this, Richard set up a guard around Westminster, under the supervision of John Nesfield, 'and the whole neighbourhood took on the appearance of a castle and a fortress'.[6]

At London's actual fortress, the public was beginning to see less and less of Edward V and his brother. Mancini reports that the former king's old attendants were forbidden access to him – a claim confirmed by records which show that they had been paid off on (18 July) – and he and his brother 'day by day began to be seen more rarely behind the bars and windows [of the Tower], till at length they ceased to appear altogether'. John Argentine, his physician and the last of Edward V's attendants to see him, reported that the youth believed that death was facing him. Edward V's forebodings were shared by others, as Mancini noted: 'I have seen many men burst forth into tears and lamentations when mention was made of him after his removal from men's sight; and already there was a suspicion that he had been done away with'.[7]

Having left England soon after the coronation, Mancini was unable to gain more information about the fate of the princes in the Tower, nor does he have any information to give us about the rest of Richard III's reign. But the suspicion that the boys had been murdered – never refuted by Richard III – took fire. With the princes believed dead, the rebels turned their sights to the little-known Henry Tudor as their future king.[8]

The rebellion seems to have come about through several interlinking strands, which eventually intertwined. Vergil reports that in London, Margaret Beaufort, having learned of the death of Edward IV's sons, sent her physician, Lewis of Caerleon, to Elizabeth Woodville in sanctuary to propose a marriage between Henry Tudor and the queen's oldest daughter. Caerleon – unlike Mistress Shore – could come and go from Elizabeth's lodgings without suspicion because of his profession. Caerleon's role in the rebellion can be substantiated through his own astronomical tables, which show that he was a prisoner in the Tower during Richard's reign.[9] Meanwhile, Crowland informs us that at his estate of Brecon in Wales, the Duke of Buckingham, 'being repentant of what had been done', took the advice of his prisoner, John Morton, Bishop of Ely and wrote to Henry Tudor, urging that he come to claim the throne.

Buckingham was a most unlikely rebel, for contrary to Shakespeare, Richard had been very much in a giving vein when it came to Buckingham. Having held no position of importance during Edward IV's reign, he had been created chief justice and chamberlain of North and South Wales. Richard also made Buckingham constable, a hereditary Bohun office, and chamberlain and granted him the coveted Bohun estates denied for so long by Edward IV. Why Buckingham joined the rebellion after receiving so much from Richard remains a mystery. Some have suggested that he aimed at the crown himself (and killed Edward IV's sons himself as a step toward that ultimate goal), others that he was manipulated by Bishop Morton and/or Margaret Beaufort, still others that he believed that Richard's reign was doomed and wanted to shield himself from reprisals by joining the rebels. Yet others believe that he was a latent Lancastrian who finally had the chance to show his true colours. The notion that he was appalled by Richard's killing of the princes has been discounted as of late, but it should not be rejected out of hand (assuming, of course, that Richard did indeed kill them). Buckingham may not have had difficulty condoning the death of grown men, but infanticide may have been an entirely different thing to him. Horror and the fear that he had imperilled his immortal soul by his complicity with Richard could explain his willingness to risk all of his long-coveted gains for an uncertain future with an obscure and untried exile. The Crowland Chronicler's statement that Buckingham was 'repentant of what had been done' may well be the truth.

Though the name often given to the uprising, 'Buckingham's Rebellion', reflects its highest-ranking conspirator, the rebels were drawn mainly from the gentry, many of them men who had flourished under Edward IV and served in his household. As Rosemary Horrox has pointed out, most of them were not embittered outsiders or unreconciled Lancastrians, but members of the Yorkist establishment who had every likelihood of prospering under the new king and every prospect of ruin if their rebellion failed. While their own motives for rebellion were no doubt multiple and complex, it is hard to escape the idea that profound revulsion at the treatment of Edward IV's sons was their core motivation, especially when it is remembered that Henry Tudor, a mere youth when he had gone into exile years before, was an unknown quantity who had never run his own estates, much less a kingdom. Still, some of the rebels did have much to gain, and nothing to lose, by rising – in particular, the Woodvilles. The Marquis of Dorset came out of hiding, and the Bishop of Salisbury out of sanctuary, to join the rebellion. Even the low-profile Richard Woodville took part.

Through spies, as Crowland tell us, Richard III had known trouble was brewing for some time. As early as 13 August, he had seized the lands of John Welles, Margaret Beaufort's half-brother, and on 28 August, he ordered a commission headed by Buckingham, not yet a suspect, to enquire into treasons and felonies in London, Surrey, Sussex, Kent, Middlesex, Oxfordshire, Berkshire, and Hertfordshire. The king's next move came on 23 September, when Richard ordered the seizure of Bishop Lionel Woodville's temporalities – i.e. his ecclesiastical possessions. He had good reason to be suspicious of the bishop, who is recorded as being at one of Buckingham's manors, Thornbury, on the day before the king issued his order. While Lionel was Buckingham's brother-in-law, it is probable that he was not at Thornbury merely for a family visit.[10] On 24 September, according to the 1484 Act of Attainder against the rebels, Buckingham wrote to Henry Tudor to ask him to invade England.

By 11 October, if not sooner, Richard had learned, as he wrote to the city of York, that Buckingham had turned traitor. His anger was still raw the next day when, in a postscript to a letter to his chancellor, he described the duke as 'the most untrue creature living whom with God's grace we shall not be long till we will be in those parts and subdue his malice'.[11]

Probably around 18 October, Buckingham and his Woodville duchess, leaving their two daughters at Brecon Castle, travelled with their sons, Edward and Henry, to Weobley in Herefordshire.[12] Shortly after they left, members of the Vaughan family (not to be confused with the Vaughan executed alongside Rivers and Richard Grey), who were loyal to the king, seized Brecon Castle, robbed it, and took Buckingham's daughters and their gentlewomen to the Vaughan house at Tretower. Meanwhile, for about a week, Buckingham remained at Weobley, the home of Sir Walter Devereux, Lord Ferrers. There, he called the men of the country to him, presumably to gain support for his rebellion.

Meanwhile, Richard issued a proclamation against the rebels, in which he offered a reward of £1,000 in money or £100 in land for anyone who captured the duke; 1,000 marks in money or 100 marks in land for whoever captured Dorset or the three rebel bishops (Lionel Woodville, John Morton, and Piers Courtenay, Bishop of Exeter); and 500 marks in money or 40 marks in land for the rebels of lower rank. Peculiarly, the 'Proclamation for the Reform of Morals', as it was officially titled, opens with a stern reminder of Richard's desire that his subjects 'be reconciled and reduced to the way of Truth and Virtue, with the abiding in good disposition', then launches into a spirited and alliterative denunciation of the sex life of Dorset, 'which not fearing God, nor the Peril of His Soul, hath many Maids, Widows, and Wives damnably and without Shame Devoured, Defloured, and Defouled, holding the unshameful and mischievous Woman called Shore's Wife in Adultery'.[13] Since Richard himself was the father of two illegitimate children, who may or may not have been conceived before his marriage and who may or may not have had the same mother, one can be forgiven for thinking the king protested too much.

Back at Weobley, Buckingham, '[r]ealising that he was hemmed in and could find no safe way',[14] decided to flee in disguise. First, however, he had a 'frieze coat' – a coat of a coarse fabric that would not ordinarily touch a noble skin – made for his 5-year-old heir, Edward Stafford, and delivered the boy to a retainer, Sir Richard Delabere, to be kept until Buckingham sent for him with a token.[15] Young Edward lived a colourful existence during the next few weeks. To shield him from discovery by the king's men, Elizabeth Mores, who later married Delabere and was then a servant in his household, shaved the boy's forehead and dressed him as a maiden; when travelling about, the boy rode pillion like a proper young lady. As children of traitors were not generally ill-treated, but would usually be allowed to stay with their mothers or be handed over to guardians, it is telling that Buckingham and his retainers were so determined to hide young Edward. If they had learned that Richard had ordered the murder of his nephews, this might explain their fear.

Buckingham, of course, never had a chance to send the token to recover his son. Ralph Bannister, a retainer who had given Buckingham shelter, betrayed the duke, either out of fear or out of greed for the price on Buckingham's head. Buckingham was taken to Shrewsbury, where, on 31 October, he was handed over to James Tyrell and Christopher Wellesbourne, who took him to Salisbury. There, his pleas for an audience with Richard III were refused, leaving what he meant to say or do had he been admitted to the king's presence as yet another mystery to ponder. On 2 November, All Souls' Day, Buckingham was beheaded in Salisbury marketplace.

Buckingham's defeat, hastened by his failure to gain widespread support from his own retainers in Wales and the torrential rains which had flooded the Severn and prevented him and his men from crossing that river, was emblematic of the fate of the rebellion as a whole, thwarted by Richard III's able network of spies and his quick reaction. Although a hardy group of rebels had proclaimed a new king, presumably Henry Tudor, at Bodmin on 3 November, the day after Buckingham's death, Bodmin Castle fell in mid-November.[16]

Dorset escaped to Brittany, while Lionel Woodville sought sanctuary in Beaulieu Abbey. Probably Richard Woodville took sanctuary as well, as he was pardoned in 1485. Others were less fortunate: Thomas St Leger, the widower of Richard III's own sister, Anne, Duchess of Exeter, was beheaded, as were two others in the Exeter group of rebels. Six of the Kentish rebels were put to death. As for the would-be king, although Henry Tudor had managed to raise a small force and cross over to England, he became separated from the rest of his ships and decided to await their arrival before venturing onto English soil. Having sent a boatload of men to communicate with the soldiers lining the shore, he rightfully suspected a trap when they effusively assured him that Buckingham was on his way at the head of an army. Henry sailed back to the continent, thereby leaving himself to fight another day.

Meanwhile, with Buckingham dead, a search began for his wife and sons. While young Edward Stafford in his 'maiden's raiement' avoided capture, Katherine and her other son, Henry, were found at Weobley by Christopher Wellesbourne, who, with the brother of John Huddleston, probably Richard Huddleston (married to Queen Anne's half-sister, an out-of-wedlock child of the Earl of Warwick), took the Duchess of Buckingham to the king in London.[17]

Katherine's status after she was brought to Richard III is unclear. Some writers have claimed that she was allowed to join her sister Elizabeth in sanctuary, but there is no evidence for this. On 19 December, however, Richard III issued an order allowing the duchess to convey her children and servants from Wales to 'these parts', meaning London, from where the order emanated.[18] This suggests that Katherine was living under close supervision. Perhaps she was placed in a house of religion or required to reside with one of Richard's supporters, as was often the case for noblewomen whose husbands ran afoul of kings.[19]

Margaret Beaufort's punishment put Richard in a quandary; her husband had been loyal to him during the revolt, and he could not afford to forfeit his good will by attainting his wife and leaving both of the couple to suffer the consequences. Margaret's treason, however, could not go unpunished. As a compromise, Margaret was stripped of all her lands, but her husband was allowed to enjoy the revenues during her lifetime. Vergil claims that Stanley was required by the king's council to take all of Margaret's servants from her and keep her 'so strait with himself' that she was unable to send messages to her son or to her friends.[20] As for Elizabeth Woodville, she remained unmolested in sanctuary with her daughters. The 1484 attainders do not name her as a plotter; perhaps Richard III was unaware of her communications with Margaret Beaufort.

Aside from those executed, more than 100 men were attainted in Richard III's parliament for their role in the rebellion.[21] Richard had met the first serious challenge to his reign, and had survived it.

But the genie of Henry Tudor could not be so easily put back in the bottle, especially with a fresh infusion of English refugees, including Bishop Morton and Dorset, joining the band of exiles. On Christmas Day, 1483, the exiles came together at the Cathedral of Rennes, where Henry swore that he would marry Elizabeth of York as soon as he became king.[22] He lost no time obtaining the necessary papal dispensation, which was issued on 27 March 1484 for Henry 'Richemont' and Elizabeth 'Plantageneta'.[23]

The dispensation had not yet been signed, however, when Richard at last persuaded Elizabeth ('urged by frequent intercessions and dire threats', Crowland tells us) to allow her five daughters to leave sanctuary. On 1 March 1484, the king swore an oath, in front of a distinguished company of lords, churchmen, and the mayor and aldermen of London, that if the girls left sanctuary, he would see to it that they would be in 'surety of their lives' and not be 'imprisoned within the Tower of London or other prison'. Rather, they would be put in 'honest places of good name & fame' and would be married to 'gentlemen born'; the king would provide dowries for them of 200 marks per year. Elizabeth herself (here called 'Elizabeth Gray late calling herself Queen of England') was to receive 700 marks per year, to be paid by John Nesfield, who was put in charge of her.[24] The references to the princesses being in surety of their lives, and the promise not to imprison them, says volumes about what was believed to have befallen their brothers, who are nowhere mentioned in the oath.

Why did Elizabeth allow her daughters to leave sanctuary? For Elizabeth's modern-day detractors, and Richard III's modern-day defenders, her actions have variously been interpreted as proof of her indifference to her children's fate or, more commonly, as proof of Richard's innocence of the death of his nephews. Paul Murray Kendall, for instance, writing from the comfort of his study in mid-twentieth-century America, thunders:

> That she came to terms with the man who had bastardized and deposed the Princes, driven her son the Marquess into exile, and executed her other son Grey and her brother Rivers is difficult enough to understand; but that she came to terms knowing also that he had murdered the Princes well-nigh passes belief, or is at least incomprehensible.[25]

In fact, the queen's actions are neither beyond belief nor incomprehensible (to cover both of Kendall's bases). There were several options open for Elizabeth in March 1484. The first, and safest, would have been for her and her daughters to each take the veil. But that would foreclose any other alternatives if the political situation in England later changed, and it would have likely been anathema to Elizabeth's older daughters, who had grown up expecting to make grand matches, not to immure themselves in convents. Probably, too, it would have been an admission of total defeat for Elizabeth. Indeed, no source suggests that such a course of action was ever considered.

The second option was to remain in sanctuary. This was an option, however, that was growing more unpalatable each day. Westminster was heavily guarded, a situation that must have been extremely irritating to the monks there, who may have also been tiring of providing sustenance for Elizabeth and her brood. Undoubtedly the abbot and his flock were eager to get back to normal and to get their relations with the Crown back on a good footing. Add to that the fact that six females, two of them adolescents, were cooped up together in a small space, with little to keep them occupied, and the situation must have been a bleak one indeed. With the king a healthy man in his early 30s, and the rebellion of 1483 having failed, the women could be facing a stay of decades in sanctuary.

Flight abroad was the third option. But it would have required help for Elizabeth to leave Westminster undetected, and how easy would it have been for a woman and five girls, ranging from age 3 to age 18, to leave the heavily guarded sanctuary undetected in the first place? Nor could such a party have likely boarded a boat or a ship without being noticed.

The fourth option was to accept Richard's offer of a pension and good marriages for the girls, with guarantees, sworn under oath in front of numerous witnesses, that Richard would not harm the women or imprison them. This option, the one that Elizabeth ultimately chose, was not without risk. Whatever the fate of the princes in the Tower, it was beyond question that Richard had executed Elizabeth's son Richard Grey and her brother Anthony Woodville, and oaths could be broken. But the chances of the girls coming to harm were slim. Richard might have put down the rebellion of the previous autumn, but his position was still a delicate one. He was in no position to break his oath that he would not maltreat his five nieces. Moreover, with Henry Tudor vowing to marry Elizabeth of York, it behoved Richard to take her off the marriage market by finding her a partner of his own choosing, which could not be accomplished while she and her sisters languished in sanctuary.

In the end, Elizabeth, faced with a stark choice between a bleak future in sanctuary and a chance for her daughters to make good marriages and recover their footing in society, chose to take the option that carried more risks, but promised more gains. One wonders what some of her detractors, faced with the same dilemma, would have done in her place.

Where Elizabeth Woodville and her daughters stayed – or indeed, whether Elizabeth herself left the confines of Westminster at all – is unknown. Audrey Williamson has related a Tyrell family legend, told to her by a member of that family, that Elizabeth and her royal sons – not her daughters – lived at Gipping Hall, the home of James Tyrell, 'by permission of the uncle' at some unspecified time.[26] This begs the question, however, of why, if Elizabeth and the princes were living at Gipping Hall, did Richard III make no mention of the boys in his 1 March oath? And where were the daughters? And since Nesfield was specifically named by Richard III as the man to be Elizabeth's attendant, how did Tyrell come into the picture? The legend may be an appealing one, but there seems little of substance to back it up. A purely speculative, but perhaps more likely, residence for Elizabeth and her girls is Hertford Castle, of which Nesfield had been made constable on 31 August 1483. The castle had formed part of the queen's jointure, so it would have been both familiar and suitable, and having the queen there would have been administratively convenient for Nesfield, as he had been placed in charge of the queen's annuity.[27]

By 24 April 1484, Richard had also granted Katherine, Duchess of Buckingham, an annuity of £200 per annum, to be taken out of the revenues of Tonbridge in Kent.[28] Possibly Katherine and her four children joined Elizabeth and her brood, but there is no evidence of the duchess's whereabouts for the rest of Richard III's reign.

The king, meanwhile, had suffered a tragedy of his own. In April, close to the anniversary of Edward IV's death, Richard's only legitimate son died at Middleton Castle, sending the king and queen 'almost out of their minds for a long time when faced with the sudden grief'.[29] Richard and Anne had had only one surviving child together, and their prospects looked bleak for having any more.

The king's enemies did not do Richard the courtesy of letting him mourn in peace. In July 1483, a Richard Edgecombe was charged with attempting to send money to some of the exiles. Meanwhile, in London, William Collingbourne was conspiring to send a messenger to Henry Tudor to advise him to invade on 18 October. More famously, on 18 July, he pinned his well-known ditty to the door of St Paul's:

> The cat, the rat, and Lovell our dog
> Rule all England under a hog

The 'cat, rat, and dog' were William Catesby, Richard Ratcliffe, and Francis, Viscount Lovell; the 'hog' referred to Richard's emblem of the white boar. Edgecombe fled to Brittany, but Collingbourne was not so lucky, being arrested in the autumn of 1484. On 29 November, a commission of oyer and terminer (the members of which included 'Lovell our dog') was set up to try him. In addition to urging Henry Tudor to invade,

Collingbourne was accused of 'devising certain bills and writing in rhyme, to the end that the same being published might stir the people to a commotion against the king'. Sometime in early December, Collingbourne was convicted at the Guildhall of high treason and was sentenced to a traitor's death. He was drawn on a hurdle to Tower Hill, hanged at a brand new gallows, and cut down while still alive. While he was being disembowelled, he managed to say either 'Jesus, Jesus' or the rather understated 'Oh, Lord Jesu, yet more trouble' before dying. The *Great Chronicle of London* reported that he was 'greatly mourned of the people for his goodly personage and favor of visage'.[30]

While England simmered, Henry Tudor and his friends remained dependent on Francis Duke of Brittany, who granted Dorset and his men 400 livres a month and Edward Woodville 100 livres a month.[31] In September 1484, Richard saw the opportunity to solve his Henry Tudor problem. Duke Francis had fallen ill, leaving his treasurer, Pierre Landais, free to negotiate with Richard.[32] It seems to have been agreed that Henry Tudor would be seized and taken to England, where it is safe to say he would not have had a long life expectancy. John Morton, however, who was staying in Flanders, got wind of the agreement and warned Henry, who fled to France, evading his would-be captors by just hours.

Henry's flight left the rest of the exiles, about 410 of them, stranded in Vannes. Francis, however, recovered sufficiently to finance their own passage to France. He summoned Edward Woodville, John Cheyne, and Edward Poynings to him and gave them 100 livres for the expenses. Soon the entire band of exiles was in France. Instead of capturing Henry Tudor, Richard had catapulted him into the arms of England's traditional enemy, and, it would prove in the long run, ensured the downfall of his own dynasty.

Ironically, Edward IV's old enemy, Louis XI, had died in August 1483, just a few months after the death of his English rival. He too had been succeeded by a minor, the 13-year-old Charles VIII, who unlike Edward V was neither deposed nor imprisoned, but reigned under the regency of his sister, 22-year-old Anne of Beaujeu.[33] The French themselves harboured no doubts about the fate of their king's English counterpart. On 15 January 1484, its chancellor had told the Estates-General, 'Look [at] what has happened in [England] since the death of King Edward [IV]: how his children, already big and courageous, have been put to death with impunity, and the royal crown transferred to their murderer by the favour of the people'.[34]

The formidable Anne of Beaujeu, herself facing a challenge to her authority from her cousin the Duke of Orléans, quickly realised the value of the newcomers. Assisting Henry Tudor to take the throne would deprive Orléans, who had associated himself with Pierre Landais in Brittany, of the ally he sought in Richard III. Moreover, while Richard had reached a truce with Scotland that September, hostilities between the French and the English at sea continued. It therefore suited the French very well to assist Henry Tudor, even though all they did for now was to lodge about 400 of the exiles at Sens and grant him 3,000 livres to clothe his followers. Charles VIII issued a letter to Toulon on 3 November announcing that the English were in 'marvellous and great division' and describing Henry Tudor, strangely, as the son of Henry VI; this is more likely a simple error than a concerted attempt by Henry and the French to misrepresent his lineage, as has been recently claimed. Henry himself never described himself in this manner, and would have made a laughing stock of himself among his prospective subjects, most of whom would have remembered Henry VI's reign all too well, if he had tried.[35]

The autumn of 1484 brought, in William Collingbourne's words, yet more trouble for Richard III. Since 1474, the Lancastrian stalwart John de Vere, Earl of Oxford, had been imprisoned at Hammes Castle near Calais.[36] In 1478, he had leapt into the moat, either to escape or to kill himself – opinions differed. If Oxford had indeed given into a sense of despair and attempted to take his own life, he would soon have enormous cause for gratitude toward whoever had fished him out of the chin-deep water, for in late October or early November 1484, he suddenly found himself a free man.

Richard III, perhaps concerned about the activities of Oxford's former associates in England, had ordered William Bolton to bring Oxford to England, presumably to move him to the greater security of the Tower or possibly to try and execute him for treason. Instead of handing over his charge, James Blount, the custodian of Hammes, simply walked away from his post, taking his erstwhile prisoner with him. Soon, the pair were greeting a delighted Henry Tudor.

Thus encouraged, Henry began to write letters to his potential subjects in England. One undated letter, in which Henry describes Richard as 'that homicide and unnatural tyrant', likely belongs to this period.[37] On 6 December, Richard in turn issued a letter to the Mayor of Windsor, and presumably to other officials around the country as well, complaining that 'rebels and traitors, now confedered with our ancient enemies of France' were tending writings [...] to provoke and stir discord between us and our lords'.[38]

The next day, 7 December, Richard followed up with a royal proclamation:

> Forasmuch as the king our sovereign lord hath certain knowledge that Piers, Bishop of Exeter, Thomas Grey, late Marquis Dorset, Jasper late Earl of Pembroke, John late Earl of Oxford and Sir Edward Woodville with others divers his rebels and traitors, disabled and attainted by the authority of the High Court of Parliament, of whom many be known for open murderers and adulterers and extortioners, contrary to the pleasure of God and against all truth honour and nature hath forsaken their natural country taking them first to be under the obeisance of the Duke of Brittany and to him promised certain things which by him and his council were thought things to be greatly unnatural and abominable for them to grant observe keep and perform. And therefore the same utterly refused they seeing that the said duke and his council would not aid and succor them nor follow their ways privily departed out of his countries into France, there taking them to be under the obeisance of the king's ancient enemy Charles calling himself king of France and too abuse and blind the commons of this said realm the said rebels and traitors have chosen to be their captain one Henry late calling himself Earl of Richmond which of his ambitious and insatiable covetousness stirred and excited by the confederacy of the king's said rebels and traitors encroaches upon him the name and title of royal estate of this realm of England, whereunto he hath no manner interest right or colour as every man well knoweth.[39]

Richard went on to accuse Henry Tudor and his confederates of agreeing to give up the English claim to France and, more generically, of 'coming to do the most cruel murders slaughters robberies and disherisons that ever were seen in any Christian realm'. He hastened to assure his subjects, however, that 'our said sovereign lord as a well willed diligent and courageous prince will put his most royal person to all labor and pain necessary' to subdue the threat.

One Woodville was not around to hear the proclamation: Lionel, Bishop of Salisbury. Since Lionel's entrance into sanctuary at Beaulieu Abbey the previous autumn, Richard had been attempting to prise him out. On 15 December 1483, he had sent a letter to the abbot demanding that he produce documents supporting his right to offer a sanctuary (although

Richard's own mother-in-law had taken sanctuary there herself following the Earl of Warwick's death at Barnet in 1471). He followed up this inquiry with a demand on 13 February 1484 that his two chaplains be allowed to bring Lionel into his presence; J.A.F. Thomson has suggested that Richard meant to allow Lionel to answer the charges against him that had been brought in Parliament in connection with the 1483 rebellion. Nonetheless, Lionel remained in sanctuary. By 1 December 1484, however, he was dead, as indicated by a letter where Richard III authorised the election of a successor. His cause of death is unrecorded. A seventeenth-century manuscript stated that he was buried at Beaulieu, while another source claims that a damaged tomb at Salisbury Cathedral is his.[40] Five of Jacquetta's sons had reached adulthood; now only two, Richard and Edward, remained.

At Westminster, Richard III put his worries aside and celebrated Christmas in high style, attracting the censure of the Crowland Chronicler: 'during this Christmas feast too much attention was paid to singing and dancing and to vain exchanges of clothing between Queen Anne and Lady Elizabeth, eldest daughter of the dead king, who were alike in complexion and figure'.[41] But more than mere gown-swapping was going on, according to Crowland: 'it was said by many that the king was applying his mind in every way to contracting a marriage with Elizabeth either after the death of the queen, or by means of a divorce for which he believed he had sufficient grounds'. A few days after the Christmas festivities, Richard's queen fell seriously ill. On 16 March 1485, she died.

Was Richard, whose queen fell seriously ill after Christmas, thinking of marrying his niece? Crowland goes on to tell us that although Richard later publicly denied wishing to wed Elizabeth of York, he had had to be dissuaded from the plan by Sir Richard Ratcliffe and William Catesby, who feared that such a match would lead to accusations by the northerners that Richard had caused the death of Queen Anne in order to marry his nubile niece. Crowland adds that Catesby and Ratcliffe also feared that as queen, Elizabeth might use her influence to avenge the death of Earl Rivers and Richard Grey upon those who had advised Richard to carry out the executions. To persuade Richard against such a match, his councillors brought in over a dozen theologians who claimed that the Pope could not issue a dispensation for such a match. The story seems a very specific and detailed one to have been fabricated by Crowland solely to malign Richard.

That there were rumours that Richard had poisoned his queen so that he could marry Elizabeth of York was confirmed by Richard himself. The Mercers' Company Records contain his denial, made on 30 March:

> the king sent for and had before him at St John's as yesterday the mayor and aldermen whereas he in the great hall there in the presence of many of his lords and of much other people showed his grief and displeasure aforesaid and said it never came in his thought or mind to marry in such manner wise nor willing or glad at the death of his queen but as sorry and in heart as heavy as man might be.[42]

A further, but very uncertain, piece of evidence exists in the form of a letter that was supposedly written by Elizabeth to John Howard, Duke of Norfolk. The letter, which exists only in paraphrase, was supposedly seen by Sir George Buck, a seventeenth-century apologist for Richard III, in a cabinet belonging to Norfolk's descendant Thomas Howard, Earl of Arundel and Surrey. Buck may well have seen such a letter – as Arundel was living, it would have ill behoved Buck to fabricate its existence – but Buck's *History of King Richard the Third*, in which the paraphrased letter appears, has a tangled and nightmarish editorial history, which includes revisions by the author, revisions by other parties, and fire damage. Out of this muddle, Arthur Kincaid reconstructed the paraphrased letter, supplying gaps in the text (indicated by Kincaid's brackets below) with emendations in later versions of Buck's work:

> First she thanked him for his many courtesies and friendly [offices, an]d then she prayed him as before to be a mediator for her in the cause of [the marriage] to the k[i]ng, who, as she wrote, was her only joy and maker in [this] world, and that she was his in heart and in thoughts, in [body,] and in all. And then she intimated that the better half of Fe[bruary] was past, and that she feared the queen would nev[er die.][43]

As one can see (especially when the material in brackets is removed), the paraphrased letter lends itself to multiple interpretations. Is Elizabeth referring to her marriage at all? If so, is she referring to a marriage between herself and the not-yet-widowed king, or to a marriage she hopes the king to arrange for her? If the word 'die' is correct, is Elizabeth callously hoping Queen Anne will die to make way for the king to take her as his wife, or is she hoping that the queen will soon be released from her suffering? Do her references to the king being her 'only joy and maker' in this world, and to her being his 'in heart and in thoughts' reveal a lovesick teenager, or are they merely the florid conventions of medieval letter writing? Assuming the actual letter is close in substance to the paraphrased version as it appears here, all that one can say for certain is that it appears that as of February 1485, Elizabeth was eager for something to happen.

In contrast to the rumours that Richard had designs on his niece, we have some evidence that after Anne's death, he entered into negotiations for the hand of Joanna, the sister of John II of Portugal. Barrie Williams points out that on 22 March 1485, six days after Anne's death, Sir Edward Brampton set off on an embassy to Portugal – although as Doreen Court notes in a follow-up article, it is by no means certain that Brampton's original brief was to propose a marriage between Richard and Joanna, or even that the proposal originated with the English government. In any case, at some point, one side or the other suggested that Richard III marry Joanna and that Elizabeth of York marry Manuel, Duke of Beja, who was John II's cousin. Joanna, who at 33 was eight months Richard's senior, had spent much of her adulthood in a convent and appeared to prefer the cloistered life to that of a royal wife. In August, the story goes, having been given an ultimatum by her brother's government, she entered into prayer and meditation, during which she had a vision which told her that Richard was dead. The next morning, she duly told her brother that if Richard were alive, she would marry him; if he was dead, her brother was not to urge her again to marry. Richard, in fact, had just been killed in battle.[44]

Richard's desire to marry his niece and the Portuguese negotiations may not be mutually incompatible. Although marriage to a niece Richard himself had declared illegitimate had its obvious disadvantages, it was not without its appeal. Assuming that Edward V and Richard, Duke of York, were dead, and everyone at this point had been behaving as if they were, placing their eldest sister on the throne as his queen was the one form of amends Richard could make to Edward IV's disgruntled supporters. If the match were fertile – and Elizabeth's mother and grandmother had been quite fecund – there was the likelihood that a grandson of Edward IV would sit on the throne. Such a marriage would also put paid to Henry Tudor's plans to marry Elizabeth of York himself. Certainly Henry, as Vergil reported, was 'pinched [...] by the very stomach' when the rumour of Richard's plan to marry his niece made its way abroad.[45]

If Richard were planning marriage to Elizabeth of York, it would also explain an odd episode that happened around this time: Dorset's attempted defection from Henry's cause. According to Vergil, Elizabeth Woodville had advised Dorset, then staying in Paris, 'to forsake earl Henry, and with all speed convenient to return into England, where he should be sure to be called of the king unto high promotion'. Dorset, 'partly despairing for that cause of Earl Henry's success, partly suborned by King Richard's fair promises', absconded under cover of darkness to Flanders, to the dismay of his fellow exiles, to whose plans he was privy. They launched a search for him, and Humphrey Cheyney tracked him to Compiègne and persuaded him to return to the fold.[46] Promises of pardon and restoration might have been enough to persuade Elizabeth Woodville to urge her only remaining son to return to England, of course, but if she knew that Richard was proposing to marry her eldest daughter, it would have been an even stronger incentive for Elizabeth to send for Dorset.

If Richard had indeed been contemplating marrying his niece, but was talked out of the idea by his advisors, it is likely that it was only at this point that he turned his attention to negotiations for a foreign bride. The warrant authorising Brampton's 22 March journey to Portugal does not specify the purpose of his mission. It is entirely possible, then, that Brampton went to Portugal initially not to negotiate a marriage but to enter into a treaty, and that the marriage later entered the picture – as it inevitably would have when the Portuguese realised that the king was now an eligible widower. Certainly the Portuguese seem to have been quite eager for the marriage, as they feared that Richard would otherwise make an alliance with Spain.[47]

With Richard having made his public denial of his plans to marry Elizabeth of York, the girl was sent, for propriety's sake, to Richard's castle of Sheriff Hutton, which had decidedly gloomy associations with the imprisonment of her uncle Anthony Woodville. There she had the company of Edward, Earl of Warwick, son of the executed Duke of Clarence, and probably his sister, Margaret, as well. Ten miles from the city of York, Sheriff Hutton was a grand castle, but moving from the royal court to Yorkshire must have been a jar for young Elizabeth.[48]

In the meantime, on 30 March, Richard III had brought yet another Woodville in from the cold by issuing a pardon to Richard Woodville, who on 12 January had bound himself for 1,000 marks to bear himself well and faithfully'.[49] His activities and whereabouts during the rest of

Richard III's reign are unknown, although he would have been in straitened circumstances, as there is no indication that he had any of his lands restored to him.

While Elizabeth of York waited at Sheriff Hutton to see what the future might bring her, the invasion plans of the exiles in France were progressing, leading Richard III to establish himself in June at Nottingham. On 22 June he sent out commissions of array, requiring the commissioners to have knights, squires, and gentlemen ready to meet a call to arms at one hour's notice. On 23 June, the king issued another proclamation against Henry Tudor, with the now familiar language denouncing his associates as 'open murderers, adulterers, and extortioners'. This time, however, Dorset was omitted from the named 'rebels and traitors', suggesting that Richard still had hopes of his defection. The June proclamation also contains a genealogical discourse impugning the legitimacy of Henry's grandfather, Owen Tudor, though not, interestingly enough, that of Henry's own father Edward Tudor, son of Owen Tudor and Katherine of Valois.[50]

On 1 August 1485, Henry Tudor at last left Harfleur with around 4,000 men, most of them French but some of them Scots in French employ, funded by a grant from Charles VIII of 40,000 livres and loans obtained by Henry himself. Ironically, Philippe de Crèvecoeur, whose piratical fleet Edward Woodville had been fighting back in the spring of 1483, supplied about 1,500 of the men. Among Henry Tudor's 'chief men' was Edward Woodville, singled out by Crowland for praise as 'a most valiant knight'. Dorset, whose attempted defection had not been forgotten, remained in France as human collateral for Henry's borrowed funds.[51]

On 22 August 1485, Richard III's forces, totalling around 8,000 to 10,000 men, and Henry Tudor's forces, totalling about 5,000 after picking up new recruits during the march from Henry's landing point in Wales, faced each other, probably on the plain southwest of Ambion Hill. The forces of Lord Stanley – Margaret Beaufort's husband – and his brother Sir William stood nearby, committed to neither side.[52] While Edward Woodville and his fellow rebels no doubt hoped that God would judge the rightness of their cause by granting them a victory, Edward could not have been a little daunted as he assessed the odds. If Henry Tudor lost the day and he managed to escape, he faced life in permanent exile, perhaps hiring himself out as a mercenary like many of the Frenchmen and Scots who stood beside him. If he fell alive into Richard III's hands, he could expect a summary execution by beheading after the battle. If Richard were minded to give his subjects an especially strong warning of the costs of rebellion, Edward might even be facing the traitor's death of hanging, drawing, beheading, and quartering.

Instead, a few hours later, a horse trotted away from the battlefield. It bore the naked and battered body of Richard III.[53]

13

Won and Lost Causes

For William Catesby, the reign of Henry VII got off to a particularly bad start: his own execution. Catesby was the only major figure from Richard III's reign to be put to death in the aftermath of the Battle of Bosworth: two others, a now obscure yeoman of the crown named William Bracher and his son, were hanged immediately after the battle. Why these three men in particular suffered is unknown; perhaps Catesby at least, as Peter Hammond suggests, had made enemies on the king's side.[1]

On 25 August 1483, probably the date of his execution in Leicester, Catesby was allowed to make his will, which included this bequest: 'that my lady of Buckingham have [£100] to help her children and that she will see my lord's debts paid and his will executed'.[2] Catesby, among others, had been granted lands by Richard III in order to settle the debts of the executed Duke of Buckingham;[3] evidently he had been dilatory in this task and was now trying to set things right for the duchess, who under Richard III had been living on what for her was a small annuity.

But Katherine, Duchess of Buckingham, would soon be in no need of the unfortunate Catesby's well-intended bequest. On 28 October 1485, Henry VII had created his uncle, Jasper Tudor, Duke of Bedford.[4] Having been restored to the lands associated with the earldom of Pembroke, Bedford was now in want only of a duchess. Katherine, who once her jointure and dower were restored would be a rich young widow, suited the purpose nicely. Some time before 7 November 1485, when the pair are mentioned as married in an Act of Parliament, the two were wed. On 7 November, the new Duchess of Bedford and Buckingham was granted the 1,000 marks jointure which Buckingham had left her in his will, as well as her dower lands. She brought her husband thirty-five lordships and manors. The couple were probably virtual strangers at the time of their marriage, unless Jasper had met Katherine during his brief stay in England in 1470. Since the young Duke of Buckingham had visited Margaret Beaufort on 28 October 1670, while Jasper and her son were visiting, it is possible that Buckingham brought his wife along with him.[5]

Katherine, of course, was not the only Woodville to benefit from the change of regime. On 16 September 1485, Edward Woodville was granted the castle and lordship of Carisbrooke and was made keeper of the castle and town of Porchester. He was now the Captain of the Isle of Wight.[6] In the parliament that opened on 7 November, Richard Woodville was recognised as his brother Anthony's heir; he now became the third Earl Rivers. Edward and Richard's nephew, Dorset, who had proven fickle to Henry Tudor's cause, did not come out of Parliament so well. While his attainder was reversed, he was not summoned to Parliament, and he was restored only to the lands he had acquired by inheritance or marriage, thereby losing the grants and wardships he had acquired under Edward IV. Elizabeth Woodville was restored to her 'state, dignity, pre-eminence and name' and was granted certain lands, though the delicate question of her landed endowment as queen was not settled. Most important, perhaps, from her point of view and her daughters', the 1484 Act of Parliament declaring her marriage to Edward IV invalid and her children by Edward IV illegitimate was repealed and, indeed, ordered destroyed. Parliament also reversed the attainder of the Lancastrian royal family, the ill-fated Henry VI, his tenacious queen, Margaret of Anjou, and their son, though none, of course, were alive to appreciate their vindication. The rhyming William Collingbourne also earned a posthumous pardon.[7]

Henry VII had been crowned on 30 October. On 10 December, the Commons, through their speaker, Thomas Lovell, requested:

> the same royal highness should take to himself that illustrious lady Elizabeth, daughter of King Edward IV, as his wife and consort; whereby, by God's grace, many hope to see the propagation of offspring from the stock of kings, to comfort the whole realm. And thereupon the lords spiritual and temporal being in the same parliament, rising from their seats and standing before the king sitting on the royal throne, bowing their heads, voiced the same request; to which the same king answered by his own mouth that he was content to proceed according to their desire and request.[8]

This was likely not, as has been suggested by some, an indication that Henry VII, having achieved the throne, had to be pushed by Parliament into fulfilling his vow to marry Elizabeth of York; rather, as Arlene Okerlund and others have pointed out, the request was probably simply a formality designed to emphasise Parliament's approval of the match. The five-month interval between Henry's victory on 22 August 1485 and his marriage on 18 January 1486 was hardly an unseemly delay, given the need for Henry to get settled in as king, repeal the act slandering the legitimacy of his prospective bride, and obtain a papal dispensation to replace the one issued in 1484, which evidently was considered inadequate.[9] Elizabeth had spent the months leading up to the marriage in her future mother-in-law's Thames-side residence of Coldharbour, where Margaret Beaufort ordered furnishings and repairs for the rooms she was to occupy.[10]

Little is known of the wedding ceremony, other than that it was conducted by Thomas Bourchier, Archbishop of Canterbury, who had made the tragic mistake of asking Elizabeth Woodville to hand over her youngest son to Richard III's custody.[11] The septuagenarian archbishop had crowned Edward IV, Elizabeth Woodville, Richard III and his queen, and Henry VII; the wedding was the last great ceremony over which he presided before his death in May 1486.[12] Presumably the ceremony was followed by the 'great jousting' which had been promised when the wedding plans were announced.[13]

Edward Woodville did not linger long at the new king's court or at his castles of Porchester and Carisbrooke. Early in 1486, possibly in fulfilment of a vow made during his exile, he departed for Spain to fight the infidels – ironically, an ambition that Richard III himself had cherished.[14] By 1 March, he was at Seville, accompanied by 300 men. From there, he rode to Cordoba, where King Ferdinand and Queen Isabella were assembling an army to fight the Moors. On 14 May, they arrived outside of the city of Loja, which the Spanish rulers aimed to capture from the Moors.

Edward – called 'Lord Scales' in the contemporary accounts of the campaign – made a considerable impression on his companions. The Italian Peter Martyr described him as 'young, wealthy, and high-born' and as 'attended by a beautiful train of household troops, three hundred in number, armed after the fashion of their land with long-bow and battle-axe'.[15] He and other eyewitnesses give us a rare description of a member of the Woodville family in battle. Fernando del Pulgar wrote that 'the Englishman, the Conde de Escalas with the bowmen and foot soldiers he brought ventured into dangerous situations and places'.[16] Andrez Bernaldez, chaplain to the Archbishop of Seville, wrote, as translated by W.H. Prescott:

> Having asked leave to fight after the manner of his country [...] he dismounted from his good steed, and, putting himself at the head of his followers, armed like himself en blanco, with their swords at their thighs, and battle-axes in their hands, he dealt such terrible blows around him as filled even the hardy mountaineers of the north with astonishment.[17]

The Castilians followed Edward's charge as the Moors fled. Edward and his men fought their way through the suburbs to the city walls. As he was mounting a scaling ladder, he was struck with a stone, knocking out two front teeth and sending him sprawling senseless on the ground. The surgeons saved his life, but not his teeth. When King Ferdinand and Queen Isabella later offered their sympathies, Edward quipped of his missing teeth, 'Our Lord, who reared this fabric, has only opened a window in order to discern the more readily what passes within'.[18]

The Moors surrendered Loja on 28 May, after which the Spaniards moved to Illora, which also fell. There, on 11 June, Queen Isabella herself, along with her daughter the Infanta, arrived to celebrate the victories. Edward, minus two teeth but resplendent in a French surcoat of black brocade and a 'white French hat with extravagant plumes', greeted the queen and the Infanta and, having made his reverence to the king, showed off his horsemanship, to the delight of the royal family.[19]

From Illora, the Spanish went on to capture Moclin, then Montefrio, before the council of war determined to return to Cordoba. From there, Edward, his crusading vow fulfilled, set off for England. He did not return empty-handed. Queen Isabella presented him with twelve Andalusan horses, two beds with rich hangings (medieval beds being valuable items), linen, and pavilions. Later, Ferdinand would praise him as the 'remarkable Count of Scales'.[20]

Edward stopped in Portugal on his way home; earlier, he had written a letter of apology to King John for not calling on him when passing through Lisbon previously; he had received a gracious royal reply.[21] Now he made good his omission and paid his respects. There, the king's secretary reported, he was 'very well received' and enjoyed a round of feasts, bullfights, cane-fights, plays, and pageants. At one point, he even engaged in some matchmaking: At a meal where the king honoured his guest by refusing to take his water while seated, Edward proposed that one of Edward IV's daughters marry the Duke of Beja – continuing, evidently, the negotiations that had been broken off by the death of Richard III the previous year. In the end, however, nothing came of the proposal.[22]

When Edward returned to England, the court was anxiously awaiting the birth of the king's and queen's first child, who arrived on 20 September 1486.[23] Born eight months after the wedding, the infant, named Arthur, may have been slightly premature – or his parents, having received Parliament's blessing for their marriage, may have anticipated the formal ceremony by a few weeks. Given the ease with which a valid marriage could be contracted, it would not have shocked morality if the couple had exchanged private vows and then consummated their marriage. On the other hand, since the christening was postponed to await the arrival of John de Vere, Earl of Oxford, an intended godfather, who was on his estates instead of being lodged nearby in anticipation of an imminent birth, it may indeed be that Arthur's arrival caught everyone by surprise.[24]

At Arthur's christening, held at Winchester on 24 September, the Woodvilles were prominent.[25] The dowager queen, Elizabeth Woodville, served as the infant's godmother; she presented her grandson with a 'rich cup of gold'. The prince, wearing a mantel of crimson cloth of gold furred with ermine, was carried by Elizabeth of York's sister Cecily, who was assisted by the Marquis of Dorset and by the Earl of Lincoln, whose heart, as it will soon appear, may not have been entirely in his task. The Marchioness of Dorset bore the infant's train, and Edward Woodville and three other men carried the canopy over the baby.

The christening would in fact be Elizabeth Woodville's last major ceremonial appearance. On 10 July 1486, she had agreed with the Abbot of Westminster to lease a mansion within the abbey called 'Cheyne gate'.[26] Was she looking for seclusion, as suggested by Arlene Okerlund, or was she simply interested in obtaining a residence convenient to the court when it was at Westminster? Whatever her reasons, it is not clear whether she actually stayed there and, if so, how long she remained there, for sometime later, she moved to Bermondsey Abbey, a Cluniac monastery on the banks of the Thames.

Elizabeth's removal coincided with, and has often been linked to, a conspiracy against Henry VII which had been building since the previous autumn. The conspiracy, which arose in Ireland, took the unlikely form of recruiting a boy, Lambert Simnel, to impersonate Edward, Earl of Warwick, the young son of the Duke of Clarence. In fact, the unfortunate Warwick was shut up fast in the Tower of London, to which the cautious Henry VII had moved him shortly after winning his crown at Bosworth.

On 1 May 1487, Henry VII, for what is described in classically vague bureaucratic terms as 'divers considerations', transferred Elizabeth Woodville's real properties to her daughter, the queen.[27] According to Polydore Vergil, the decision to 'deprive' the dowager queen of her possessions was taken in the midst of a council meeting called at Sheen to discuss the rebellion. Yet the reason Vergil gives has nothing to do with the nascent rebellion, but with her 1484 agreement with Richard III to leave sanctuary.[28] The Tudor historian Hall follows Vergil in ascribing Elizabeth's loss of her properties to her long-ago deal with Richard, adding, 'By this folly and inconstancy of the queen, she incurred the hatred and displeasure of many men, and for that cause lived after in the Abbey of Bermondsey beside Southwark'.[29] As Elizabeth's rapprochement with Richard III was old news in 1487, this hardly seems a plausible explanation.

It was not until the seventeenth century, when Francis Bacon wrote his history of Henry VII's reign, that Elizabeth was explicitly linked to the Lambert Simnel conspiracy:

> That which is most probable [is] that it was the Queen Dowager from whom this action had the principal source and motion. For certain it is, she was a busy negotiating woman [...] and was at this time extremely discontent with the King, thinking her daughter (as the King handled the matter) not advanced but depressed: and none could hold the book so well to prompt and instruct this stage-play, as she could. Nevertheless it was not her meaning, nor no more was it the meaning of any of the better and sager sort that favoured this enterprise and knew the secret, that this disguised idol should possess the crown; but at his peril to make way to the overthrow of the King; and that done, they had their several hopes and ways. That which doth chiefly fortify this *conjecture* is, that as soon as the matter brake forth in any strength, it was one of the King's first acts to cloister the Queen Dowager in the nunnery of Bermondsey ...[30]

Bacon's admitted conjecture, arrived at more than a century after the events in question, has for some taken on the aura of historical fact. Yet, as others have pointed out, it defies credibility that Elizabeth would support supplanting her daughter's husband (and their heir, her new grandson) in favour of the Earl of Warwick, the son of the man who had aided in the death of her father and her brother, John. An alternative explanation is that Elizabeth believed that Simnel was not Warwick, but the vanished Edward V, her son.[31] While such a belief certainly would give Elizabeth a motive, the argument is undermined by the failure of any contemporary or near-contemporary source to mention such a claimed identity for the pretender. Moreover, as the rebellion attracted close associates of Richard III such as Francis, Viscount Lovell, it is difficult to imagine any of them fighting to restore Edward V to the throne when they themselves had helped remove him from it in the first place.

It is possible, however, that Henry VII's seizure of Elizabeth's properties was linked to his suspicions of her son, Dorset. According to Vergil, the king, preparing to meet the rebels in battle, arrived at Bury St Edmunds, where, believing Dorset to be privy to the conspiracy, he arrested him and sent him to the Tower.[32] Bacon amplified the story:

> And being come to St Edmund's-bury, he understood that Thomas Marquis Dorset [...] was hasting towards him to purge himself of some accusations which had been made against him. But the king, though he kept an ear for him, yet was the time so doubtful, that he sent the Earl of Oxford to meet him and forthwith to carry him to the Tower; with a fair message nevertheless that he should bear that disgrace with patience, for that the King meant not his hurt, but only to preserve him from doing hurt either to the King's service or to himself; and that the King should always be able (when he had clared himself) to make him reparation.[33]

Unlike his mother, Dorset did stand to gain from putting Warwick upon the throne: Dorset had been Warwick's guardian during Edward IV's reign and had probably hoped to marry him to one of his many daughters. That old tie, combined with Dorset's defection from him during exile, might have been enough to awaken the suspicions of the jittery king, who after all had good reason to know how easily a ruler could be pushed off his throne. That Dorset was indeed under a cloud at this time is confirmed by the king's failure to summon him to Parliament that autumn.[34]

Nonetheless, whatever reservations the king had against Dorset's loyalty, they did not extend to the whole of the Woodville family: as we shall see, Edward Woodville not only fought for the king against the rebels but held high command in the king's army. Furthermore, if Henry did suspect Elizabeth of plotting, Bermondsey, an abbey conveniently located on the

Thames, seems an odd place to stow her; there were more secure and more remote locations to which she might have been sent.

It is quite possible that Elizabeth's removal to Bermondsey was prompted chiefly by financial concerns on the part of the king. The order transferring Elizabeth's estates is sandwiched in among a number of routine matters of royal business, suggesting that the order had likewise been an administrative matter rather than a security measure. Due to chance and political upheavals, it had been a century since a married king had faced the situation of maintaining a queen dowager while assuring his own queen of her proper landed endowment. Henry solved this problem by transferring Elizabeth Woodville's lands to her daughter; in recompense, Elizabeth received an annuity of 400 marks, raised on 19 February 1490 to £400.[35] While a different king might have treated Elizabeth Woodville more generously, the events of the past few years had left England on shaky financial ground, and Elizabeth could at least console herself that her daughter was receiving a suitable endowment. Moreover, Henry may have thought that Elizabeth would soon have no need of an endowment in England, because on 28 November 1487, he and the Scottish king, James III, agreed that the latter would marry Elizabeth. The negotiations had been carried on pursuant to the three-year truce that the English and the Scots had formed the previous July. James's death in June 1488, however, kept Elizabeth from becoming the Queen of Scots.[36]

The Lambert Simnel conspiracy had gained fresh blood when John de la Pole, Earl of Lincoln, Edward IV's nephew by his sister Elizabeth, Duchess of Suffolk, fled the country for Burgundy. There he began raising an army to support the pretended Earl of Warwick.[37] Hitherto, Lincoln had given no sign of disloyalty, even dutifully playing his role at Prince Arthur's christening and attending a council meeting in February 1487. As his own claim to the throne was quite strong, he may have been planning to replace Henry VII with himself rather than either the real or the feigned Warwick. His aunt Margaret, the Dowager Duchess of Burgundy, and her step-son-in-law Maximilian of Austria, the Regent of Burgundy, supplied him with an army of 2,000 mercenaries, led by Martin Schwarz. In May 1487, Lincoln and his forces arrived in Dublin.

Henry VII was well prepared for them. Having been apprised of a possible invasion in March, he had left on a progress through East Anglia, apparently in the expectation of a landing on the east coast. On 22 April, however, he moved abruptly to Coventry, probably after receiving news of possible trouble on the west coast as well. On 13 May at Kenilworth, learning that the rebels had landed in Ireland, he wrote to Elizabeth of York's chamberlain, the Earl of Ormond, asking that the earl bring 'our dearest wife and [...] our dearest mother' to him there – an indication, perhaps, of the affection he had for both women.

On 24 May at Christchurch Cathedral in Dublin, the pretender's supporters, who included Lincoln, Richard III's old ally Francis, Viscount Lovell, and Garrett Fitzgerald, Earl of Kildare, had crowned the boy as 'Edward VI'. With the new king in tow, the group soon sailed from Dublin and landed on 4 June at the Cumbrian coast.

At Kenilworth, Henry VII had appointed his commanders: Jasper, Duke of Bedford, the mainguard, John de Vere, Earl of Oxford, the vanguard, and George, Lord Strange, the rearguard. The vanguard was divided into two wings, the right of which was commanded by Edward Woodville.

Edward's first duty was to ride to York and stall the invaders by harassing them. According to Molinet, the only chronicler to record Edward's actions, he had 2,000 horsemen; Christopher Wilkins, however, estimates that he had only 500, given Molinet's fondness for large numbers.[38] For three days outside Doncaster, Edward and his men made life thoroughly miserable for 'King Edward's' army, although Molinet, a Burgundian chronicler, shines his best light on the pretender's forces: '[Edward] was so closely pursued from encampment to encampment and driven back for three days on end that he was forced to fall back in great haste through the forest of Nottingham'.[39] As Christopher Wilkins points out, however, the purpose of Edward's mission was to impede the advance of the invaders which he achieved by cutting their miles travelled per day by half.[40]

Mission accomplished, Edward rejoined the main army south of Nottingham. On 16 June, the two armies met at Stoke Field. King Henry had about 12,000 men, the rebels only 8,000 to 9,000.

The battle was over in about an hour. The Irish in the rebel army were ill-equipped, and there were no timely defections to save the day for the invaders. The Earl of Lincoln was killed in battle, as was the mercenary leader Martin Schwarz. Francis, Viscount Lovell, disappeared; whether he was killed in battle or fled abroad remains a mystery to this day, although there is a grisly legend that a skeleton found in a bricked-up room in one of his manors was his remains.[41] The young pretender, Lambert Simnel, was captured and set to work turning a spit in the royal kitchens; eventually, he rose to the position of royal falconer and according to Vergil was still alive in 1534.[42] The real Warwick was far less fortunate. The rebellion, and the arrival of a new pretender, Perkin Warbeck, on the scene a few years later, put paid to any chances he had had of being freed from the Tower. Warwick spent the rest of his life in captivity and was executed in 1499 for plotting with Perkin Warbeck; he may well have been entrapped in entering into communications with the pretender.

Having beaten back the first major challenge to his kingship, Henry could now turn his thoughts to a happier matter: the coronation of his queen, which took place on 25 November 1487.[43] There were two notable Woodville absences: the dowager queen and her son, Dorset. Custom might have prevented Elizabeth Woodville, a crowned queen herself, from taking part in the ceremony, but she is not listed as being present even at the feast afterward, unlike the king's mother, who observed the ceremony from a private spot and dined with the queen. Was she prevented from coming, or did she choose not to come? Some very awkward guests were present at the coronation, these being the Duke and Duchess of Suffolk, whose son the Earl of Lincoln had died at Stoke fighting against Henry, and Margaret Pole, the sister of the imprisoned Warwick. Given their presence, it seems unlikely that Elizabeth Woodville would have been kept away. Perhaps the imprisonment of her son, Dorset, had soured her relations with the king. Dorset himself may have still been in the Tower, according to Bacon, who informs us that he was released after the coronation, 'to show that it was now fair weather again, and that the imprisonment of Thomas Marquis Dorset was rather upon suspicion of the time than of the man'.[44]

These two absences did not keep other family members away. During the traditional procession from the Tower to Westminster that took place the day before the coronation, Katherine, Duchess of Bedford and Buckingham rode in the first chariot following the queen. With her was Elizabeth of York's younger sister, Cecily. A few places back, the duchess's ladies followed in their own chariot. At the feast after the coronation, the duchess sat at the left hand of the queen, who was served such dishes as hart, pheasant, capons, lamprey, crane, pike, carp, perch, and custard, preceded and followed by an elaborate 'subtlety', a decorative dish that was as much a feast for the eyes as it was for the mouth. Kneeling on either side of the queen were the Countess Rivers – Anthony's widow – and the Countess of Oxford, who were required to hold a kerchief before the queen at 'certain times', i.e. if she needed to spit out her food or perhaps use a toothpick. The Countess Rivers, still a young woman, probably found the kneeling easy enough to endure, but one's bones ache in sympathy for the Countess of Oxford, well into middle age, whose knees had to pay the price for royal protocol. The Woodville men were represented by Richard, Earl Rivers.

Edward Woodville is not recorded as being at the coronation, but he was certainly not in royal disfavour. The following year, on 27 April 1488, he was invested with the highest chivalric honour in England – the Order of the Garter.[45] Described by S.B. Chrimes as 'the ultimate mark of honour favoured by Henry VII', the Garter was an honour Edward's father and his brother Anthony had also achieved.[46] The queen and the king's mother, along with other ladies including Countess Rivers, were among the company assembled at Windsor for the feast of St George. The ceremonies, which included a requiem mass at which Edward offered the helm and crest of a deceased knight, John, Lord Dudley, inspired a burst of poetry:

> O knightly order, clothed in robes with garter:
> The queen's grace, thy mother in the same;
> The nobles of thy realm, rich in array, after;
> Lords, knights and ladies unto thy great fame.
> Now shall all ambassates know thy noble name.
> By they feast royal. Now joyous may thou be,
> To see thy king so flowering in dignity!

Edward had other concerns than the new garter adorning his calf, however. Francis, Duke of Brittany, who had offered succour and support to Edward as well as the king during their exile, was threatened with a French invasion.[47] As Henry VII owed his very crown to the aid of France, he was in a difficult position.

Edward longed to help his old friend. As Vergil tells it:

> Edward Woodville, a stout and courageous man […], either to avoid the tedium of peace or moved by his love of the duke, earnestly beseeched King Henry that by his permission he might go to Britanny with some band of soldiers to aid his friends. And, lest the King of France could reproach Henry for this, he said he would go secretly with no supplies, which would give a show of unfeigned flight. The king, who hoped that a peace would be arranged by his ambassadors, was so far from indulging Edward's ardor that he strictly forbade him to undertake any scheme of the kind, thinking it foreign to his dignity to offend Charles, to whom he hoped to ingratiate himself in a matter of little importance which he thought would do nothing to aid the

> Duke of Britanny. But Edward, when the king had forbidden him to do as he wished, decided to act without his knowledge, and quickly and secretly went to the Isle of Wight, of which he was lieutenant. And from there, having gathered a band of soldiers to the number of approximately four hundred, he crossed over to Britanny and joined with them against the French.[48]

Edward crossed the seas with his 400 men in ships provided by the Breton ambassadors. Meanwhile, his preparations had inspired others to follow suit. Writing to his brother, John Paston III, William Paston III reported:

> [W]hereas it was said that the Lord Woodville and others should have gone over into Brittany to have aided the Duke of Brittany. I cannot tell you of nonesuch aid. But upon that saying there came many men to Southampton, where it was said that he should have taken shipping to have waited upon him over, and so when he was countermanded those that resorted there to have gone over with him tarried there still, in hope that they should have been licenced to go over, and when they saw no likelihood that they should have licence there was two hundred of them that got them into a Breton ship the which was come over with salt, and bade the master set them a land in Brittany. And they had not sailed past six leagues but they espied a Frenchman, and the Frenchman made over to them, and they feared as though they would not have meddled with them, and all the Englishmen went under the hatches so that they showed no more but those that came to Southampton with the ship, to cause the Frenchmen to be the more gladder to meddle with them. And so the Frenchmen boarded them, and then they were under the hatches came up and so took the Frenchmen and carried the men, ship, and all into Brittany.[49]

Edward had sparked an international incident. Vergil tells us that the French suspected a trick on King Henry's part and that the English ambassadors in France feared for their own safety, although 'international law prevailed'. To mollify King Charles, Henry wrote a letter declaring that Edward had been expressly forbidden to make the trip to Brittany and that he had arrested the Earl of Arundel's younger brother when he tried to follow Edward's example. For good measure, Henry added, most of the men had gone without armour and were in any case low-lives who had taken asylum for their crimes and misdemeanours. It would soon be apparent, Henry concluded smugly, that Edward had been 'badly counselled' in making such a foolish attempt.[50] King Charles, Vergil tells us, did not put much credence in the king's letter, but put a good face on things. Meanwhile, Edward was enjoying the hospitality of Rennes, which welcomed him on 5 June by breaking open two barrels of claret and two barrels of white wine.

King Charles instructed his commander, General de la Trémoille, on 5 July to 'make war as vigorously as you can', an order which the general followed with enthusiasm. On 14 July, King Henry signed a peace treaty with France. The next day, Ferdinand and Isabella, whose ambassadors were discussing the possibility of a marital alliance with England, put in a good word for Edward, describing him as their faithful servant and asking Henry to forgive him.[51]

By this time troops had streamed into Rennes, including contingents contributed by Emperor Maximilian and King Ferdinand. On 25 July, Duke Francis, after meeting with a council of war that included Edward, determined to go to the relief of Fougères and St Aubin, both under siege. Although it turned out to be too late to save the fortresses, which had surrendered, the Bretons determined, as reported by Molinet, 'to engage the French […] as best they could'.[52]

The Marshal de Rieux was in overall command of the Breton forces, Trémoille in charge of the French. To fool the French into believing that there were a large number of English troops, the Breton army dressed 1,700 Bretons in surcoats bearing the red cross of St George, like the men of Edward's forces.

As reported by Hall:

> When both the armies were approaching to the other, the ordinance shot so terribly and with such a violence, that it sore damaged and encumbered both the parties. When the shot was finished, both the vanguards joined together with such a force that it was marvell[ous] to behold. The Englishmen shot so fast, that the Frenchmen in the forward, were fain to recule to the battle where their horsemen were. The rearward of the Frenchmen, seeing this first discomfiture began to flee, but the captains retired their men together again, & the horsemen set fiercely on the Bretons, and slew the most part of the footmen. When the forward of the Bretons perceived that their horsemen nor the Almaines carne not forward they provided for themselves & fled, some here, and some there, where they thought to have refuge or succour. So that in conclusion the Frenchmen obtained the victory, & slew all such as wore red crosses, supposing them all to be Englishmen. In this conflict were slain almost all the Englishmen, & six thousand Bretons, Amongst whom were found dead the lord Woodville […].[53]

Molinet reports that Edward fell 'near a wood called Selp'.[54]

On 20 August, the Duke of Brittany signed a treaty with France in which he acknowledged himself as its vassal. Three weeks later, he died, leaving his 12-year-old daughter, Anne, as his heir. Anne would ultimately marry Charles VIII of France.

Legend has it that only one of the numbers who had left with Edward returned to the Isle of Wight: a page named Diccon Cheke. A ballad tells his story:

> Fight on, fight on, my Island men
> Still gallant Wideville cried.
> Ah, how he fought till stricken sore
> Our Captain fell to rise no more
> Within these arms he died.
>
> Of all that sturdy Island band
> Who stern refused to flee,
> Knights and squires thirty and ten,
> Twenty score of stout yeomen,
> There is returned but me.[55]

When the Knights of the Garter met again in 1489, they would hold a requiem mass and offer the swords, helms, and crests of two fallen knights, Henry Percy, Earl of Northumberland (murdered during a tax revolt) and Edward Woodville. It was left for the same heralds who had recorded Edward's presence at his one and only Garter feast to write his epitaph: 'a noble and a courageous knight'.[56]

14

The Last of the Blood

On 31 October 1489, Queen Elizabeth went into confinement to await her coming child (Margaret, born on 29 November). Normally, once a pregnant queen 'took to her chambers', men would be barred until the child was born, but in this case, four ambassadors from France, one of whom, Francois of Luxembourg, was related to the queen, managed to be admitted into this all-female sanctum. When the men saw the queen, she was with not only the king's mother, but with her own mother as well.[1]

This rare glimpse of Elizabeth Woodville belies Bacon's later claim that she had been 'banished [from] the world into a nunnery; where it was almost thought dangerous to visit her or see her'.[2] Clearly, she had not been shut off from all contact with her family, although the extant records furnish no clue as to how often she saw or heard from them. Elizabeth of York's privy purse expenses, which would give us an idea as to whether messages or visits were exchanged between mother and daughter, do not survive for this period (or indeed for any other period other than the last year of the queen's life), and heraldic accounts by their very nature were concerned only with court ceremonies, not day-to-day interactions.

But there were fewer members of the Woodville family for the dowager queen to see. With Edward's death in battle, only one of Elizabeth's brothers, Richard, Earl Rivers, survived. Two Woodville sisters, Jacquetta, Lady Strange, and Mary Herbert, had died some years before.[3] Anne, who had married George Grey after the death of her first husband, Sir William Bourchier, died on 30 July 1489 and was buried at Warden Abbey in Bedfordshire.[4] Margaret, Lady Maltravers, died some time before 6 March 1491.[5] Joan, Lady Grey of Ruthin, was alive as of 24 September 1485, when Edward Woodville mentioned her as one of his heirs, but had died by 4 August 1492, when a post-mortem inquisition on her brother Richard was taken.[6]

It is possible, however, that Elizabeth Woodville had another brother living – an illegitimate one. Anthony Woodville's surviving papers show payments of wages to a Richard Woodville.[7] This is unlikely to be his legitimate brother Richard, who had his own estates to occupy his time; illegitimate sons, by contrast, could often be found in the service of their legitimate brothers. Moreover, a Richard Woodville attended Prince Arthur's christening in 1486 as an esquire for the king's body.[8] This again would not be the legitimate Richard Woodville, who had become Earl Rivers after Richard III's defeat at Bosworth and thus would have been referred to as such. The surname could be coincidence, of course, but given the prominence of the queen's relations at Arthur's christening, it seems far more likely that there was a family connection between them and this esquire. Finally, following the death of Edward Woodville, Henry VII had continued to send English forces to assist the Bretons. One of the commanders he sent was a Sir Richard Woodville, who was killed at Nantes in 1490.[9] Taken together, these references strongly suggest that before his marriage to Jacquetta, or even during it – perhaps during one of Jacquetta's many pregnancies – the elder Richard Woodville fathered an illegitimate son, who took up his brother Edward's Breton cause and died in it.

As for Richard, 3rd Earl Rivers, he had lived as quietly as an earl as he had as a knight. He played his part at court ceremonies, and had joined the king on his northern progress of early 1486.[10] During Henry VII's reign, he served on commissions of the peace in Bedfordshire and Northamptonshire and was among those commissioned to take musters of archers. Richard was also commissioned to investigate treasons, felonies, and conspiracies in Hereford in 1486 and to try petitions presented to Parliament in 1487.[11] Even as an earl, he seems to have made no effort to look for a wife.

The third Earl Rivers died on either 6 March 1491 or 25 April 1491; as he had made his will on 20 February 1491, the earlier date appears more likely.[12] He named his nephew the Marquis of Dorset as his heir and ordered that he be buried at St James at Northampton in a place made ready. Rivers asked that Dorset be a good lord to one William Hartwell, apparently Rivers's deputy as keeper of Sawcey (Sausy) Forest, 'for he had never none advantage by me but ever labour and pain'.[13] Finally, he asked that Dorset sell as much underwood at Grafton as was needed to purchase a bell 'for a remembrance of the last of the blood'.

On 28 June 1491, Henry VII and Elizabeth of York's second son, Henry, was born. The arrival of the future Henry VIII into the world did not excite much comment, and it is not known whether Elizabeth Woodville attended his birth. He would never come to know his maternal grandmother, for her own eventful life was drawing to a close.

The dowager queen wrote her will on 10 April 1492.[14] Styling herself as 'by the grace of God Queen of England, late wife to the most victorious Prince of blessed memory Edward the Fourth', she asked that she be buried next to the king at Windsor, 'without pompous entering or costly expenses'. Elizabeth requested that her 'small stuff and goods' be disposed to satisfy her debts and to provide for the welfare of her soul. Having 'no worldly goods to do the Queen's grace, my dearest daughter, a pleasure with, neither to reward any of my children, according to my heart and mind', she left Queen Elizabeth, and her other children, her blessing.

Elizabeth died at Bermondsey on 8 June 1492.[15] Two days later, her body was taken by water to Windsor, in accordance with her wishes; according to the herald's report, the late queen was buried immediately. The late queen was accompanied by two of her executors, John Ingleby, the Prior of the Charterhouse at Sheen, and Dr Thomas Brent, her chaplain; by her cousin, Edward Haute; by an unnamed gentlewoman; and by Grace, described as an illegitimate daughter of Edward IV. Nothing is known about Grace other than this single mention of her in the account of Elizabeth's funeral, but her presence suggests that Elizabeth did not greatly resent the products of her husband's extramarital flings.

The next day, workers constructed a hearse – a structure built around a coffin (or, here, a burial site) which could hold candles and banners as well as accommodate the most important mourners. Elizabeth's hearse, the herald noted, was:

> such as they use for the common people, with four wooden candlesticks above it and a cloth of black cloth of gold over it, with four wooden candlesticks of silver and gilt every each having a taper of no great weight, and two escutcheons of her arms pinned on that cloth.

Elizabeth's three unmarried daughters, Anne, Katherine, and Bridget, arrived at Windsor on 12 June. Anne would later marry Thomas Howard, then Earl of Surrey, while Katherine would marry William Courtenay, the heir to the earldom of Devon. Bridget was a nun at Dartford Priory. Queen Elizabeth, who would bear a short-lived daughter, Elizabeth, on 2 July 1492, had already taken to her chamber and could not attend the funeral. Also absent from the funeral was the queen's second daughter, Cecily, who was married to John, Viscount Welles, a half-brother of Margaret, Countess of Richmond. Perhaps the viscountess was attending the pregnant queen. The Duchess of Bedford and Buckingham did not attend but was represented by one of her two daughters. The dowager queen's daughter-in-law, Cecily, Marchioness of Dorset, was present, as was her niece Elizabeth Herbert, daughter of her sister Mary.

On 13 June, Anne, Katherine, and Bridget attended a requiem mass for their mother. That same day, the men arrived. They included Dorset; Henry Bourchier, Earl of Essex, the dowager queen's nephew by her late sister Anne; Viscount Welles; and Charles Somerset, the illegitimate son of Henry Beaufort, Duke of Somerset (and the new husband of Elizabeth Herbert). That night, a dirge was sung. The herald who recorded the funeral ceremonies grumbled that there were no new torches or poor men in black gowns, only 'a dozen divers old men holding old torches and torches' ends'. Elizabeth Woodville's wishes of a simple funeral were being followed, apparently too well for the herald's taste.

The next day, John Vaughan, a canon at Windsor, sang the mass of our Lady, at which Dorset offered a gold piece. A ceremony of offering followed, at which the Lady Anne, acting in lieu of her sister, the queen, offered the mass penny. Lady Katherine Grey bore Anne's train. The other daughters, carrying their own trains, offered pieces of gold, after which Dorset offered his own piece of gold, followed by the rest of the company. The ceremony concluded with the giving of alms.

Of Jacquetta and Richard Woodville's children, only the youngest, Katherine, now remained. Little is known about her life with Jasper Tudor, Duke of Bedford. In his study of Bedford, R.S. Thomas notes that the duke spent most of his last years at Thornley and Sudeley in Gloucestershire and at Minster Lovell in Gloucestershire. In January 1494, the king visited and was treated to ginger, oranges, lemons, and marmalade; sadly, whether the duchess was present is unknown.[16] Probably Katherine enjoyed taking possession of Minster Lovell, the former home of Richard III's vanished ally Francis, Viscount Lovell.

Jasper died on 21 December 1497 at Thornbury, having made his will on 15 December, and was buried at his request in Keynsham Abbey.[17] His businesslike will makes only one mention of Katherine, in the form of a request to his executors that 'my Lady my wife and all other persons have such dues as shall be thought to them appertaining by right law and conscience'. He did not name Katherine as an executor. Whether he thought she was not suited to the task, or whether he simply preferred men for the job, is unknown. Katherine in any event might have had her mind on something else, because by 25 February 1496, just two months after Jasper's death, she married her third husband, Richard Wingfield, who was about twelve years younger than the duchess, then in her late 30s.[18] The eleventh of the twelve sons of Sir John Wingfield of Leatheringham, Suffolk, and his wife, Elizabeth, he could have hardly had great material prospects, so presumably it was either personal attraction or a desire to forestall a political marriage that brought the duchess so precipitately into his bed. Henry VII fined the impetuous couple £2,000 for marrying without royal licence, although ultimately it was Katherine's oldest son, Edward Stafford, Duke of Buckingham, who had to come up with the fine once he entered into his inheritance.[19] Katherine would have probably known Richard for some time, as there were already ties between the Wingfields and the Woodvilles. Richard's mother, Elizabeth FitzLewis, was connected to Mary FitzLewis, Anthony Woodville's second wife.[20] Two of Richard's brothers, and perhaps Richard himself, had served in Katherine's household, and some family members had rebelled against Richard in 1483 and fought for Henry VII at Bosworth.[21]

Katherine did not enjoy her youthful husband for long; she died just over a year later on 18 May 1497.[22] It is tempting to speculate that she died from the effects of a late-life pregnancy, but there is no evidence that either of her last two marriages produced children. Her burial place is unknown. In his will made many years later, Wingfield, who remarried and was to enjoy a distinguished career in Henry VIII's diplomatic service, remembered to order masses for the soul of his 'singular good Lady Dame Katherine'.[23]

For all the turmoil and carnage of the fifteenth century, it was not violence that finished off the Woodville family, but an accident of biology: the failure of Jacquetta and Richard's five adult sons to beget legitimate male heirs. Thus, with the death of Katherine, the story of the Woodvilles became absorbed into the stories of the noble families into which Jacquetta's and Richard's daughters married – indeed, into the story of England itself.

As their blood became diluted over the years, so too did the sense of the Woodvilles as individuals. They became an amorphous mass, and an unsympathetic one at that as political propaganda, unsubstantiated legend, and myth collected about them. Yet although the Woodvilles, like our own families, shared collective triumphs and tragedies, they were as individual as we are. Even with the blurring effect of time, we can still pick out distinct personalities amid the whole of the Woodvilles: the knight who dared marry a duchess, the widow who captivated a king, the jouster who went to his death wearing a hairshirt, the young knight who charmed Ferdinand and Isabella and who died fighting for a cause not his own, the men and women who quietly went about their daily duties. We should not do them the disservice of forgetting them.

Appendix

The Wills of the Woodvilles

THE WILL OF THOMAS WOODVILLE

(Source: *History and Antiquities of Northampton*)

To the worship of God of our Lady and of all the company of Heaven, this is the will of me Thomas Widevill of Grafton in the county of Northampton Squire as it sheweth more plainly beneath by parcels made at Grafton. Abovesaid the 12th day of the month of October the year of the reign of King Henry the Sixth after the conquest the thirteenth.

In the first, I will that my feoffees of my lands make no estate of them to no manner Aman unto the time that my debts been paid, my will and my testament fully performed, and [this] done, I will that my said feoffees of my lands make a lawful estate to my brother Richard Widevill and to the heirs males of his body lawfully begotten in and of my manor and all other my lands and tenements rents reversions and services with all their appurtenances whatsoever they be in Grafton beside Aldrynnton with the hundred of Cleyle in the said county of Northampton. And if the said Richard my brother die without issue male of his body lawfully begotten then I will that all the said manor lands and tenements rents reversions and services with all other their appurtenances whatsoever they be in Grafton abovesaid together with the said hundred of Cleyle reverting wholly to my right heirs. Also I will that my said feoffees make a lawful estate to my right heirs in and of all my lands and tenements as well of my purchases of fee simple rents reversions and services with all other their apurtenances whatsoever they be in Westpury in Hertwell in the said county of Norhampton in Hulcote in the county of Bedford in Burton milles in the county of Buckingham to holden to them and to the right heirs of their bodies lawfully begotten for evermore in party of recompensation of the said manor of Grafton with the appurtenances. And if my said right heirs die without heirs of their bodies lawfully begotten then I will that all the said lands and tenements of my purchase and fee simple with rents reversions and services with all other their appurtenances whatsoever they be revert to the right heirs of John Wideville my father. Also I will that after my debts be paid my will and my testament fully performed that then my said feoffees make a lawful estate to my right heirs and to the heirs of their bodies lawfully begotten in and of all my manors lands and tenements rents reversions and services with all other their appurtenances whatsoever they be in the towns and in the fields of Northampton, Horton, Easton, Hulcote, Thurneby, Asshen, Roade, Hertewell, and Quinton or in any other place the which be undevised with in the said county of Northampton. And if my said right heirs die without issue of their bodies lawfully begotten then I will that the said lands and tenements rents reversions and services with all other their appurtenances wholly revert to the right heirs of my said father John Wideville. Also I will that my said feoffees keep the manor of Stoke Brewerne and Aldryngton and all other lands and tenements meadows leases and pastures rents reversions and services with the avowsons of the church of the said Stoke and Aldryngton, and all other appurtenances in the said Stoke, Aldryngton, and Shittehanger in the county of Northampton still in their hands unto the time that they have reserved thereof 200 marks [133 *6s 8d*] and paid it to my executors to perform with my will or else until the time that they pretenden title to inherit the said maner of Stoke with the appurtenances tail as it is abovesaid have paid to my said executors the said 200 marks and this payment of this 200 marks in the form of abovesaid had and an annuity of an 100 shilling, be my said feoffees to be granted to the father and the mother of Master John Aylewurd now parson of the church of the said Stoke in case that the said parson die leaving his said father and his mother or one of them, may be made secure to him yearly to be taken of the said manor of Stoke with the appurtenances to them or to one of them longest living to the term of their lives at the terms specified in a deed thereof to them to be made by said feoffees, all this truly and effectually performed then I will that my said feofees make estate to them that pretend to have the inheritance of the said manor be tail according thereto. Also it is my will that my said feofees make estate to the abbot of Saint James beyond Northampton to the convent of the same place and to their successors, in the Hermitage of Grafton, Schawe Woode, and in the manor of Avescote and all other lands and tenements rents reversions and services in Evescote, Patteshull, Derlescote, and Escote, with all their appurtenances wheresoever and whatsoever they be in the county of Northampton and in Fighelden in the county of Wiltshire or oughtwhere else to the term of fifty winter after the date of the deed by my said feoffees there of to them made, and if the same lands may be enpropered to them in the meantime forevermore for to find with five poor men and a keeper for them and for to do other certain observances in the said abbey to the worship of God and for the health of the souls of me the said Thomas Widevill my wives Elizabeth and Ales my father my mother my grandsire Thomas Lyons, Margaret his wife, and all other my friends and all Christian dewryng the said term of fifty winter and forevermore if the said Hermitage wood and manor with the appurtenances may be enpropered to the said abbot and his successors and my said feoffees. Also I will that my said feoffees and my executors purchase as much land as they may have for 200 marks and give it to my said right heirs of their bodies lawfully begotten in full recompensation of the said manor in Grafton aforesaid, and if my said right heirs die without heirs of their bodies lawfully begotten then I will that the said lands by my feoffees and executors with my goods so purchased revert to the right heirs of my father John Widevill. Also I will that my said feofees grant to John Beck my old servant a place and six acres of land with the appurtenances in Grafton abovesaid, in the which he is possessed now and an annuity of one mark be give by deed to be taken to him term of his life of my said manor and all my lands in Grafton at usual terms in the said deed contented with a clause of distress for default of payment. Also I will that my said feoffees grant to Robert Packer my servant a place and six acres of land with the appurtenances in Grafton above said and an annuity of 20 shillings by year by deed to be taken to him term of his life of my manor [and] my lands in Grafton above said at usual terms in the said deed contented with a clause of distress for default of payment. Also I will that my said feofees grant to John of the Botery my servant a place and all the lands and tenements with their appurtenances the which I purchased of John Warwick squire in Westpury to him term of his life yielding thereof yearly a rose flower to my said feofees at the feast of midsummer term of his life and bearing all other charges to the said place and land belonging during the said term. Also I will that my said feofees grant to my niece Elizabeth Holwell an annuity of six marks to be taken to her term of her life of my manor in Hertwell with the appurtenances called Morwelles manor and of all other my lands and tenements in the said town with the appurtenances where so ever they be with a clause of distress for default of payment. Also I will that my said feofees grant to Margaret Broke my servant an annuity of twenty shillings to be taken to her term of her life of my maner and all my lands and tenements in Roode with the appurtenances where so ever they be with a clause of distress for default of payment. In the witness of the which thing to this part of my will tripartite indentured my seal I have put to. Given the day and the year and the place above said. Also I will that my executors shall receive and have to perform my will all manner of rents and pfytes coming of my lands tenements reversions and services the which my feofees shall hold in their hands until my said will be fully performed. Also I will that my said feofees grant to William Butler my servant all my lands and tenements with the appurtenances in Horton by deed to be taken to him term of his life. Also I will that my said feofees grant to Thomas Barbour my servant estate in all my lands and tenements with the appurtenances in Quynton to term of his life. Also I will that my said feoffees grant to William Manning my servant all the lands and tenements that I have in Estneston and Hulcote beside Towcester in the county of Northampton to term of his life.

THE WILL OF RICHARD WOODVILLE, ESQUIRE

(Source: *Register of Henry Chichele, Archbishop of Canterbury*. Translated from the Latin by Hannah Kilpatrick)

In the name of God, Amen. Vigil of Saint Andrew the Apostle [Nov. 30], year of the Lord 1441, I, Richard Woodville the elder, compose my testament as follows. Firstly, I bequeath my soul to God and my body to be buried in the church of Maidstone. Also I give and bequeath all my movable property to Joan my wife that she, together with my other executors named below, may honestly arrange for my burial and for the payment of all my servants' wages and of all my other debts. And in order that these and other payments may be faithfully made in full I wish, ordain, and decree that my manor of Shalford in county Bedford be sold, by the said Joan my wife and my other executors, as advantageously as possible, such that all other expenses and payments may be met in full from the resulting money. And as for the remainder of my assets, after all debts have been paid and every other will and order of mine expressed by myself to my executors has been faithfully and wholly carried out, I wish, ordain, and decree that the whole be settled upon my wife Joan in perpetuity. And I name her my principal executor, and Sir Richard my son, William Haute, lord Robert Abbot of Graciis, and Richard Barbour of Maidstone, to carry out this my will. And I ask Sir Richard my son, and firmly instruct him, that he be faithful to Joan my wife, his mother, and that he protect her and aid her throughout all her life, as he wishes to come before

God with my blessing. Given on the day and year abovementioned, witnessed by William Manning, John Warburton, John Lange, and others, etc.

THE WILL OF ANTHONY, EARL RIVERS

(Source: PROB 11/8. Transcribed by Simon Neal)

In the name of our Lord amen I Antony Widevile etc In hole mynd and Fressh memory in the Castell of Shwyshoton the xxiij day of Juyn and the vigill of seint John Baptyst the yere of our lord m^{l} cccclxxxiij make my testament and last will in the fo[ur]me folowyng Furst I bequeith my soule unto the grete m[er]cy of J[esus] Crist and to his dere moder our Lady seint Mary and to the glorious company of Hevyn And my hert to be had to our Lady of Pewe beside seint Stephyns College at Westmynster there to be buried by thadvyse of the deane and his brethern And If I dy be yend trent than to be buried be fore our Lady of Pewe aforseid Also I will that all such Land as was my Lord my faders Remayne Holy to his right heyres w[i]t[h] my cupp of gold of Colombyne which was Lefte me by bequest to that entent it shuld remayne to the right heires of my seid Lord my Faders and such londes as were the Lady Scalis my fyrst wyfe be unto my brother Syr Edward and to his heyris male For faut of such heyres male unto the right heyres of my seid lord my fadre / This is my will and entent therin to take effecte as ferre as consciens and Law will / And that to be sene and determyned by ij doctours of London and ij of Oxford and of Cambrigge / or docto[ur]s at the lest w[i]t[h] ij of the chefe Juges and ij of theldest s[er]vauntes of the Lawe And if they fynde that this myn entent may not with conscience and Lawe and any part therof that it be guydid after their demyng And if they think that my seid brother may have it all / or for fawt of hym ony of my seid Lord my fadre heires he that shalhave the lond to pay or he have possession v^{c} marcas that to be employed for the soules of my Last wyfe Lady Scalys and Thom[a]s hyr brother and the soules of all the scales blode in helping and refresshing hospitalles and other dedes charitable / And if all the Land may not be so had than to pay but aft[er] the Rate of such lond as I may bequeith. Also I will that all my goodes goo to the paying of my dettes And all my fee simpill Lond that is to sey the maner of Tyrington Hall In Middylton with the Hundreth of Frebrigge / the man[er] of Wolv[er]ton w[i]t[h] thadvowson in the Counte of Norfolke the Maner of Rokey in Barway in the Counte of Hertford to be sold to the same entent and for to make an hospitall at Rowchestyr for xiij pou[er] folkes and other dedes of Charite as to pay prisoners fees and small dettes to visett the prisones of London and help to bury the dede w[i]t[h] other werkes of mercy And as for my dettes I knowlege I owe to the bisshop of Worcester lx[li] which I will he be truly paid Also I knowlege that I owe a somme of mony to Loumer Mercer of London as it wele apperith both by his billes and by my boke in my closett at London which I wyll be content after consciens Also I knowlege that I owe abowght xl[li] to Coles Mayce goldsmyth as Butsyde of London and Griffith my servaunt can tell which Coles I wilbe truly content Also I knowlege that I owe to the Mayor of Lynne and to divers creditours in Norfolk And to Abrey Drap[er] of Norwich s[er]teyn sommes of money as apperith by warauntes signid by my hand to Fynch[a]m myn receyvo[ur] which shuld pay theym of my Lyvelode and fees in Norfolk and Suffolk growing from Mychelmas Last passid which warantes I wilbe paid in any wyse Also I Remember there was a preest claymid to be executor to a boucheer of London callid Lamye As Andrew Dymmok knowith and that I shuld owe the same bocheer money which I will in any wyse be paid And that ther be a preest founde a yere at our Lady of Pewe to pray for the sowle of the seid brocherer and all cristen soules And an other for the sowles of Syr Henry Lowes And a preest to be fow[n]de to syng at the Chapell of the Redes in Grenewich to pray for my soule and all [Christ]en sowlys And that my wyfe have all such plate as was the same Henry Lowes And other of my plate to the valiwe of asmuche thing as I hadd of his Also that she have all such plate as was geven hyr at our mariage and the sparver of white sylke w[i]t[h] iiij peyre of shetes ij payre of fustians a federbed j chambring of gresylde And except that stuffe all other stuffe of howsehold in the mote and at my place in the Vyntree to be to my seid lord my faders heyres advising theym on goddes behalve that thabbot of Seint Jamys beside Northampton And the Nonnes beside Caunturbury be allwey dewley answerd of their Claymes And Syr John Gilford to content it as it apperith by the evidences that Richard Haute hath Also I will that Seint Mary of York have my grete gilt basons And such a somme of money as myn executours shall think goode to p[r]ay for my soule Also I owe to Syr Thomas Vaugh[a]n cc marc wherof I have paid xx[ti] marc here in the north And he hath to plegge my balys in Colombyne with v perles Also I will that all my household serv[a]ntes in the Chekyr Roll have trewly ther wages for Mydsom[er] quarter And every one a blak gowne And as I Remembyr I owe Willi[a]m Butler xx[s] which I will he be paid And as for myn evidences Andrewe Dymmok knowyth them And canne shewe how all my lond standith And if Willi[a]m Aubrey which was coferer to the kyng which now is whan he was prince Thomas Wytman the seid Andrew Dymmok Butsyde and John Gryffyth know any moo dettes that I shuld owe I require them for to shew it And I will myn executours in any wyse to pay to whom it be owyng And I desire on goddes behalve that no man int[er]rupt my seid executours in fulfilling this my will as they will answere at the dredefull day of Dome geving to my seid executours power by this my seid will to take a Rekenyng and Levy all such sommes of money as is owyng me of my lyvelod fees annuitees or otherwyse And they to employe such goodes as shall come to their handes after this will and moost conscient for the wele of my soule And I will that all myn Aray for my body and my horse harnes be sold And with the money therof be bought shyrtes and smokkes to pouer folkes And my gowne of Tawney cloth of gold I geve to the priour of Royston / my trapper of blakk cloth of gold I geve to our Lady of Walsingham Also I desire and charge on goddes behalve and upon payne of damnac[i]on that my feeffes make none Astate nor Relese Ne my tenauntes make no recov[er]e but acording to theffect of this my Last will Also I will that all such lond as I purchasid by the meane of Syr Jamys Molaynes preest Remayn still w[i]t[h] the Man[er] of Grafton toward the fynding of the preest of thavuntage Also the londes that I purchased beside the mote to Remayne to my lord my faders heyres / Also I will that my Lady Willoughby late the wyfe of Syr Gerveis Clyfton be co[m]mond w[i]t[h] all by myne executours towching such stuff as syr Ewan p[ar]son of Wolverton and other my serv[a]ntes had awey from hyr place and she to be delt w[i]t[h] therin and Answerid acording to goode right and conscience And I will in no wyse that the Nonnes of Blakborough be hurt in such Londes of theires as Lieth w[i]t[h]in the Roche Fenne of Myddylton which I late closid Also I will that Syr Jamys Molaynes and Emson late Attorney of the Duchie of Lancastre be co[m]mond w[i]t[h] And that it be sene if so be that I have occupied bradon w[i]t[h]out good Right that myn executours se the contentacion and Refo[ur]myng therof acording to right and conscience And I will that thadvowson of the parissh church of Bewdeley Remayne the Patronacion therof to the right heires of my lord my fadre Theym to present to the benefice whan it shall fawle voyde an able preest to pray for the sowles of my seid Lord my fadre my Lady my modre my brother S[ir] John me and all Cristen sowles Also I wull that Wyttyngton College of London have a somme of money to pray for my soule and myn executours see that such tythes as I owt to have made be Answerid in the moost behofefull wyse for my sowle Also I will that Tybold my barbo[ur] have v mark And I will my s[er]v[a]nt Jamys [*blank*] have xl[s] Also I make myn executours the Bisshop of Lincoln Chaunceler of Englond the bisshopp of

Worcestyr / Husy the Chefe Juge of the Kinges benche / Bryan the chefe Juge of the Comyn place Willi[a]m Tunstall Robert Poynz Richard Hawte Willi[a]m Catesby Andrew Dymmok and Thom[a]s Thorysby To which all And at the Lest to thre of them I geve full auctorite and power And prey them at the Reverence of J[esus] to see this my will may be fulfillid Over this I besech humbly my Lord of Gloucestyr in the Worshipp of Cristes passhion and and for the meryte and wele of his sowle to Comfort help and assist as sup[er]visors for very trust of this testament that myn executours may w[i]t[h] his pleasur fulfill this my Last will which I have made the day aboveseid In wittenes Syr Thomas Gower Knyght Willi[a]m Tunstall Doctor Lovell Syr John Esingwold vicar of Shyryshton Syr Willi[a]m Teysedale Thomas Wawer preestes and Richard Lepton gentylman / My will is now to be buried before An Image of our blissid Lady Mary w[i]t[h] my Lord Richard In Pomfrete And J[esus] have mercy of my soule etc

THE WILL OF RICHARD, THIRD EARL RIVERS

(Source: PROB 11/8. Transcribed/translated by Simon Neal)

In dei nomine amen the xx day of February the yere of our Lord god m[l] ccccIxxxx I Richard Wydevile Erle of Ryvers being in hole mynd Lovid be all myghty god make and ordeigne this my present testament in the man[er] and forme here folowyng First I bequeith my soule to allmighty god and to his blessid moder seint Mary and to all the holy company of heven my body to be buried at seint Jamys Abbey at North[a]mpton in a place made redy therfor It[e]m I bequeith to Syr John p[ar]son of Lee the lesse fetherbed that was there and ij kene of Rede colour Also I will that such hogges that been there quick and dede be sold by the oversight of the Mayor of London and Hugh Pemberton Shreve of London to thentent that the money receyved for them be bestowed abowte the reparacion of our Lady chapell in the seid p[ar]isch church of Lee It[e]m I bequeith to the parissh church of Grafton all such catell as I have at Grafton that is to sey ij oxon v kene ij bolokes to thentent that they shall yerely kepe an obite for my soule that is to sey dirige and Masse of requiem w[i]t[h] the curatt iiij preestes and iiij clerkes w[i]t[h] an heerse and iiij tapers every preest takyng for his wagis v[d] and every clerk iij[d] And the residewe that shall comyn of them ov[er] shall goo yerely to the reparacion of the same church of Grafton moost necessary It[e]m I bequeith to the p[ar]issh church of Wylmyngton viij kene that been there to thentent that they shall yerely kepe for my soule an obite dirige and masse of requiem w[i]t[h] the curatt and iiij preestes and iiij clerkes every preest taking for his wages v^{d} and every Clerk iij^{d} And the residew of the seid Catall to goo to the reparacion of the same church moost necessary It[e]m I bequeith to the Roode church a bay mare and ij foolys Also I will that all the evidences concernyng a ward callid Elisabeth Gripon be deliverd to Martyn Hawte and his felowes Fearis for and upon this condicion that the seid Elisabeth wilbe rewlyd after them Item I forgeve all such money as it [...] me so that they medill not w[i]t[h] the howse in stony stratford in the which Thomas Edy died this I bought and paid for Also I will that my Lord Thomas Markes Dors[et] be myn exe[cutor] And I will and graunt to hym all such Londes and tenementes as I may geve whersoev[er] they be The residew of all my goodes moveable and unmoveable not bequist I bequeith to the seid Lord Thomas Markes Dors[et] Willi[a]m H[...]wod of Preston and John Pekk if Kyngthorpe whom I make and ordeign myn executours they to execute my seid will in the man[er] and forme above rehersid after an Inventory made of the seid goodes Also I beseche my seid Lord Markes that ther may be as muche underwode sold in the wodys of Grafton as shall by a bell to be teno[ur] at Grafton to the bellys there nowe for a remembrance of the last of the blode Also I beseche the seid Lord that all such grauntes made by my lettyrs patent to theis or to any of them that is to sey Willi[a]m Goddeley Thomas Maynard John Addington John Ware and John Walley for terme of lyfe or for terme of yeres may be confermid and admittyd by hym they to pray for my soule Also I beseche the seid Lord Markes that he will soe to the av[a]ntage of Grafton and conf[ir]me the evidences of the old enheritaunce that I have of it be thought of conscience that thabbot of Seint Jamys shuld have any thing therof I wold that my lord Markes and myn executours wold relese of Shaw Woode the which they have yerely whan it is sold Also I beseche my seid Lord Markes to be goode Lord to thaforseyd Willi[a]m Hartwell in his office of Sausy for he had never non avauntage by me but ever Labo[ur] and payne

Translation of the Probate

The before-written will was proved before the archbishop at Lamehith on the 23rd day of the month of March in the year of the lord 1491 by the oath of William Hertwell, the executor named in this will, who refused to take up the charge of the execution of the same upon himself then and there, and it was approved, etc. And the administration of all and singular the goods and debts of the said deceased was committed to the very powerful master lord Thomas, marquess of Dorset, the executor, named in the said will, in the person of Master John Reed, notary public, the proctor, etc, sworn, etc, well, etc, and concerning a full inventory, etc, before the feast of Holy Trinity next, etc, and also concerning a plain and true account, etc.

THE WILL OF ELIZABETH, QUEEN TO EDWARD IV

(Source: PROB 11/9. Transcribed by Simon Neal)

In dei Nomine Amen the xth daie of Aprill the yere of oure lord gode m^{l}cccclxxxxij I Elsabeth by the grace of god Quene of Englond late wif to the most victoriouse prince of blessed memorie Edward the fourth being of hole mynde seyng the worlde so transitorie and no creature certayne whanne they shall departe frome hence havyng Almyghty gode fressh in mynde in whome is all mercy and grace bequeith my sowle in to his handes beseching him of the same mercy to accept it graciously and oure blessed Lady quene of comforte and all the holy company of hevyn to be good meanes for me It[e]m I bequeith my body to be buried w[i]t[h] the bodie of my Lord at Windessore according to the will of my saide Lorde and myne without pompes entreing or costlie expensis donne there a bought It[e]m where I have no wordely goodes to do the quenes grace my derest doughter a pleaser with nether to reward any of my children according to my hart and mynde I besech almyghty gode to blisse here grace with all her noble issue and w[i]t[h] as good hart and mynde as is to me posible I geve her grace my blesing and all the forsaide my children It[e]m I will that suche smale stufe and goodes that I have be disposed treuly in the contentac[i]on of my dettes and for the helth of my sowle as farr as they will extende It[e]m yf any of my bloode wilbie any of my saide stufe or goodes to me p[er]teyning I will that they have the prefermente be fore any other And of this my present testament I make and ordeyne myne executores that is to sey John Ingilby priour of the Chartour House of Shene William Sutton and Thomas Brente docto[ur]s and I besech my said derest doughter the quenes grace and my Sone Thomas Marques Dorsett to putto there good willes and help for the p[er]forma[n]s of this my testamente In witnesse wherof to this my present testament I have sett my seale these witnesses John Abbot of the Monast[er]y of Sainte Saviour of Bermondesley and Benedictus Cun Doctor of Fysyk Yeven the day and yere abovesaid

Bibliography

Unprinted Primary Sources

British Library Additional Manuscripts
Eton College Archives: ECR 60/3/2
The National Archives

Printed Primary Sources

Ancient Songs and Ballads ..., Collected by Joseph Ritson, vol. II. (London, 1829).

Annales Rerum Anglicarum, in Joseph Stevenson, ed., *Letters and Papers Illustrative of the Wars of the English in France during the Reign of King Henry VI*, vol. II, pt. 2, pp. 743 et seq. (London, 1864).

Bacon, Francis, *The History of the Reign of King Henry the Seventh*, F.J. Levy, ed. (Indianapolis and New York, 1972).

The Bedford Inventories: The Wordly Goods of John, Duke of Bedford, Regent of France (1389–1435), Jenny Stratford, ed. (London, 1993).

'The Book of Howth,' in J.S. Brewer and William Bullen, eds, *Calendar of the Carew Manuscripts Preserved at the Archiepiscopal Library at Lambeth*, pp. 1 *et seq*. (London, 1871).

British Library Harleian Manuscript 433, Rosemary Horrox and P.W. Hammond, eds, 4 vols. (London, 1979–83).

Buck, George, *The History of King Richard the Third*, Arthur Noel Kincaid, ed. (Gloucester, 1979).

Calendar of the Carew Manuscripts Preserved at the Archiepiscopal Library at Lambeth, 1575–1588, J.S. Brewer and William Bullen, eds (London, 1868).

Calendar of the Close Roll, preserved in the Public Record Office, Edward II to Henry VII (London, 1891–1916).

Calendars of Patent Rolls, preserved in the Public Record Office, Edward II to Henry VII, 45 vols (London, HMSO, 1844–1916).

'The Captivity of a Royal Witch: The Household Accounts of Queen Joan of Navarre, 1419–21', A.R. Myers, ed., in *Bulletin of the John Rylands Library*, 24 (1940).

The Cely Letters 1472–1488, Alison Hanham, ed. (Oxford, 1975).

Chronicles of London, Charles L. Kingsford, ed. (Oxford, 1905).

The Chronicles of the White Rose of York, John A. Giles, ed. (London, 1845).

Commynes, Philippe de, *Memories*, ed. J. Calmette and G. Durville, 3 vols (Paris, 1923–25).

The Coronation of Elizabeth Wydeville: Queen Consort of Edward IV on May 26th, 1465, George Smith, ed. (Cliftonville, 1975).

The Coronation of Richard III: The Extant Documents, Anne Sutton and P.W. Hammond, eds (Gloucester and New York, 1983).

The Coventry Leet Book, Mary Dormer Harris, ed. (London, 1907).

The Crowland Chronicle Continuations, 1459–1486, Nicholas Pronay and John Cox, eds (London, 1986).

Edward IV: A Source Book, Keith Dockray, ed. (Stroud, 1999).

Edward IV's French Expedition of 1475, Francis Pierrepont Barnard, ed. (Gloucester Reprints: 1975).

An English Chronicle: 1377–1461, William Marx, ed. (Woodbridge, 2003).

English Historical Documents, vol. IV, 1327–1485, A.R. Myers, ed. (London, 1969).

English Historical Literature in the Fifteenth Century, Charles L. Kingsford, ed. (New York, 1913).

Excerpta Historica, or, Illustrations from English History, Samuel Bentley, ed. (London, 1833).

Fabyan, Robert, *The New Chronicles of England and France,* Henry Ellis, ed. (London, 1811).

Fifteenth Century Prose and Verse, Alfred W. Pollard, ed. (Westminster, 1903).

Foedera, conventiones, literae et cujuscunque gemeris Acta Publica, Thomas Rymer, ed., vol. XII (Burlington, Ontario, 2003).

The Forty-Eighth Annual Repast of the Deputy Keeper of the Public Records (London, 1887).

Grants, etc. from the Crown during the Reign of Edward the Fifth, John G. Nichols, ed. (London, 1854)

The Great Chronicle of London, A.H. Thomas and I.D. Thornley, eds. (Gloucester, 1983).

Hall's Chronicle, Henry Ellis, ed. (London, 1809).

Henry VI, Margaret of Anjou, and the Wars of the Roses: A Source Book, Keith Dockray, ed. (Stroud, 2000).

The Heralds' Memoir 1486–1490: Court Ceremony, Royal Progress and Rebellion. Emma Cavell, ed. (Donington, 2009).

Historie of the Arrivall of Edward IV in England and the Finall Recouerye of His Kingdomes from Henry VI, John Bruce, ed. (London, 1838).

The Household Books of John Howard, Duke of Norfolk, 1462–1471, 1481–1483. Anne Crawford, ed. (Stroud, 1992).

'The Household of Queen Elizabeth Woodville, 1466–7', A.R. Myers, ed., *Bulletin* of the John Rylands Library, 50 (1967–68), pp. 207–35, 443–81.

'The Household of Queen Margaret of Anjou, 1452–3', A.R. Myers, ed., *Bulletin* of the John Rylands Library, 40 (1957–58), pp. 79–113, 391–431.

Illustrations of Ancient State and Chivalry, W.H. Black, ed. (London 1840).

The Itinerary of King Richard III 1483–1485, Rhoda Edwards, ed. (London, 1983).

Leland, Joannis, *De rebus brittanicis collectanea,* Thomas Hearn, ed., vol. II (Oxford, 1770).

Letters and Papers, Henry VII, 16 December 1533, item 1528; 3 November 1534, item 1368.

Letters and Papers Illustrative of the Reigns of Richard III and Henry VIII, James Gairdner, ed., 2 vols. (London, 1861, 1863).

Letters of the Kings of England, James O. Halliwell, ed., vol. I (London, 1846).

The Logge Register of PCC Wills, 1479 to 1486, Lesley Boatwright, Moira Habberjam, and Peter Hammond, eds, 2 vols (Knaphill, 2008).

London and the Kingdom, Reginald R. Sharpe, ed., vol. III (London, 1895).

Mancini, Dominic, *The Usurpation of Richard III*, C.A.J. Armstrong, ed. (Gloucester, 1989).

The Manuscripts of the Corporations of Southampton and King's Lynn, Historical Manuscripts Commission, 11th Report, Appendix, pt. III (London, 1878).

Marche, Olivier de la, *Mémoires de l'Olivier de la Marche*, Henri Beaune and J. D'arbaumont, eds, vol. III (Paris, 1885).

The Marcher Lordships of South Wales, 1415–1536: Select Documents, T.B. Pugh, ed. (Cardiff, 1963).

Materials for a History of the Reign of Henry VII, W. Campbell, ed., 2 vols (London, 1873 and 1877).

Monstrelet, Enguerran de, *La chronique d'Enguerran de Monstrelet*, L. Douët-D'Arcq., ed., vol. V (Paris, 1861).

More, St Thomas, *The History of King Richard III*, Richard S. Sylvester, ed. (New Haven and London, 1976).

Original Letters Illustrative of English History, H. Ellis, ed. second series, vol. I (London, 1827).

The Paston Letters, James Gairdner, ed. (Gloucester, 1986).

Paston Letters and Papers of the Fifteenth Century, Norman Davis, ed. (pts. I and II), Richard Beadle and Colin Richmond, eds (pt. III) (Oxford, 2004–05).

The Plumpton Letters and Papers, Joan Kirby, ed. (Cambridge, 1996).

Political Poems and Songs Relating to English History, Thomas Wright, ed., vol. II (London, 1861).

The Prologues and Epilogues of William Caxton, W.J.B. Crotch (New York, 1971).

Privy Purse Expenses of Elizabeth of York; Wardrobe Accounts of Edward the Fourth, Nicholas H. Nicolas, ed. (London, 1830).

The Reburial of Richard Duke of York 21–30 July 1476, Anne F. Sutton and Livia Visser-Fuchs, eds, with Peter Hammond (London, 1996).

The Register of Henry Chichele, Archbishop of Canterbury, 1414–1443, vol. 2, E.F. Jacob, ed. (Oxford, 1938).

Reliques of Ancient English Poetry, Thomas Percy, ed., vol. II (London, 1839).

Richard III: A Source Book, Keith Dockray, ed. (Stroud, 1997).

Richard III: The Road to Bosworth Field, Peter Hammond and Anne F. Sutton, eds. (London, 1985).

Rotuli Parliamentorum, John Strachey, ed., vol. VI (1777).

Rous, John, *Historia Regum Angliae*, T. Heame, ed. (2nd edition, Oxford, 1765).

Rous, John, *The Rous Roll*, intro. Charles Ross (reprinted, Gloucester, 1980).

The Royal Funerals of the House of York at Windsor, Anne F. Sutton and Livia Visser-Fuchs, eds, with R.A. Griffiths (London, 2005).

Six Town Chronicles of England, Ralph Flenley, ed. (Oxford, 1911).

'Some Ancient Indictments in the Kings Bench Referring to Kent, 1450–1452', in R. Virgoe, ed., *Documents Illustrative of Medieval Kentish Society* (Kent Archaeological Society 18, 1964).

Stonor Letters and Papers: 1290–1483 (Kingsford's Stonor Letters and Papers 1290–1483). Christine Carpenter, ed., (Cambridge, 1996).

John Stow, *Annales, or a General Chronicle of England* (London, 1631).

Three Catalogues, describing the Contents of the Red Book of the Exchequer, of the Dodsworth Manuscripts in the Bodleian Library, and of the Manuscripts in the Library of the Honourable Society of Lincoln's Inn, Joseph Hunter, ed. (London, 1838).

Three Chronicles of the Reign of Edward IV (Gloucester, 1988).

The Travels of Leo of Rozmital, Malcolm Letts, ed. and trans. (Cambridge 1957).

Vergil, Polydore, *Three Books of Polydore Vergil's English History*, Henry Ellis, ed. (New York and London, 1968).

Visitations of the North, Part III: A Visitation of the North of England Circa 1480–1500, C.H. Hunter Blair, ed. (Durham and London, 1930).

Warkworth, John, *Chronicle of the First Thirteen Years of the Reign of King Edward IV*, James O. Halliwell, ed. (1839).

Waurin, Jehan de, *Recueil des Chroniques et anchiennes istories de la Grant Bretaigne*, William Hardy and Edward Hardy, eds., vols IV,V (London, 1884, 1891).

Waurin, Jean de, *Anchiennes Chroniques de l'engleterre*, ed. E.L and M.E. Dupont, eds (Paris, 1858–63).

York House Books 1461–1490, Lorraine C. Attreed, ed., 2 vols (Stroud, 1991).

Secondary Sources

Books

Ames, Joseph, and Herbert, William, *Typographical Antiquities* (London, 1810).

Arthurson, Ian, *The Perkin Warbeck Conspiracy 1491–1499* (Stroud, 1994).

Ashdown-Hill, John, *Eleanor, the Secret Queen: The Woman Who Put Richard III on the Throne* (Stroud, 2009).

Ashdown-Hill, John, *The Last Days of Richard III* (Stroud, 2010).

Aston, Margaret, and Horrox, Rosemary, eds, *Much Heaving and Shoving: Late-Medieval Gentry and Their Concerns; Essays for Colin Richmond* (Chipping, 2005).

Baldwin, David, *Elizabeth Woodville: Mother of the Princes in the Tower* (Stroud, 2002).

Barker, Juliet, *Conquest: The English Kingdom of France* (London, 2009).

Barnwell, Edward Lowry, *Perrot Notes, or, Some Account of the Various Branches of the Perrot Family* (London, 1867).

Beauchesne, Marquis de, *L'Expedition d'Edward Wydeville en Bretagne* (Vannes, 1911).

Bellamy, J.G., *The Law of Treason in England in the Later Middle Ages* (Cambridge, 1970).

Bennett, Michael, *The Battle of Bosworth* (New York, 1985).

Bennett, Michael, *Lambert Simnel and the Battle of Stoke* (New York, 1987).

Blomfield, Francis, *An Essay Towards a Topographical History of the County of Norfolk*, vol. 9 (London 1808).

Boardman, Andrew, *The First Battle of St Albans: 1455* (Stroud, 2006).

Brindley, David, *Richard Beauchamp: Medieval England's Greatest Knight* (Stroud, 2001).

Britton, John, *The History and Antiquities of the Cathedral Church of Salisbury* (London, 1814).

Calmette, J., and Perinelle, G., *Louis XI et L'Angleterre* (Paris, 1930).

Carson, Annette, *The Maligned King* (Stroud, 2008).

Catto, J.I., and Evans, Ralph, eds, *The History of the University of Oxford*, vol. II, *Late Medieval Oxford* (Oxford, 1992).

Cavill, P.R. *The English Parliaments of Henry VII 1485–1504* (Oxford, 2009).

Chrimes, S.B. *et al.*, eds, *Fifteenth-Century England 1399–1509: Studies in Politics and Society* (New York: Mancester University Press, 1972).

Chrimes, S.B. *Henry VII* (New Haven and London, 1999).

Cokayne, G.E. *et al.*, *The Complete Peerage of England, Scotland, Ireland, Great Britain and the United Kingdom* (London, 1910–39).

Colvin, H.M., gen. ed., *The History of the King's Works* (London, 1963–73).

Crawford, Anne, *The Yorkists: The History of a Dynasty* (London and New York, 2007).

Crawford, Anne, *Yorkist Lord* (London and New York, 2010).

Davis, Virginia, *William Waynflete, Bishop and Educationalist* (Woodbridge, 1993).
Doyle, James William Edmund, *The Official Baronage of England* (London, 1886).
Evans, H.T., *Wales and The Wars of the Roses* (1915; repr. Stroud, 1998).
Gairdner, James, *The History of the Life and Reign of Richard the Third* (London, 1879).
Gill, Louise, *Richard III & Buckingham's Rebellion* (Stroud, 2000).
Goodman, Anthony, *The Wars of the Roses* (New York, 1981).
Griffiths, Ralph, *King and Country: England and Wales in the Fifteenth Century* (London, 1991).
Griffiths, Ralph, *The Reign of King Henry VI* (Stroud, 1998).
Griffiths, Ralph, and Sherborne, James, eds, *Kings and Nobles in the Later Middle Ages* (New York, 1986).
Griffiths, Ralph and Thomas, Roger S., *The Making of the Tudor Dynasty* (Stroud, 1998).
Gunn, Steven and Janse, Antheun, eds, *The Court as a Stage: England and the Low Countries in the Later Middle Ages* (Woodbridge, 2006).
Hammond, Peter, *Richard III and the Bosworth Campaign* (Barnsley, 2010).
Hammond, Peter, *The Battles of Barnet and Tewkesbury* (New York, 1990).
Hanham, Alison, *Richard III and his Early Historians 1483–1535* (Oxford, 1975).
Harris, Barbara J. *Edward Stafford: Third Duke of Buckingham, 1478–1521* (Stanford, 1986).
Harvey, I.M.W., *Jack Cade's Rebellion of 1450* (Oxford, 1991).
Hellinga, Lotte, *Caxton in Focus: The Beginning of Printing in England* (London, 1982).
Helmholz, R.H., *Marriage Litigation in Medieval England* (Cambridge, 1994).
Hepburn, Frederick. *Portraits of the Later Plantagenets* (Woodbridge and Dover, 1986).
Hicks, M.A., *False, Fleeting, Perjur'd Clarence: George, Duke of Clarence 1449–78* (Gloucester, 1980).
Hicks, Michael, *Anne Neville: Queen to Richard III* (Stroud, 2007).
Hicks, Michael, *Edward V: The Prince in the Tower* (Stroud, 2003).
Hicks, Michael, *The Wars of the Roses* (New Haven and London, 2010).
Hicks, Michael, *Warwick the Kingmaker* (Oxford, 2002).
Hicks, Michael, *Richard III: The Man Behind the Myth* (London, 1991).
Hicks, Michael, *Richard III and His Rivals: Magnates and their Motives in the Wars of the Roses* (London and Rio Grande, 1991).
Horrox, Rosemary, *Richard III: A Study in Service* (Cambridge, 1991).
Horrox, Rosemary, ed., *Richard III and the North* (Hull, 1986).
Hughes, Jonathan, *Arthurian Myths and Alchemy: The Kingship of Edward IV* (Stroud, 2002).
Hutton, William, *The Battle of Bosworth Field* (London, 1813).
Johnson, P.A. *Duke Richard of York 1411–1460.*(Oxford, 1988).
Jones, Michael K., *Bosworth 1485: Psychology of a Battle* (Stroud, 2003).
Jones, Michael K. and Underwood, Malcolm G., *The King's Mother: Lady Margaret Beaufort, Countess of Richmond and Derby* (Cambridge, 1992).
Kekewich, Margaret Lucille *et al.*, eds, *The Politics of Fifteenth Century England: John Vale's Book.* (Stroud, 1995).
Kendall, Paul Murray, *Richard the Third* (New York and London, 1955).
Lander, J. R., *Crown and Nobility 1450–1509* (Montreal, 1976).
Lander, J. R., *Government and Community: England, 1450–1509* (Cambridge, 1980).
Lander, J. R., *The Wars of the Roses* (New York, 1990).
Laynesmith, J.L., *The Last Medieval Queens* (Oxford, 2005).
Lee, Sidney, *Dictionary of National Biography* (London and New York, 1909)
Levine, Mortimer, *Tudor Dynastic Problems* (London and New York, 1973).
Loades, David, *The Tudor Queens of England* (London, 2009).

MacGibbon, David, *Elizabeth Woodville (1437–1492): Her Life and Times* (London, 1938).

Maurer, Helen E., *Margaret of Anjou: Queenship and Power in Late Medieval England* (Woodbridge, 2003).

Mercer, Malcolm, *The Medieval Gentry: Power, Leadership, and Choice during the Wars of the Roses* (London and New York, 2010).

Mitchell, R.J., *John Tiptoft (1427–1470)* (London, 1938).

Morant, P., *The History and Antiquities of the County of Essex*, vol. II (London 1768).

Muller, James Arthur, *Stephen Gardiner and the Tudor Reaction* (New York, 1970).

Okerlund, Arlene, *Elizabeth: England's Slandered Queen* (Stroud, 2006).

Okerlund, Arlene, *Elizabeth of York* (New York, 2009).

Petre, J., ed., *Richard III: Crown and People* (Gloucester, 1985).

Pierce, Hazel, *Margaret Pole, Countess of Salisbury, 1473–1541* (Cardiff, 2009).

Pollard, A.J., *Richard III and the Princes in the Tower* (Stroud, 1991).

Pollard, A.J., *Warwick the Kingmaker: Politics, Power, and Fame* (London and New York, 2007).

Pollard, A.J., *The Worlds of Richard III* (Gloucestershire and Charleston, 2001).

Prescott, William H., *History of the Reign of Ferdinand and Isabella the Catholic*, vol. I (Philadelphia, 1868).

Rawcliffe, Carole, *The Staffords, Earls of Stafford and Dukes of Buckingham 1394–1521* (Cambridge, 1978).

Rhodes, Dennis E., *John Argentine: Provost of King's: His Life and His Library* (Amsterdam, 1967).

Ross, Charles. *Edward IV* (New Haven and London, 1997).

Ross, Charles. *Richard III* (Berkeley and Los Angeles, 1981).

Ross, James. *John de Vere, Thirteenth Earl of Oxford (1442–1513): 'The Foremost Man of the Kingdom'* (Woodbridge, 2011).

Sanceau, Elaine, *The Perfect Prince: A Biography of the King Dm Joao II, Who Continued the Work of Henry the Navigator* (Porto, 1959).

Scofield, C.L., *The Life and Reign of Edward the Fourth*, 2 vols (London, 1923).

Scott, Kathleen, *Later Gothic Manuscripts: 1390–1490* (London, 1996).

Seabourne, Gwen, *Imprisoning Medieval Women: The Non-Judicial Confinement and Abduction of Women in England, c. 1170–1509* (Farnham and Burlington, 2011).

Shaw, William A., *The Knights of England*, 2 vols (London, 1906).

Spont, Afred, *La marine Française sous le règne de la Charles VIII, 1483–1493* (Paris, 1894).

Sutton, Anne F. and Visser-Fuchs, Livia, *Richard III's Books* (Stroud, 1997).

Weightman, Christine, *Margaret of York: Duchess of Burgundy 1446–1503* (New York, 1989).

Wilkins, Christopher, *The Last Knight Errant: Sir Edward Woodville and the Age of Chivalry* (London and New York, 2010).

Williams, Ethel Carleton, *My Lord of Bedford, 1398–1435* (London, 1963).

Williamson, Audrey, *The Mystery of the Princes* (Chicago, 1978).

Wingfield, John M., ed., *Some Records of the Wingfield Family* (Athens, Georgia, 1991).

Essays and Articles

Anglo, Sydney, 'Anglo-Burgundian Feats of Arms: Smithfield, June 1467', *Guildhall Miscellany*, 2 (1965).

Anglo, Sydney, 'Financial and Heraldic Records of the English Tournament', *Journal of the Society of Archivists*, 2 (1960).

Antonovics, A.V., 'Henry VII, King of England, "By the Grace of Charles VIII of France"', in Ralph Griffiths and James Sherborne, eds, *Kings and Nobles in the Later Middle Ages* (New York, 1986).

Archer, Rowena, 'Rich Old Ladies: The Problem of Late Medieval Dowagers', in A.J. Pollard, ed., *Property and Politics: Essays in Later Medieval English History* (Gloucester and New York, 1984).

Archer, Rowena, 'Testamentary Procedure with Special Reference to the Executrix', in *Medieval Women in Southern England*, Reading Medieval Studies, 15 (1989).

Armstrong, C.A.J., 'The Piety of Cicely, Duchess of York: A Study in Late Medieval Culture', in his *England, France and Burgundy in the Fifteenth Century* (London, 1983).

Armstrong, C.A.J., 'Some Examples of the Distribution and Speed of News in England at the Time of the Wars of the Roses', in his *England, France and Burgundy in the Fifteenth Century* (London, 1983).

Arthurson, Ian and Nicholas Kingwell, 'The Proclamation of Henry Tudor as King of England, 3 November 1483', *Bulletin of the Institute for Historical Research*, 63 (1990).

Ashdown-Hill, John, 'Walsingham in 1469: The Pilgrimage of Edward IV and Richard, Duke of Gloucester', *The Ricardian*, 11 (1997).

Ashdown-Hill, John and Annette Carson, 'The Execution of the Earl of Desmond', *The Ricardian*, 15 (2005).

Brown, A.L. and Bruce Webster, 'The Movements of the Earl of Warwick in the Summer of 1464 – a Correction', *English Historial Review*, 81 (1966).

Clarke, Peter D., 'English Royal Marriages and the Papal Penitentiary in the Fifteenth Century', *English Historical Review*, 120 (2005).

Cosgrove, Art., 'The Execution of the Earl of Desmond, 1468', *Journal of the Kerry Archaeological and Historical Society*, 8 (1975).

Court, Doreen, 'The Portuguese Connection: A Communication', *The Ricardian*, 6 (1983).

Cron, B.M., 'Margaret of Anjou and the Lancastrian March on London, 1461', *The Ricardian* (1999).

Currin, John M., '"The King's Army into the Partes of Bretaigne": Henry VII and the Breton Wars', *War in History*, 7 (2000).

Dockray, Keith, 'The Yorkshire Rebellions of 1469', *The Ricardian*, 6 (1983).

Driver, John T., 'Sir Thomas St Leger, *c*1439–83: The Rise and Fall of a Royal Servant during the Reigns of Edward IV and Richard III', *Surrey Archaeological Collections*, 94 (2008).

English Heritage Battlefield Report: Towton 1461 (1995).

Fahy, Conor, 'The Marriage of Edward IV and Elizabeth Woodville: A New Italian Source', *English Historical Review*, 76 (1961).

Farrar, Peter B., and Anne F. Sutton, 'The Duke of Buckingham's Sons, October 1483–August 1485', *The Ricardian*, (1982).

F.M., 'The Children of King Edward IV', *Gentleman's Magazine*, vol. 101, January 1831.

Freeman, Jessica, 'Sorcery at Court and Manor: Margery Jourdemayne, the Witch of Eye next Westminster', *Journal of Medieval History*, 30 (2004).

Friedrichs, Rhoda Lange, 'Rich Old Ladies Made Poor: The Vulnerability of Women's Property in Late Medieval England', *Medieval Prosopography*, 21 (2000).

Gillespie, James L., 'Ladies of the Fraternity of Saint George and of the Society of the Garter', *Albion*, 17 (Autumn 1985).

Grant, Alexander, 'Foreign Affairs Under Richard III', *Richard III: A Medieval Kingship*, 1993.

Griffiths, Ralph, 'Duke Richard of York's Intentions in 1450 and the Origins of the Wars of the Roses', *Joumal of Medieval History*, 1 (1975).

Griffiths, Ralph, 'Funeral of Prince George', in Anne F. Sutton and Livia Visser-Fuchs, eds., *The Royal Funerals of the House of York at Windsor* (London, 2005).

Grummit, David, 'William, Lord Hastings and the Defence of Calais', in T.J. Thornton, ed., *Social Attitudes and Political Structures in the Fifteenth Century*, (Stroud, 2000).

Hampton, W.E., 'A Further Account of Robert Stillington', (1976).

Hampton, W.E., 'Witchcraft and the Sons of York', (1980).

Hanham, Alison, 'Sir George Buck and Princess Elizabeth's Letter: A Problem in Detection', *The Ricardian*, 7 (1987).

Harriss, G.L., 'The Struggle for Calais: An Aspect of the Rivalry Between Lancaster and York', *English Historical Review*, 75 (January 1960).

Harper, April, and Caroline Proctor, eds., *Medieval Sexuality: A Casebook*. H-German, H-Net Reviews, (September, 2009).

Harrod, Henry, 'Queen Elizabeth Woodville's Visit to Norwich in 1469', *Norfolk Archaeoogy*, 5 (1959).

Harris, Graham, 'The Dicts and Sayings of the Philosophers', *The Ricardian*, 3 (1975).

Haward, Winifred I., 'Economic Aspects of the Wars of the Roses in East Anglia', *English Historical Review*, 41 (1926).

Helmholz, Richard H., 'The Sons of Edward IV in Peter Hammond, ed., *Richard III: Loyalty, Lordship, and Law*, (London: Richard III and Yorkist History Trust, 2000).

Hicks, Michael, 'The Case of Sir Thomas Cook, 1468', *English Historical Review*, 93 (1978).

Hicks, Michael, 'The Changing Role of the Wydevilles in Yorkist Politics to 1483', in Charles Ross, ed. *Patronage, Pedigree, and Power in Later Medieval England*, (Gloucester: Alan Sutton and Rowman & Littlefield, 1979).

Hicks, Michael, 'Descent, Partition and Extinction: The Warwick Inheritance', in his *Richard III and His Rivals: Magnates and their Motives in the Wars of the Roses* (London and Rio Grande, 1991).

Holland, P., 'Cook's Case in History and Myth', *Historical Research*, 61 (1988).

Horrox, Rosemary, ed., 'Financial Memoranda of the Reign of Edward V', *Camden Miscellany*, 29 (1987).

Ives, E.W., 'Andrew Dymmock and the Papers of Antony, Earl Rivers, 1482–3', *Bulletin of the Institute of Historical Research*, 41 (1968).

Jones, Michael K., 'Richard III as a Soldier', in John Gillingham, ed., *Richard III: A Medieval Kingship* (New York, 1993).

Kelly, H.A., 'English Kings and the Fear of Sorcery', *Pontifical Institute of Mediaeval Studies*, 39 (1977).

Kibre, Pearl, 'Lewis of Caerleon, Doctor of Medicine, Astronomer, and Mathematician (d. 1494?)', *Isis*, 43 (1952).

Kincaid, Arthur, 'Buck and the Elizabeth of York Letter: a Reply to Dr Hanham', *The Ricardian*, 8 (1988).

Kingsford, C.L., 'On Some London Houses of the Early Tudor Period', *Archaeologia*, second series, 71 (1921).

Kleineke, Hannes, 'Gerhard von Wesel's Newsletter from England, 17 April 1471', *The Ricardian*, 16 (2006).

Leland, John, 'Witchcraft and the Woodvilles: A Standard Medieval Smear?', in *Reputation and Representation in Fifteenth-Century Europe*, ed. by Douglas L. Biggs, Sharon D. Michalove and A. Compton Reeves (Leiden: Brill, 2004), pp. 267–88.

Lewis, Barry, 'Battle of Edgecote or Banbury (1469) Through the Eyes of Contemporary Welsh Poets', in Anne Curry and Adrian Bell, eds, *Journal of Medieval Military History*, 9 (2011).

Lowe, D.E., 'The Council of the Princes of Wales and the Decline of the Herbert Family during the Second Reign of Edward IV (1471–1483)', *Bulletin of the Board of Celtic Studies*, (1982).

Lowe, D.E., 'Patronage and Politics: Edward IV, the Wydevills, and the Council of the Prince of Wales, 1471–83', *Bulletin of the Board of Celtic Studies*, 29 (1980–82).

Marques, Antonio S., 'Alvaro Lopes de Cheves: A Portuguese Source', *Ricardian Bulletin*, Autumn 2008.

Merriman, Roger B., 'Edward Woodville – Knight-Errant', *Proceedings of the American Antiquarian Society*, 16 (1903–04).

Moorhen, Wendy E.A., 'William, Lord Hastings and the Crisis of 1483: An Assessment. Part 2 (conclusion)', *The Ricardian*, 9 (1993).

Moreton, C.E., 'Anthony Woodville, Norwich and the Crisis of 1469', in Margaret Aston and Rosemary Horrox, eds, *Much Heaving and Shoving: Late Medieval Gentry and Their Concerns; Essays for Colin Richmond* (Chipping, 2005).

Muller, James Arthur, *Stephen Gardiner and the Tudor Reaction* (New York, 1970).

Orme, Nicholas, 'The Education of Edward V', *Bulletin of the Institute of Historical Research*, 57 (1984).

Palliser, David, 'Richard III and York', in Rosemary Horrox, ed., *Richard III and the North* (Hull, 1986).

Pascual, Lucia Diaz, 'Jacquetta of Luxembourg, Duchess of Bedford and Lady Rivers (*c.* 1416–1472)', *The Ricardian*, 21 (2011).

Phillipps, Thomas, 'Account of the Ceremonial of the Marriage of the Princess Margaret, in 1468', *Archaeologica*, 31 (1846).

Pidgeon, Lynda, 'Antony Wydeville, Lord Scales and Earl Rivers: Family, Friends, and Affinity', *The Ricardian*, 15, 16 (2005, 2006).

Pollard, A.J., 'Elizabeth Woodville and her historians', in D. Biggs, S.D. Michalove, and A. Compton Reeves, eds., *Traditions and transformations in late medieval England* (Leiden: Brill, 2002), pp.145–158.

Pugh, T.B., 'Richard Plantagenet (1411–60), Duke of York, as the King's Lieutenant in France and Ireland', in J.G. Rowe, *Aspects of Late Medieval Government and Society* (Toronto, 1986).

Rawcliffe, Carole, 'The Inventory of a Fifteenth-Century Necromancer', *The Ricardian*, 13 (2003).

Roskell, J.S., 'The Office and Dignity of Protector of England, with Special Reference to Its Origins', *English Historical Review*, 68 (1953).

Roskell, J.S., 'William Catesby, Counsellor to Richard III', *Bulletin of the John Rylands Library*, 42 (1959).

Routh, Pauline E., 'Princess Bridget', *The Ricardian*, 3 (1975).

Sanituste, David, '"Putting Downe and Rebuking of Vices": Richard III and the Proclamation for the Reform of Morals', in April Harper and Caroline Proctor, eds., *Medieval Sexuality: A Casebook* (2007).

Scofield, Cora, 'The Capture of Lord Rivers and Sir Anthony Woodville, 19 January 1460', *English Historical Review*, 37 (1922).

Scofield, Cora, 'Elizabeth Wydevile in the Sanctuary at Westminster, 1470', *English Historical Review*, 24 (1909).

Shaw, William A., 'The Early English School of Portraiture', *The Burlington Magazine for Connoisseurs*, 65 (October 1934).

Smith, Gordon, 'Lambert Simnel and the King from Dublin', *The Ricardian*, 10 (1996

Smith, Herbert, 'Notes of Brasses Formerly Existing in Dover Castle, Maidstone, and Ashford Churches', *Archaeologia Cantiana*, 1 (1858).

Stuart, Dorothy Margaret, 'The Marriage of Margaret of York and Charles Duke of Burgundy July 1468', *History Today*, 8 (1958).

Sutton, Anne F., 'Sir Thomas Cook and his 'troubles': an Investigation', *English Historical Review*, 93 (1978).

Sutton, Anne F., and Visser-Fuchs, Livia, 'Choosing a Book in Late Fifteenth-century England and Burgundy', in Caroline Barron and Nigel Saul, eds, *England and the Low Countries in the Late Middle Ages* (Stroud, 1995).

Sutton, Anne F., and Visser-Fuchs, Livia, 'The Entry of Queen Elizabeth Woodville over London Bridge, 24 May 1465', *The Ricardian*, 19 (2009).

Sutton, Anne F., and Visser-Fuchs, Livia, 'A "Most Benevolent Queen": Queen Elizabeth Woodville's Reputation, her Piety and her Books.', *The Ricardian*, 10 (1995).

Sutton, Anne F., and Visser-Fuchs, Livia, 'The Provenance of the Manuscript: The Lives and Archive of Sir Thomas Cooke and His Man of Affairs, John Vale', in Margaret Lucille Kekewich, *et al.*, eds. *The Politics of Fifteenth Century England: John Vale's Book* (Gloucestershire: Alan Sutton Publishing Limited, 1995).

Sutton, Anne F., and Visser-Fuchs, Livia, 'The "Retirement" of Elizabeth Woodvile and Her Sons' (in Research Notes and Queries), *The Ricardian*, 11 (1999).

Sutton, Anne F., and Visser-Fuchs, Livia, 'Richard III's Books: Mistaken Attributions', *The Ricardian*, 9 (1992).

Sutton, Anne F., and Visser-Fuchs, Livia, 'Richard III's Books: XI Ramon Lull's *Order of Chivalry* translated by William Caxton', *The Ricardian*, 9 (1991).

Thomson, J.A.F., 'Bishop Lionel Woodville and Richard III', *Bulletin of the Institute of Historical Research*, 59 (1986).

Vale, Malcolm, 'An Anglo-Burgundian Nobleman and Art Patron: Louis de Bruges, Lord of la Gruthuyse and Earl of Winchester', in Caroline Barron and Nigel Saul, eds, *England and the Low Countries in the Late Middle Ages*, (Stroud, 1995).

Visser-Fuchs, Livia, 'The Debate: Elizabeth of York's Letter', *Ricardian Bulletin*, Winter 2004.

Visser-Fuchs, Livia, 'English events in Caspar Weinreich's Danzig Chronicle, 1461–1495', *The Ricardian* 7, (1986), pp. 310–20.

Visser-Fuchs, Livia, 'Richard Was Late', *The Ricardian*, 11 (1999).

Waters, Gwen, 'Richard III and Ireland', *The Ricardian*, 6 (December 1984), pp. 398–409.

Williams, Barrie, 'The Portuguese Connection and the Significance of 'the Holy Princess', *The Ricardian*, 6 (1983).

Williams, Barrie, 'The Portuguese Marriage Negotiations: A Reply', *The Ricardian*, 6 (1983).

Williams, Barrie, 'Rui de Sousa's Embassy and the Fate of Richard, Duke of York', *The Ricardian*, 5 (1981).

Williams, Daniel, 'The Hastily Drawn Up Will of William Catesby, Esquire, 25 August 1485', *Leicestershire Archaeological Society Transactions*, 1975–76.

Unpublished Dissertations

Jones, M.K., 'The Beaufort Family and the War in France, 1421–1450', Bristol, 1982.

Thomas, D.H., 'The Herberts of Raglan as Supporters of the House of York in the Second Half of the Fifteenth Century', University of Wales, 1967.

Thomas, Roger Stuart. 'The Political Career, Estates and "Connection" of Jasper Tudor, Earl of Pembroke and Duke of Bedford (d. 1495)', University of Wales, University College, Swansea, 1971.

Online Sources

Calendar of Papal Registers Relating to Britain and Ireland (British History Online).

Calendar of State Papers and Manuscripts in the Archives and Collections of Milan – 1385–1618 (British History Online).

Calendar of State Papers Relating to English Affairs in the Archives of Venice (British History Online).

English Heritage Battlefield Report: Towton 1461 (1995).

'*Gregory's Chronicle: 1461–1469*', *The Historical Collections of a Citizen of London in the fifteenth century* (British History Online).

Letters and Papers, Foreign and Domestic, Henry VIII (British History Online)

Oxford Dictionary of National Biography

Records of the Parliaments of Scotland to 1707 (University of St Andrews).

Rymer's Foedera, vols. 8-10 (British History Online)

Vergil, Polydor, *Anglica Historia* (1555 version), ed. Dana F. Sutton (The Philological Museum).

Victoria County History: A History of the County of Derby (British History Online).

Victoria County History: A History of the County of Northampton (British History Online).

CD-ROM Materials

The Parliament Rolls of Medieval England, ed. C. Given-Wilson (General Editor), P. Brand, A. Curry, R. E. Horrox, G. Martin, W. M. Ormrod, J. R. S. Phillips (Scholarly Digital Editions, 2005).

Notes

Abbreviations:

CPR: Calendar of Patent Rolls
Harleian 433: British Library Harleian Manuscript 433
Milan: Calendar of State Papers and Manuscripts in the Archives and Collections of Milan
ODNB: Oxford Dictionary of National Biography (online edition)
PL: Paston Letters, 2004-05 edition.
PROME: Parliament Rolls of Medieval England
VCH: Victoria County History
Venice: Calendar of State Papers Relating to English Affairs in the Archives of Venice

1 The Duchess and the Knight

1 *PL*, no. 88, part I, p. 162; Fabyan, p. 635; Gregory, *1451–1460*; Scofield, 'Capture of Lord Rivers'.
2 Monstrelet, vol. 5, p. 56.
3 *Coronation of Elizabeth Wydeville*, p. 43; Waurin, vol. 4, p. 37; *Bedford Inventories*, p. 116.
4 *Bedford Inventories*, p. 18.
5 *Bedford Inventories*, pp. 18–19; E. Carleton Williams, p. 228.
6 Pascual, p. 70.
7 *Great Chronicle*, p. 171.
8 *Coventry Leet Book*, p. 52
9 Gillespie, p. 272.
10 E. Carleton Williams, p. 237.
11 E. Carleton Williams, p. 247.
12 *Bedford Inventories*, p. 25.
13 *Bedford Inventories*, pp. 29–30.
14 *Bedford Inventories*, pp. 25, 365.
15 Jones, 'Beaufort Family', p. 318 n.1.
16 Hicks, 'Changing Role' p. 62.
17 For this and the above, see Jones, 'Beaufort Family', pp. 317–20.
18 *CPR*, 1436–41, p. 53.
19 Cokayne, vol. XI, p. 16, 'Rivers'.
20 *PL*, no. 88, part I, p. 162.
21 *Excerpta Historica*, pp. 249–50.
22 Leland, vol. ii, p. 491.

23 Lee, *Dictionary of National Biography* vol. XXI, p. 88; Doyle, vol 3, p. 141; Rymer's *Fœdera*, vol. 10, January–March 1430; Cokayne, vol. XI, p. 19 & n.i.
24 *Letters and Pages Illustrative of the Wars of the English in France*, vol. 2, pt. 2, p. 436.
25 *Chronicles of London*, p. 138; 48th Report, p. 312.
26 Monstrelet, vol. 5, p. 272.
27 PROME, January 1437, item 16.
28 *CPR* 1436–1441, p. 53; Pascual, pp. 72–73. A pardon was issued on 24 October 1437. Rymer's *Fœdera*, vol. 10, 1437, pp. 661–81.
29 *CPR* 1436–1441, p. 72.
30 Waurin, vol. 4, p. 257.
31 48th Report, p. 347; Waurin, vol. iv, p. 326; *Chronicles of London*, pp. 147–48.
32 *Chronicles of London*, p. 146.
33 Anglo, 'Financial and Heraldic Records', p. 193; *Chronicles of London*, p. 148.
34 *Visitations of the North*, p. 58.
35 TNA: C 140/42/49.
36 *Annales Rerum Anglicarum*, quoted in *Edward IV: A Source Book*, p. 48.
37 *Calendar of Papal Registers*, vol. XIII, 7 January 1482.
38 TNA: C 142/7/2. Though some secondary sources have ascribed an earlier birth date to Katherine, without citation, a later rather than an earlier birth date is corroborated by Elizabeth Woodville's coronation records, which show that she and her young husband, Henry Stafford, Duke of Buckingham, were young enough in 1465 to be carried around on the shoulders of squires, and by Elizabeth Woodville's household records. *Coronation of Elizabeth Wydeville*, p. 16; 'Household of Queen Elizabeth Woodville', pp. 471, 475.
39 TNA: C 142/1/36; Scofield, *Edward IV*, vol. 1, p. 178 n. 1.
40 *CPR* 1436–1441, p. 426.
41 VCH Northampton, vol. 5, 'Grafton Regis'.
42 Smith, 'Notes of Brasses', p. 178 and plate.
43 *Register of Henry Chichele*, vol. 2, p. 608.
44 *Coronation of Elizabeth Wydeville*, p. 46, citing Add. MS 23938, Computs J. Breknoke.
45 Loades, pp. 16–19; R.S. Thomas, pp. 18–21.
46 Pascual, p. 76.
47 Cokayne, vol. XI, p. 20; *Coronation of Elizabeth Wydeville*, p. 46.
48 For an excellent account of these events, see Juliet Barker, *Conquest: The English Kingdom in France*.
49 Harvey, pp. 81, 82.
50 'Some Ancient Indictments', pp. 215–16.
51 Harvey, pp. 91–95; Griffiths, *Henry VI*, p. 615.
52 Griffiths, 'Duke Richard of York's Intentions', p. 192.
53 Pugh, 'Richard Plantagenet', p. 126.
54 Pidgeon, 'Antony Wydevile', pt. 1, p. 10.
55 Johnson, p. 91–92 & n. 81.
56 Griffiths, *Reign of King Henry VI*, p. 707 n. 108.
57 Harriss, 'Struggle for Calais', pp. 31–32.
58 *Three Catalogues*, pp. 277–78.
59 Gardiner, *Paston Letters*, vol. II, pp. 297.
60 Griffiths, *Reign of King Henry VI*, pp. 730–32, Harriss, 'Struggle for Calais', pp. 34–39. It seems likely that Richard and Jacquetta's son Lionel was born during this period, judging from his name.

61 For what follows see Hicks, *Wars of the Roses* (2010), pp. 107–12; Hicks, *Warwick*, pp. 115–17. An excellent account of the battle itself is Andrew Boardman, *The First Battle of St. Albans 1455*.
62 *PL*, no. 1029, part III, p. 162.
63 Maurer, pp. 128–29.
64 *Coventry Leet Book*, p. 300.
65 *Coventry Leet Book*, p. 292.
66 Maurer, p. 144; Hicks, *Warwick*, p. 132; Pollard, *Warwick*, p. 201.
67 Hicks, *Warwick*, pp. 132–34; *Six Town Chronicles*, p. 160.
68 *Great Chronicle*, p. 190.
69 Hicks, *Warwick*, pp. 147–48.
70 Hicks, *Warwick*, p. 151; Okerlund, *Slandered Queen*, p. 47.
71 Okerlund, *Slandered Queen*, p. 47.
72 Hicks, *Wars of the Roses*, pp. 140–43; Pollard, *Warwick*, pp. 38–42.
73 Goodman, *Wars of the Roses*, p. 29.
74 Gregory, 196–210; *PL*, no. 88, part I, p. 162; Fabyan, 635–36; Scofield, 'Capture', 253–54.
75 Gregory, 196–210.
76 *PL*, no. 88, part I, p. 162.
77 *PL*, no. 888, part 2, p. 540.
78 Pollard, *Warwick*, pp. 44–45.
79 Hicks, *Warwick*, p. 180.
80 Johnson, p. 211.
81 *Gregory*, http://www.british–history.ac.uk/report.aspx?compid=45559#n17.
82 Whethamsted's Register, in *Henry VI: A Source Book*, p. 99.
83 PROME, October 1460, Introduction and item 30.
84 Gregory, pp. 146–210.
85 Cron. pp. 597–99.
86 *Chronicles of London*, p. 173; Milan, no. 65, 22 February 1461. Anthony Woodville had married Elizabeth Scales, the daughter of Thomas, Lord Scales, and his wife Esmania. Scales had been murdered by a London mob in July 1460, after which Anthony had succeeded to his title in right of his wife; he is called Lord Scales in a letter of 4 April 1461 and in a dispatch by the Earl of Salisbury on 7 April 1461. 'Lady Scales', then, likely refers to Elizabeth, rather than her mother, who may not have survived her husband. *PL*, no. 90, part I, p. 165; Milan, 1461, no. 80; Pidgeon, *Antony Wydeville*, part 2, p. 18.
87 English Heritage, p. 3.
88 *PL*, no. 90, part I, p. 165.
89 Milan, 1461, nos 80 and 91.
90 Scofield, *Edward IV*, vol. 1, p. 178 n. 1.
91 Milan, 1461, no. 120.
92 *PL*, no. 320, part 1, p. 523.

2 The King and the Widow

1 Shaw, 'Early English School of Portraiture', p. 184.
2 Hepburn, pp. 54–60.

3 Hall, p. 365; More, p. 61.
4 *Coronation of Elizabethy Wydeville*, p. 27.
5 'Household of Queen Margaret of Anjou', p. 182 n.2.
6 'Household of Queen Margaret of Anjou', p. 182 n.2; *CPR*, p. 353; *Coronation of Elizabethy Wydeville*, pp. 27–28.
7 *Coronation of Elizabeth Wydeville*, p. 28; Baldwin, p. 133; MacGibbon, pp. 15–17.
8 Cokayne, vol. V, pp. 359–61.
9 Cokayne, vol. V, p. 362 n. *c*; TNA: C 142/7/2; Shakespeare Birthplace Trust Record Office DR37/2/73/34.
10 Hall, p. 264. Caspar Weinreich, writing in far-off Danzig, recorded later gossip about the fate of John Grey: 'People say that [he] was killed in battle; some said he was pushed off the bridge at Rochester; some said that he, too, had been beheaded during the previous parliament'. Visser-Fuchs, 'English Events', p. 313.
11 Hicks, *Edward V*, pp. 44–45.
12 Lander, *Crown and Nobility*, p. 210.
13 Okerlund, p. 59.
14 Lander, *Government and Community*, 237–38 n. 4.
15 Waurin, vol. V, pp. 352–53; Visser-Fuchs, 'English Events', p. 313
16 More, pp. 61–62.
17 MacGibbon, pp. 32–33.
18 Mancini, p. 61; *Chronicles of the White Rose*, p. 15–16.
19 Hall, p. 379.
20 Laynesmith, *Last Medieval Queens*, p. 52 & n. 126.
21 Josephine Tey, *The Daughter of Time*, Chapter 16.
22 *Crowland Chronicle, First Continuation*, quoted in *Edward IV: A Source Book*, p. 10.
23 Scofield, *Edward IV*, vol. 1, p. 127 n. 2.
24 Fahy, pp. 663–64.
25 Mancini, p. 61.
26 More, p. 62.
27 Gregory, pp. 210–239.
28 Hicks, *Edward V*, p. 47.
29 Fabyan, p. 654.
30 Baldwin, p. 11.
31 Laynesmith, p. 66.
32 Hicks, *Edward V*, pp. 45–46.
33 Hicks, *Edward V*, p. 41.
34 *Chronicles of the White Rose*, p. 16.
35 Hicks, *Edward V*, p. 47.
36 Fabyan, p. 654.
37 Milan no. 138; *Crowland Chronicle, First Continuation*, quoted in *Edward IV: A Source Book*, p. 44.
38 Mancini, p. 61–63.
39 Crawford, *Yorkist Lord*, pp. 43–44.
40 Lander, *Crown and Nobility*, p. 119; Brown and Webster, pp. 80–82.
41 Ross, *Edward IV*, pp. 91–92.
42 Ross, *Edward IV*, p. 92; Lander, *Wars of the Roses*, pp. 105–06.
43 Scofield, *Edward IV*, vol. 1, p. 364.
44 *CPR*, 1446–1452, pp. 311–12.

45 *Annales Rerum Anglicarum,* p. 783; Lander, *Wars of the Roses*, p. 105; *PL*, no. 742, part II, p. 375.
46 *Annales Rerum Anglicarum*, p. 785; *CPR* 1467–1477, p. 25.
47 *Annales Rerum Anglicarum*, p. 785; Rosemary Horrox, 'Grey, Edmund, first earl of Kent (1416–1490)'; *ODNB*, 2004.
48 *Annales Rerum Anglicarum*, p. 786; Thomas, 'Herberts of Raglan', pp. 279–83.
49 *Annales Rerum Anglicarum*, p. 785; *Coronation of Elizabeth Wydeville*, pp. 11, 16, 21.
50 *Annales Rerum Anglicarum*, p. 783.
51 *Annales Rerum Anglicarum*, p. 786.
52 *Annales Rerum Anglicarum*, translated from the Latin in Lander, *Wars of the Roses*, pp. 106–07.
53 Ross, *Edward IV*, p. 94.
54 Archer, 'Rich Old Ladies', p. 22; Lander, *Crown and Nobility*, p. 111.
55 Ross, *Edward IV*, p. 93.
56 Archer, 'Testamentary Procedure', p. 19.
57 Mancini, p. 75.
58 Lander, *Crown and Nobility*, p. 114 n. 111; Rawcliffe, *The Staffords*, p. 28. As Lander also points out, the word 'forced' is misleading: 'His marriage had been disposed of like that of any other child of the feudal classes whether in wardship or not.'
59 Rawcliffe, p. 28.
60 *Coronation of Elizabeth Wydeville*, p. 15.
61 Laynesmith, p. 211.
62 Hicks, 'Changing Role', pp. 67–70.
63 'Household of Queen Elizabeth Woodville', pp. 451, 473.
64 *Annales Rerum Anglicarum*, p. 791.
65 For the following see *Coronation of Elizabeth Wydeville*, pp. 7–25, 61–64, and Laynesmith, pp. 87–110.
66 *Herald's Memoir*, p. 140.
67 *Coronation of Elizabeth Wydeville*, p. 12.

3 The Black Legend of the Woodvilles

1 *Annales Rerum Anglicarum*, p. 785.
2 Jacquetta came to Windsor on 16 July 1467, probably to be with her pregnant daughter. MacGibbon, pp. 67–68, 85; Scofield, *Edward IV*, pp. 428, 482–83.
3 Milan, 12 April 1469, no. 169.
4 For this and what follows see *Travels of Leo of Rozmital*, pp. 45–47.
5 *Travels of Leo of Rozmital*, p. 47 n. 1.
6 *English Historical Literature*, p. 386.
7 Art Cosgrove in 'The Execution of the Earl of Desmond, 1468' offers the most through exploration of the reasons for Desmond's execution and concludes that they 'should be sought in his own conduct'. Cosgrove, p. 26.
8 Cosgrove, pp. 22–23.
9 *Calendar of the Carew Manuscripts*, vol. 2, pp. cv–cvii.
10 Ashdown-Hill and Carson, p. 85 n. 41.

11 Cosgrove, p. 20; *CPR*, 1461–1467, p. 340.
12 Ashdown-Hill and Carson, pp. 85–86.
13 Ashdown-Hill and Carson, p. 85.
14 *Book of Howth*, pp. 186–87.
15 Cosgrove, p. 25.
16 Mitchell, pp. 124–25.
17 Okerlund, pp. 162–63.
18 Mitchell, pp. 132–33.
19 The instructions concerning Desmond and other Irish lords can be found in *Harleian* 433, vol. III, pp. 108–14, as well as in *Letters and Papers Illustrative of the Reigns of Richard III*, vol. I, pp. 67–78.
20 Kendall, *Richard the Third*, p. 522 n. 21 and p. 532 n. 8.
21 Waters, p. 402. The elder Desmond's father, in fact, was Clarence's godfather. Ashdown-Hill and Carson, p. 72 n. 7.
22 Ashdown-Hill and Carson, p. 82.
23 As we shall see, after Jacquetta's husband and son were murdered in 1469, certainly by men acting under the direction of the Earl of Warwick, she brought an action not only against the earl, but against his followers. These are the sort of men whom Richard likely was allowing the younger Desmond to prosecute.
24 Ashdown-Hill and Carson, p. 82.
25 Pollard, 'Elizabeth Woodville', pp. 154–56.
26 Sutton, 'Sir Thomas Cook', p. 97.
27 Hicks, 'Case of Sir Thomas Cook', pp. 82, 94; Sutton, 'Sir Thomas Cook', pp. 93–94; Sutton and Visser-Fuchs, 'Provenance', p. 95; Holland, 'Cook's Case', pp. 23–24. Cook was not ruined by this affair, as some accounts have it; when he died in 1478, he was still very wealthy.
28 Sutton, 'Sir Thomas Cook', p. 101–02.
29 Sutton and Visser-Fuchs, 'Provenance', p. 89 n. 87.
30 Sutton and Visser-Fuchs, 'Provenance', p. 89; Hicks, 'Case of Sir Thomas Cook', p. 94.
31 Sutton, 'Sir Thomas Cook', p. 89–90.
32 E.W. Ives, 'Markham, Sir John (b. after 1399, d. 1479)', *ODNB*, 2004.
33 'Household of Queen Margaret of Anjou', p. 141; Kendall, *Richard the Third*, p. 79. Kendall also increases the fine from 8,000 marks to a whopping £8,000.
34 Hicks, 'Case of Sir Thomas Cooke', p. 95–96; Crawford, *The Yorkists*, p. 83.
35 Holland, 'Cook's Case', p. 29; Hicks, p. 96.
36 Holland, 'Cook's Case', pp. 34–35.

4 Murder at Coventry

1 *Great Chronicle*, p. 208.
2 *Crowland*, p. 115.
3 Weightman, p. 37, 39; Lander, *Government and Community*, p. 245; Pollard, *Warwick*, p. 60.
4 Pollard, *Warwick*, p. 60; Michael Hicks, 'Neville, George (1432–1476)', *ODNB*, 2008.
5 For what follows, see *Excerpta Historica*, pp. 171–222.
6 Anglo, 'Anglo-Burgundian Feats of Arms', p. 275.

7 Anglo, 'Anglo-Burgundian Feats of Arms', p. 282.
8 Scofield, *Edward IV*, vol. I, pp. 424–25, 428–29.
9 Pollard, *Warwick*, p. 60.
10 Scofield, *Edward IV*, vol. I, p. 430.
11 Hicks, *Warwick*, p. 265.
12 Scofield, *Edward IV*, vol. I, p. 443; Hicks, *Warwick*, p. 265.
13 For what follows see Phillipps, pp. 327–38; Marche, vol. III, pp. 106–07; *Excerpta Historica*, 223–39.
14 *PL*, no. 330, part I, p. 539.
15 *PL*, no. 330, part I, p. 539.
16 *PL*, no. 236, part I, p. 396.
17 Marche, vol. III, p. 199.
18 *PL*, no. 330, part I, p. 539; Michael K. Jones, 'Beaufort, Edmund, Styled Third Duke of Somerset (c.1438–1471)', *ODNB*, online edition, May 2009.
19 Scofield, *Edward IV*, vol. I, p. 481.
20 Kleineke, pp. 95–96.
21 Scofield, *Edward IV*, vol. 1, p. 454; *Anales Rerum Anglicarum*, pp. 789–90; *Great Chronicle*, p. 207.
22 Scofield, *Edward IV*, vol. I, pp. 481–82.
23 Hicks, *Wars of the Roses*, p. 190.
24 Dockray, 'Yorkshire Rebellions', p. 255; Ashdown-Hill, 'Walsingham', p. 4.
25 Scofield, *Edward IV*, vol. I, p. 482–83.
26 Scofield, *Edward IV*, vol. I, p. 492; Ashdown-Hill, p. 14.
27 Dockray, 'Yorkshire Rebellions', pp. 252–54; Pollard, *Warwick*, p. 65; Hicks, *Warwick*, pp. 275–76.
28 Scofield, *Edward IV*, vol. I, p. 493–95;
29 Warkworth, p. 46–51.
30 Ross, *Edward IV*, p. 71; R.A. Griffiths, 'Herbert, William, First Earl of Pembroke (c.1423–1469)', *ODNB*, January 2008.
31 Michael Hicks, 'Stafford, Humphrey, Earl of Devon (c. 1439–1469)', *ODNB*, January 2008.
32 Rosemary Horrox, 'Fogge, Sir John (b. in or before 1417, d. 1490)', *ODNB*, January 2008.
33 Ross, *Edward IV*, p. 80.
34 Pollard, *Warwick*, p. 65.
35 For what follows see Lewis, pp. 100–04; Ross, *Edward IV*, pp. 130–32.
36 For what follows see Harrod, pp. 32–36.
37 Lewis, p. 101; Ross, *Edward IV*, p. 132; Warkworth, pp. 6–7.
38 Scofield, *Edward IV*, vol. 1, p. 497 n. 4; Waurin, vol. 5, p. 580.
39 Scofield, *Edward IV*, vol. 1, p. 493; Waurin, vol. 5, p. 580.
40 *Coventry Leet Book*, p. 346; Waurin, vol. 5, p. 580..
41 Moreton, p. 64.
42 TNA: KB 27/836 m. 61d.
43 *History of the County of Derby*, vol. 2, pp. 80–81.
44 Eton College Archives: ECR 60/3/2; Waurin, vol. 5, p. 581.
45 Scofield, *Edward IV*, vol. 1, p. 498 n. 2.
46 Milan, 16 August 1469, no. 173.
47 Hicks, *Warwick*, p. 277.
48 Scofield, *Edward IV*, vol. 1, pp. 500–01.
49 Kleineke, p. 99.
50 Kleineke, pp. 99–100; Ross, *Edward IV*, p. 135.
51 Moreton, p. 63–65.

5 Witchcraft and Sorcery

1 *CPR*, 1467–77, pg. 190.
2 Sutton, 'Sir Thomas Cook', p. 103.
3 For Joan, see 'Captivity of a Royal Witch'.
4 For Eleanor see Griffiths, *King and Country*, pp. 233–52; Freeman, 'Sorcery at Court'.
5 Sutton, 'Sir Thomas Cook', p. 103; Pascual, 'Jaquetta of Luxembourg', p. 85.
6 Warkworth, p. 7; TNA: KB 27/836 m. 61d.
7 Leland, 'Witchcraft and the Woodvilles', p. 272.
8 *Rotuli Parliamentorum*, vol. VI, p. 232. This source gives the date as 20 January; *CPR*, 1467–77, pg. 190 gives the date as 19 January.
9 *CPR*, 1467–77, pg. 190.
10 *Rotuli Parliamentorum*, vol. VI, p. 232. Thomas Wake does not seem to have suffered for his role in accusing the duchess or in murdering her husband and son; he died in 1476. Hampton, 'Roger Wake of Blisworth', p. 156.
11 PROME, January 1485, item 1 [5]. The issue of whether Elizabeth might have used astrology to forecast Richard's death, as hinted at in a letter by the soon-to-be king, will be dealt with in Chapter 11.
12 Hughes, *Arthurian Myths and Alchemy*, p. 196.
13 Pascual, 'Jacquetta of Luxembourg', p. 87.
14 Sutton and Visser-Fuchs, *Richard III's Books*, pp. 224–25, 236,
15 Hughes, *Arthurian Myths and Alchemy*, pp. 172–73; Rous, *Rous Rolls*, no. 18.
16 *Coventry Leet Book*, p. 393.
17 Fabyan, p. 654.
18 Hampton, 'Witchcraft and the Sons of York', pp. 173–75.
19 Carson, p. 118.
20 Freeman, 'Sorcery at Court and Manor', p. 346.
21 Freeman, 'Sorcery at Court and Manor', p. 346, 349, 350.

6 Exile and Sanctuary

1 *PL*, no. 245, part I, p. 410.
2 Hicks, *Warwick*, p. 280.
3 Moreton, 'Anthony Woodville', pp. 64–65.
4 Warkworth, p. 9.
5 TNA: KB 27/836 m. 61d; Scofield, *Edward IV*, vol. I, p. 522.
6 Hicks, *Warwick*, pp. 287–89.
7 Hicks, *Warwick*, p. 287; Scofield, *Edward IV*, pp. 521, 526–27.
8 TNA: KB 27/836 m. 61d.
9 Ross, *Edward IV*, p. 146
10 Scofield, *Edward IV*, vol. I, p. 530 (citing Lettres de Louis XI, IV, 131).
11 Hicks, *Warwick*, p. 296.
12 Haward, p. 179; Ross, *Edward IV*, pp. 152–53; *Coventry Leet Book*, pp. 358–59. Edward's younger brother, Richard, Duke of Gloucester, probably arrived in Holland at a later date. Visser-Fuchs, 'Richard Was Late', pp. 616–17.
13 Sharpe, *London and the Kingdom*, vol. III, pp. 385–86; *Chronicles of London*, p. 182; Warkworth, p. 13; *PL*, no. 345, part I, p. 564.

14 *Original Letters*, second series, vol. I, pp. 141–42.
15 Scofield, 'Elizabeth Wydevile in the Sanctuary at Westminter, 1470', p. 91; Scofield, *Edward IV*, vol. I, p. 546.
16 *Chronicles of London*, p. 183; Scofield, *Edward IV*, vol. 1, p. 546; Hicks, *Edward V*, p. 54.
17 *CPR* 1467–1477, p. 228.
18 Hammond, *Battles of Barnet and Tewkesbury*, p. 52–54; Calmette and Perinelle, pp. 321–23.
19 Hammond, *Battles of Barnet and Tewkesbury*, p. 58; *Historie of the Arrivall of Edward IV*, pp. 2–3.
20 Haward, p. 179.
21 *Historie of the Arrivall of Edward IV*, p. 17.
22 Kleineke, 'Gerhard von Wesel's Newsletter', p. 80; *Anchiennes Chroniques*, vol. III, p. 211; *Historie of the Arrivall of Edward IV*, p. 34.
23 Hammond, *Battles of Barnet and Tewkesbury*, p. 74.
24 Kleineke, p. 81
25 *Historie of the Arrivall of Edward IV*, p. 21–23.
26 Hammond, *Battles of Barnet and Tewkesbury*, pp. 105–07.
27 The following is taken from Hammond, *Battles of Barnet and Tewkesbury*, pp. 107–08; Scofield, *Edward IV*, vol. 1, pp. 591–92.
28 *Historie of the Arrivall of Edward IV*, p. 37.
29 *Crowland*, p. 129.
30 *Political Poems and Songs*, vol. II, pp. 278–79.
31 Hammond, *Battles of Barnet and Tewkesbury*, pp. 108–13.
32 *Historie of the Arrivall of Edward IV*, p. 38.

7 A Woodville Abroad

1 *PL*, no. 373, part I, pp. 566–67.
2 Grummitt, p. 154; Scofield, *Edward IV*, vol. II, p. 4.
3 *PL*, no. 350, part I, p. 570; no. 262, part I, p. 440; no. 266, part I, p. 446.
4 Scofield, *Edward IV*, vol. II, pp. 31–32, 33–34; CPR, 1467–1477, p. 339; Ross, *Edward IV*, pp. 206–07; PL, no. 269, part. I, p. 450.
5 Ames and Herbert, vol. 1, p. 61.
6 TNA: C 142/1/36 (Cambridge); C 142/1/37 (Hertford); C 142/1/38 (Norfolk); C 142/1/39 (Suffolk).
7 'Household of Queen Margaret of Anjou', p. 182 n.1.
8 TNA: C 142/1/36 (Cambridge); C 142/1/37 (Hertford); C 142/1/38 (Norfolk); C 142/1/39 (Suffolk).
9 *PL*, no. 90, part I, p. 165.
10 *PL*, no. 574, part II, p. 175.
11 See Chapter 1.
12 *Coronation of Elizabeth of Wydeville*, p. 46.
13 Harvey, p. 81.
14 Griffiths, p. 707, n.108.
15 *English Chronicle*, p. 96.
16 Scofield, *Edward IV*, vol. I, p. 92.

17 Scofield, *Edward IV*, vol. I, p. 92; *English Chronicle*, p. 98.
18 Pidgeon, part 2, pp. 30, 35.
19 *Manuscripts of the Corporations of Southampton and Kings Lynn*, pp. 224–25.
20 Crawford, *Household Books*, pt. I, pp. 281, 480–82; Crawford, *Yorkist Lord*, pp. 41–42, 156.
21 Myers, 'Household of Queen Margaret of Anjou', p. 288.
22 Pidgeon, part 2, p. 35. The heirs in 1485 were John de Vere, Earl of Oxford, returned home after a long exile and imprisonment, and William Tyndale. James Ross, *John de Vere*, p. 91.
23 Blomefield, vol. 9, p. 26. As Blomefield confuses Anthony's brother Richard with his brother Edward, and has Anthony attempting to make a Scottish marriage several years after the match in question was suggested, his account is not entirely trustworthy; however, the identity of Anthony's mistress does not appear to have been questioned. H.T. Evans identifies Gwenllian as William's daughter and as Anthony's mistress but does not name Gwenllian's mother. Evans, p. 142 n.7.
24 Barnwell, p. 32. Barnwell gives no source for the deed.
25 Alasdair Hawkyard, 'Poyntz, Sir Robert (b. late 1440s, d. 1520)', *ODNB*, January 2008; TNA: E 315/486/57.
26 PROB 11/8; Pidgeon, part 2, p. 43.
27 Pidgeon, 'Antony Wydeville', part 2, p. 41.
28 See Appendix. Poyntz himself would remain loyal to his wife's Woodville relations; he joined the rebellion against Richard III a few months after Anthony's death and fought for Henry Tudor at Bosworth in 1485.
29 *Calendar of Papal Registers*, 1476. 5 Kal, May (27 April), St. Peter's, Rome (f. 99v.).
30 TNA: PROB 11/8; Pidgeon, pp. 43, 45.
31 Edward's younger brother Richard had been born at Shrewsbury on 17 August 1473.
32 Scofield, *Edward IV*, vol. II, p. 5; H.T. Evans, p. 116.
33 Lowe, 'Patronage and Politics', pp. 556–61.
34 *PL*, no. 273, part 1, p. 456.
35 For what follows see Orme, 'The Education of Edward V'.
36 Mancini, pp. 67–69; Lowe, *Patronage and Politics*, pp. 553–54; Ives, 216–25.
37 Friedrichs, p. 222.
38 Hicks, 'Changing Role of the Wydevilles', p. 83.
39 Lowe, 'Patronage and Politics', p. 553.
40 For what follows see Ross, *Edward IV*, pp. 205–38; Scofield, *Edward IV*, vol. II, pp. 113–51.
41 *Edward V's French Expedition*, pp. 1V–2R, 7–10, 15–19.
42 Ross, *Edward IV*, p. 237.
43 Milan, 1 October 1475, no. 315.
44 *Prologues and Epilogues of William Caxten*, p. 38.
45 *Calendar of Papal Registers*, vol. 13, *Lateran Regesta* 762: 1475–76, 1716; 5 Kal. May (27 April), f. 99v.
46 Milan, 7 March 1476, no. 324.
47 *PL*, no. 298, part 1, p. 494.
48 Venice, 10 May 1476, no. 454.
49 Venice, 13 May 1476, no. 455.
50 Milan, 9 June 1476, no. 339, 11 June 1476, no. 340.

8 Pomp and Printing

1 TNA: C 140/42/49.
2 *Calendar of Close Rolls*, 1476–1485, p. 194.
3 Sutton and Visser-Fuchs, *Royal Funerals*, p. 4 & n.6.
4 For the following see *English Historical Literature*, pp. 382–88.
5 The Duchess of Exeter's Lancastrian husband, Henry Holland, seriously wounded at the battle of Barnet, was a prisoner in the Tower. The future Richard III, who would execute three of the guests and force two of the others into sanctuary in 1483, was not named among those at table.
6 Hicks, *Edward V*, p. 63.
7 Vale, 'Louis de Bruges', p. 119. Sir Guichard d'Angle was made Earl of Huntingdon in 1377.
8 Sutton and Visser-Fuchs, *Royal Funerals*, p. 4 & n.6.
9 Scofield, *Edward IV*, vol. II, p. 60.
10 Scofield, *Edward IV*, vol. II, p. 117.
11 Shaw, *Knights of England*, pp. 136–37. Poignantly, Thomas Vaughan, chamberlain to Prince Edward, was also made a Knight of the Bath; he and his fellow knight, Richard Grey, would die together at Pontefract eight years later.
12 *Excerpta Historica*, pp. 371–72, 373
13 Scofield, *Edward IV*, vol. II, p. 163.
14 Sutton and Visser-Fuchs, *Reburial*, pp. 7–28.
15 Griffiths in Sutton and Visser-Fuchs, *Royal Funerals*, pp. 47–49.
16 For Caxton's arrival in England and the chronology of his publications, see Hellinga, *Caxton in Focus*, pp. 80–83.
17 Hellinga, *Caxton in Focus*, pp. 42–43.
18 Hellinga, *Caxton in Focus*, p. 84.
19 A. W. Pollard, *Fifteenth Century Prose and Verse*, p. 204. For translators in the fifteenth century, see Sutton and Visser-Fuchs, 'Choosing a Book', pp. 68–69.
20 Ames and Herbert, vol. 2, p. 65.
21 Sutton and Visser-Fuchs, 'Richard III's Books: XI Ramon Lull's Order of Chivalry', p. 297.
22 *Prologues and Epilogues*, pp. 20–22.
23 Sutton and Visser-Fuchs, 'Richard III's Books', pp. 113–14; Hellinga, *Caxton in Focus*, pp. 84–86.
24 Sutton and Visser-Fuchs, 'Richard III's Books', p. 114. The Duke of Clarence may have been a patron of Caxton's before the printer moved to England. Hellinga, p. 31.
25 Hellinga, p. 77; Sutton and Visser-Fuchs, 'Richard III's Books', p. 297.
26 For what follows see Illustrations, pp. 27–40. For Anne Mowbray's background see Colin Richmond, 'Mowbray, John (VII), fourth Duke of Norfolk (1444–1476)', *ODNB*, 2006.

9 The Downfall of a Duke

1 The dispute has been covered extensively, especially by Michael Hicks. A good summary can be found in his 'Descent, Partition and Extinction', pp. 327–33.

2 Hicks, *Anne Neville*, p. 104.
3 *Crowland*, p. 133.
4 Hicks, *Anne Neville*, p. 143; Clarke, 'English Royal Marriages', p. 1023. The dispensation was discovered only recently and thus is spoken of as being nonexistent in a number of sources published before 2005.
5 *PL*, part I, p. 447, no. 267.
6 Hicks, 'Descent, Partition and Extinction', p. 328; *False, Fleeting, Perjur'd Clarence*, p. 116.
7 *PL*, part I, p. 464, no. 277; Hicks, *False, Fleeting, Perjur'd Clarence*, pp. 121–22.
8 Hicks, *False, Fleeting, Perjur'd Clarence*, pp. 128, 130, 138.
9 Scofield, *Edward IV*, vol. II, pp. 184–86; Ross, *Edward IV*, pp. 250–51, Commynes, vol. II, p. 8.
10 Halliwell, *Letters of the Kings of England*, vol. I, p. 147.
11 Lander, *Crown and Nobility*, pp. 247–48; Hicks, *False, Fleeting, Perjur'd Clarence*, pp. 137–39; Scofield, *Edward IV*, vol. II, pp. 186–88.
12 Charles Ross, *Edward IV*, pp. 240–42; Hicks, *Clarence*, 133–37; Scofield, *Edward IV*, vol. II, pp. 188–90.
13 PROME, January 1478, Appendix, item 1.
14 Crowland, pp. 145–47.
15 Ross, *Edward IV*, pp. 242–43; Hicks, *False, Fleeting, Perjur'd Clarence*, 200–04; *CPR*, 1476–85, p. 115.
16 Mancini, pp. 63–65.
17 Pollard, 'Elizabeth Woodville and Her Historians', p. 156.
18 Mancini, p. 97.
19 PROME, January 1484, item 1 [5].
20 Commynes, vol. II, pp. 63–64.
21 Kendall, pp. 147, 259–60, 532 n.8, 555–56. Notably, Kendall cites Richard's letter of instructions regarding the Earl of Desmond, discussed in Chapter 3, to support his claim that the Woodvilles procured Clarence's death, despite the fact that Richard's letter regarding Desmond never mentions the Woodvilles, explicitly or implicitly.
22 Levine, *Tudor Dynastic Problems*, p. 30 & n. 66.
23 Kendall, p. 259; *Foedora* vol. 12, p. 66; *Stonor Letters and Papers*, vol. II, p. 41–42; *CPR*, 1476–85, p. 102.
24 *CPR*, 1476–85, pp. 553–54.
25 Charles Ross, *Edward IV*, pp. 253–54; Scofield, *Edward IV*, vol. II, p. 245 & n. 4.
26 *CPR*, 1476–85, pp. 553–54, 565–66, 571.

10 Before the Storm

1 For what follows see Scofield, *Edward IV*, vol. II, pp. 251–53.
2 Records of the Parliament of Scotland.
3 *York House Books*, vol. I, p. 196.
4 Scofield, *Edward IV*, vol. II, p. 253.
5 For what follows see Griffiths in Sutton and Visser-Fuchs, *Royal Funerals*, pp. 47–53.
6 Kendall, pp. 197, 254.
7 *Calendar of Papal Registers*, vol. 13, 7 January 1482.
8 John A.F. Thomson, 'Woodville, Lionel (c. 1454–1484)', *ODNB* September 2011.

9 *PL*, vol. I, p. 645, no. 403.
10 Davis, *William Waynflete*, p. 33.
11 *Calendar of Papal Registers*, vol. 13, 14 July 1479.
12 *English Historical Documents*, p. 903.
13 Morant, *History and Antiquities of the County of Essex*, vol. I, p. 252.
14 Pidgeon, 'Anthony Wydeville', part 2, p. 20; Scott, part 2, p. 170
15 Hicks, 'Changing Role', p. 221; Pidgeon, , 'Anthony Wydeville', part 2, pp. 21–22.
16 Margaret Beaufort, Countess of Richmond, had borne the future Henry VII when she was just 13, but such cases were fortunately rare; even among the nobility, where girls often wed at very young ages, consummation was often delayed until the bride was 15 or 16.
17 *Privy Purse Expenses*, pp. 163–65; Scofield, *Edward IV*, vol. II, p. 284.
18 Scofield, *Edward IV*, vol. II, p. 295–96.
19 Hellinga, pp. 29–31, 48
20 Armstrong, 'Piety of Cicely, Duchess of York', p. 85; Sutton and Visser-Fuchs, *Royal Funerals*, p. 4 n.7.
21 F.M., *Gentleman's Magazine*, 1831, p. 25; Routh, 'Princess Bridget', pp. 13–14.
22 Davis, *William Waynflete*, p. 70–71; Wood, *History and Antiquities*, vol. 1, pp. 637–38. For Richard Woodville's position, see Calto and Evans, p. 736.
23 Philomena Jones, 'Anne Mowbray', in Petre, p. 88.
24 R.G. Davies, 'Beauchamp, Richard (d. 1481)', *ODNB*, online edition, May 2009.
25 *Calendar of Papal Registers*, 7 January 1481/82.
26 Muller, Stephen Gardiner, p. 306; C.D.C. Armstrong, 'Gardiner, Stephen (c.1495x8–1555)', *ODNB*, online edition, January 2008.
27 Sutton and Visser-Fuchs, *Royal Funerals*, pp. 58–60.
28 For what follows see Ross, *Edward IV*, pp. 287–90; Ross, *Richard III*, 45–47; Jones, 'Richard III as a Soldier', p. 100; Wilkins, pp. 76–78.
29 *Coventry Leet Records*, p. 505.
30 *Crowland*, p. 149.

11 Welcome Fortune!

1 Ives, 'Andrew Dymmock', pp. 228–29. The letter bears no year, but Ives makes a strong argument for the proper year being 1483.
2 Orme, 'Education of Edward V', pp. 124–29.
3 Ives, pp. 223–25.
4 Carson, *Maligned King*, pp. 35–36
5 PROME, January 1483, Introduction.
6 In the 1450s, the future Edward IV and his brother requested that the delivery of their new bonnets – clearly not an undertaking fraught with secrecy – be by 'the next sure messenger'. Scofield, *Edward IV*, vol. 1, p. 20.
7 Ross, *Richard III*, p. 187; Ross, *Edward IV*, pp. 336–37; Driver, 'Sir Thomas St Leger', pp. 213, 216; PROME, January 1483, Introduction and items 20 and 21.
8 *Crowland*, p. 151; Mancini, pp. 59, 107 n.5; Scofield, *Edward IV*, vol. II, p. 365; Commynes, vol. II, pp. 62, 87.
9 *Crowland*, p. 149.
10 Mancini, pp. 59–61, 107–08 n. 7; *Crowland*, p. 153.
11 Palliser, 'Richard III and York', p. 56.

12 Kendall, *Richard the Third*, pp. 193–94.
13 Mancini, p. 71; *Crowland*, p. 155.
14 Armstrong, 'Some Examples of the Distribution and Speed of News', p. 450.
15 Kendall, p. 200; Ross, *Richard III*, p. 66; Roskell, 'The Office and Dignity of Protector', p. 196.
16 *The Logge Register of PCC Wills*, no. 105, p. 329.
17 *Crowland*, p. 155; Mancini, pp. 69–72.
18 More, pp. 11, 52.
19 Ives, pp. 221–22; Gairdner, *History of the Life and Reign of Richard the Third*, p. 394.
20 *Crowland*, p. 153–55.
21 Mancini, pp. 71–75.
22 *Crowland*, p. 155.
23 Pollard, *Richard III and the Princes in the Tower*, p. 97; Charles Ross, *Richard III*, p. 68 & n.18.
24 Hicks, *Wars of the Roses*, pp. 216–17.
25 Mancini, p. 75.
26 *Edward IV's French Expedition*, p. 14.
27 Jones, 'Richard III as a Soldier', p. 98.
28 Rawcliffe, *The Staffords*, pp. 30–31.
29 Harris, *Edward Stafford*, p. 21.
30 British Library Additional Manuscripts 6113, folio 74d.
31 Sutton and Visser-Fuchs, *Royal Funeral*, pp. 17–31.
32 Rous, *Historia Regum Angliae,* p. 212.
33 For what follows see Mancini, 75–79, 116 n.46; *Crowland*, pp. 155–57; More, 18–21.
34 Rivers's stay at Sheriff Hutton can be seen from his will; see Appendix. For Grey, see Pollard, *Worlds of Richard III.*
35 Mancini, p. 81; Horrox, 'Financial Memoranda', p. 211; Wilkins, pp. 87–89.
36 *Crowland*, p. 157; Mancini, p. 79.
37 Thomson, 'Bishop Lionel Woodville', p. 131; *Stonor Letters*, vol. II, p. 159; *Grants from the Crown*, p. 3; *Harleian Ms* 433, vol. III, p. 2.
38 *Crowland*, p. 161.
39 Kendall, p. 69.
40 Hicks, *Richard III*, pp. 96–97.
41 For further discussion along these lines, see Pollard, *Richard III and the Princes in the Tower*, pp. 101–06.
42 Mancini, p. 83–85.
43 *Coronation of Richard III*, p. 17; *Crowland*, p. 157–59.
44 *Grants From the Crown*, pp. 1–3; *Harleian* 433, vol. III, pp. 1–2; Wilkins, p. 75; *CPR*, 1476–1485, p. 180; Horrox, *Study in Service*, pp. 102.
45 Wilkins, pp. 88 & 205 n. 14.
46 Horrox, 'Financial Memoranda', pp. 211, 216; Horrox, *Study in Service*, pp. 102–03; Wilkins, p. 94–95, 177.
47 Mancini, pp. 85–87; Horrox, *Study in Service*, p. 103.
48 Griffiths and Thomas, *Making of the Tudor Dynasty*, p. 106.
49 Horrox, *Study in Service*, pp. 99–100.
50 Mancini, p. 81.
51 Horrox, *Study in Service*, p. 91.
52 Horrox, 'Financial Memoranda', p. 210.
53 *Cornation of Richard III*, p. 17.

54 *Crowland*, p. 159.
55 *Harleian* 433, vol. III, p. 190.
56 *Harleian* 433, vol. III, pp. 34–35.
57 Sutton and Visser-Fuchs, 'A "Most Benevolent Queen"', p. 221.
58 *Coronation of Richard III*, p. 19.
59 *Stonor Letters*, vol. II, p. 159–60, no. 330.
60 For this and the extract above see Hammond and Sutton, *Richard III: The Road to Bosworth Field*, pp. 103–04.
61 John Leland, 'Witchcraft and the Woodvilles', pp. 281–87.
62 Argentine, said by Mancini to be the last of the attendants employed to wait on Edward V, does not appear to have been regarded with any suspicion by Richard III; later, Argentine was employed by Henry VII as Prince Arthur's physician. Nandyke, described in a 1483 Act of Attainder as Buckingham's 'necromancer', was caught up in rebellion in 1484, as well as Buckingham's rebellion of 1483. Caerteon, Margaret Beaufort's physician, was also involved in Buckingham's rebellion, as we shall see in Chapter 12. Rhodes, p. 13; Rawcliffe, 'Inventory', pp. 384–85.
63 Horrox, *Study in Service*, pp. 113–16, offers a succinct discussion of the theories.
64 More, 48–49.
65 Vergil, *Three Books*, pp. 180–81.
66 Pollard, *Richard III and the Princes in the Tower*, p. 99.
67 More, pp. 48–49; Vergil, *Three Books*, pp. 180–81.
68 The daughter of John Lambert, a London mercer, Elizabeth Shore – rechristened by the dramatist Thomas Heywood in 1599 as 'Jane' – succeeded in having her marriage to William Shore annulled on account of his impotence. Thomas More casts her as Edward IV's mistress, while he and the *Great Chronicle of London* assign her to Hastings as well. Richard III allowed his solicitor, Thomas Lynom, to take her as his wife. Rosemary Horrox, 'Shore, Elizabeth [Jane] (d. 1526/7?)', *ODNB*, 2004.
69 *CPR*, 1476–85, p. 371.
70 *Stonor Letters*, vol. II, p. 161, no. 331.
71 Mancini, p. 91; Hanham, *Richard III*, p. 179. Frustratingly, the *Great Chronicle* informs us that Dorset 'escaped many wonderful dangers, whereof if I should tell all the circumstance, it would make a long book'. *Great Chronicle*, pp. 231–32.
72 *Crowland*, p. 159; Mancini, p. 89. That the men were armed is confirmed by Simon Stallworth, who writes in a private letter that there were 'great plenty of harnessed men' at Westminster.
73 *Stonor Letters*, vol. II, p. 161, no. 331.
74 Mancini, p. 95; More, p. 67; *Crowland*, pp. 159–61.
75 PROME, January 1484, item 1 [5].
76 Helmholz, 'The Sons of Edward IV', pp. 111–13.
77 This and other genealogical information is taken from Ashdown-Hill, *Eleanor*, pp. 19, 68, 88, 101.
78 Commynes, p. 63.
79 Ashdown-Hill, *Eleanor*, p. 209; *Letters and Papers, Henry VIII*, 16 December 1533, item 1528; 3 November 1534, item 1368.
80 Cavill, *English Parliaments of Henry VII*, p. 30.
81 *Crowland*, p. 161.
82 Hampton, 'Robert Stillington', pp. 163–64.
83 Ashdown-Hill, *Eleanor*, p. 92.
84 Ashdown-Hill, *Eleanor*, p. 142.

85 Ashdown-Hill, *Eleanor*, p. 171.
86 Mancini, p. 69.
87 Carson, pp. 72, 230–31; Ashdown-Hill, *Eleanor*, pp. 115, 156–57.
88 *Crowland*, pp. 169–71.
89 For what follows, see Helmholz, *Marriage Litigation*, pp. 26–31.
90 *Coronation of Richard III*, pp. 24–25; *Crowland*, pp. 159–61; Mancini, p. 97.
91 *Harleian* 433, vol. III, p. 25; Pollard, *Worlds of Richard III*, p. 5.
92 *Crowland*, p. 161; Rous, *Historia Regum Anglia*, pp. 213–14 (translated in Hanham, *Richard III and His Early Work*, 119–20).
93 *Harleian* 433, vol. III, p. 25; Pollard, *Worlds of Richard III*, p. 5.
94 Crotch, *Prologues and Epilogues*, p. 39; Percy, *Reliques*, pp. 45–47; Ritson, *Ancient Songs and Ballads*, vol. II, pp. 3–5; *Chronicles of the White Rose of York*, p. 209.

12 Under the Hog

1 For what follows see *Coronation of Richard III*, pp. 35–38, 169.
2 For what follows see Michael K. Jones and Malcolm G. Underwood, 'Beaufort, Margaret, Countess of Richmond and Derby (1443–1509)', *ODNB*, 2004.
3 For what follows see *King's Mother*, pp. 48–62.
4 Catto and Evans, eds, *History of the University of Oxford*, vol. II, p. 736; CPR, 1476–85, pp. 569–70.
5 Horrox, *Study in Service*, pp. 149–50; *Road to Bosworth Field*, p. 125; Stow, p. 450.
6 *Crowland*, p. 163.
7 *Harleian* 433, vol. II, p. 2; Mancini, p. 93.
8 For what follows see *Crowland*, pp. 163–69; Vergil, *Three Books*, pp. 192–204; Horrox, *Study in Service*, pp. 138–77; Ross, *Richard III*, 105–24; Gill, passim.
9 Kibre, 'Lewis of Caerlon', pp. 101–02.
10 Gill, *Buckingham's Rebellion*, p. 13–14; Thomson, pp. 132–33.
11 *Road to Bosworth Field*, p. 145.
12 Farrer and Sutton, 'The Duke of Buckingham's Sons', pp. 87–91.
13 D. Sanituste, '"Putting Downe"', p. 145.
14 *Crowland*, p. 165.
15 Farrer and Sutton, 'The Duke of Buckingham's Sons', pp. 87–91.
16 Arthurson and Kingwell, 'Proclamation of Henry Tudor', pp. 101–02.
17 Farrer and Sutton, 'The Duke of Buckingham's Sons', pp. 88–90.
18 *Harleian* 433, vol. I, p. 63. Farrar and Sutton suggest (p. 90) that the children were taken into Richard III's or his queen's household, but the authors appear to have been unaware of the order allowing Katherine's servants and children to be brought to her in London.
19 Seabourne, *Imprisoning Medieval Women*, pp. 42–43.
20 Vergil, *Three Books*, p. 204.
21 Charles Ross, *Richard III*, p. 118.
22 Vergil, *Three Books*, p. 203.
23 Clarke, 'English Royal Marriages', pp. 1024–25.
24 *Harleian* 433, vol. III, p. 190.
25 Kendall, p. 484.
26 Williamson, p. 122–23.
27 *CPR*, 1476–85, p. 485; *King's Works*, vol. II, p. 680.

28 *Harleian* 433, vol. I, p. 213; vol. II, p. 130.
29 *Crowland*, p. 171.
30 Horrox, *Study in Service*, pp. 275–77; *CPR*, 1476–85, pp. 519–20; Bellamy, pp. 121–22; Fabyan, pp. 671–72; *Great Chronicle*, p. 236.
31 Griffiths and Thomas, *Making of the Tudor Dynasty*, p. 106.
32 Griffiths and Thomas, *Making of the Tudor Dynasty*, pp. 110–20; Charles Ross, *Richard III*, pp. 198–200; Horrox, *Study in Service*, pp. 277–78.
33 For what follows see Grant, 'Foreign Affairs under Richard III', pp. 123–26; Chrimes, pp. 31–34; Ross, *Richard III*, pp. 198–201; Antonovics, 'Henry VII', pp. 171–73; Griffiths and Thomas, pp. 118–20
34 Quoted in Dockray, *Richard III*, p. 77.
35 Spont, *La Marine Francaise*, p. 9. Admirers of Richard III have, rather disingenuously, transferred this isolated statement by the French into Henry Tudor's own mouth. Ashdown-Hill, *Last Days of Richard III*, pp. 48, 58; Carson, pp. 244–45, Born in 1470, and therefore far too young to remember the events of 1470–71 personally, Charles VIII might have simply overlooked a clerical error.
36 For what follows see James Ross, *John de Vere*, pp. 74–84; Griffiths and Thomas, pp. 122–23.
37 Griffiths and Thomas, p. 120; Hammond, *Richard III and the Bosworth Campaign*, p. 40.
38 Hammond, *Richard III and the Bosworth Campaign*, p. 40; Hutton, *The Battle of Bosworth Field*, 190–91.
39 *Harleian* 433, vol. III, pp. 124–25.
40 *Harleian* 433, vol. I, pp. 59, 92, 177; Thomson, 'Bishop Lionel Woodville and Richard III', pp. 134–35; John A.F. Thomson, 'Woodville, Lionel (*c.* 1454–1484)', *ODNB*, September 2011; Britton, *History and Antiquities of the Cathedral Church of Salisbury*, p. 94.
41 For the following see *Crowland*, pp. 175–77.
42 Hammond, *Road to Bosworth Field*, p. 199.
43 Buck, p. 191. Kincaid's edition contains an extensive description of the textual history of Buck's manuscript. For further discussion, see Hanham, 'Sir George Buck and Princess Elizabeth's Letter', and Kincaid, 'Buck and the Elizabeth of York Letter'.
44 E 404/78/3/47. See the articles by Court, Barrie Williams, and Marques in the bibliography.
45 Vergil, *Three Books*, p. 215.
46 Vergil, *Three Books*, pp. 210, 214. Although Vergil is vague about the time for this episode, it appears to have occurred shortly before Anne's death.
47 Ashdown-Hill, *Last Days of Richard III*, pp. 27–28.
48 Vergil, *Henry VII*, online edition; Pierce, *Margaret Pole*, pp. 8–9.
49 Horrox, *Study in Service*, p. 293; *CPR*, 1476–85, p. 532.
50 *Harleian* 433, vol. II, pp. 228–30; *Paston Letters* (Gardiner), vol. VI, no. 1001, pp. 81–84.
51 Ross, *Richard III*, p. 201; Griffiths and Thomas, *Making of the Tudor Dynasty*, pp. 129–31; Hammond, *Richard III and the Bosworth Campaign*, p. 75; *Crowland*, p. 181.
52 Hammond, *Richard III and the Bosworth Campaign*, pp. 75–78, 91.
53 Vergil, *Three Books*, p. 226; *Great Chronicle*, p. 238; *Crowland*, p. 183.

13 Won and Lost Causes

1 Hammond, *Richard III and the Bosworth Campaign*, p. 108.
2 Roskell, 'William Catesby', p. 170–72; Williams, 'Hastily Drawn-Up Will of William Catesby', p. 49.
3 *Harleian* 433, vol. I, pp. 183, 241; vol. II, pp. 135, 138.
4 For what follows see Roger Stuart Thomas, p. 248–67.
5 Hicks, *False, Fleeting, Perjur'd Clarence*, p. 103; Jones and Underwood, *King's Mother*, p. 52.
6 *Materials for a History of the Reign of Henry VII*, pp. 6–7, 286.
7 PROME, November 1485, Introduction and items 7, 16 [21], 17 [22], 18 [23].
8 PROME, November 1485, item 9.
9 Okerlund, *Elizabeth of York*, pp. 48–49.
10 James and Underwood, *King's Mother*, p. 67; Kingsford, 'On Some London Houses', pp. 43–50 passim.
11 *Crowland*, p. 191.
12 Linda Clark, 'Bourchier, Thomas (*c.* 1411–1486)', *ODNB*, 2004.
13 *Plumpton Letters*, p. 63.
14 Ross, *Richard III*, p. 142. For my account of Edward's adventures in Spain I have relied on Wilkins, pp. 1–15, 134, 179–81; Merriman, 134–37; Prescott, vol. I, pp. 396–97.
15 Prescott, p. 396.
16 Wilkins, p. 7.
17 Prescott, pp. 396–97.
18 Prescott, p. 397.
19 Wilkins, p. 11.
20 Wilkins, p. 181.
21 Marques, p. 27.
22 Sanceau, *Perfect Prince*, pp. 296–97.
23 *Herald's Memoir*, p. 99 & n.202.
24 *Herald's Memoir*, pp. 100–01.
25 For the following see *Herald's Memoir*, pp. 100–06.
26 Okerlund, *Slandered Queen*, p. 245.
27 *Materials for a History of the Reign of Henry VII*, pp. 148–49.
28 Vergil, quoted by Sutton and Visser-Fuchs, '"Retirement" of Elizabeth Woodville', pp. 561–62.
29 *Hall*, p. 431.
30 Bacon, pp. 83–84 (italics mine).
31 See Gordon Smith, 'Lambert Simnel and the King from Dublin'.
32 Vergil quoted in Bennett, *Lambert Simnel*, p. 135.
33 Bacon, pp. 91–92.
34 Cavill, *English Parliaments*, pp. 111–12.
35 *Materials for a History of the Reign of Henry VII*, pp. 319–20; CPR, 1485–94, p. 302; Sutton and Visser-Fuchs, '"Retirement" of Elizabeth Woodville', p. 563. The situation of having a married king on the throne and an adult dowager queen in good standing had not occurred since Edward III's time. Queen Phillipa was dead when Richard II came to the throne; after the death in prison of Richard II, his queen, a child, was kept in Henry IV's care before being returned to France; Henry V had imprisoned Henry IV's queen on allegations of witchcraft before marrying Catherine of Valois; Henry VI's

mother, Catherine of Valois, died before Henry VI married Margaret of Anjou; Margaret of Anjou was in exile when Edward IV took the throne; and Elizabeth Woodvile, of course, was not recognised as queen by Richard III.

36 *Foedera*, vol. 12, pp. 328–39; Chrimes, *Henry VII*, p. 279.
37 For what follows see Bennett, *Lambert Simnel*; Wilkins, *Last Knight Errant*, pp. 139–46; Chrimes, *Henry VII*, pp. 75–78; Okerlund, *Elizabeth of York*, pp. 70–75.
38 Wilkins, pp. 142–43 & 213 n.18.
39 Molinet quoted in Bennett, *Lambert Simnel*, p. 130.
40 Wilkins, pp. 142–43.
41 Rosemary Horrox, 'Lovell, Francis, Viscount Lovell (b. *c.*1457, d. in or after 1488)', *ODNB*, online edition, 2004.
42 Michael J. Bennett, 'Simnel, Lambert (b. 1476/7, d. after 1534)', *ODNB*, October 2008.
43 For what follows see Cavell, *Heralds' Memoir*, pp. 120–50; .
44 Bacon, p. 97.
45 Cavell, *Heralds' Memoir*, pp. 156–60.
46 Chrimes, *Henry VII*, p. 140.
47 What follows is based primarily on Wilkins, pp. 151–64.
48 Vergil, *Anglica Historia.*
49 *PL*, no. 411, part I, p. 655.
50 Vergil, *Anglica Historia.* For a translation of Henry's letter, see Wilkins, pp. 183–84.
51 *Calendar of State Papers, Spanish*, 15 July 1488,
52 Wilkins, p. 160.
53 *Hall*, p. 441.
54 Wilkins, p. 161.
55 *Heralds' Memoir*, pp. 161, 172.
56 Beauchesne, p. 39.

14 The Last of the Blood

1 *Heralds' Memoir*, p. 175.
2 Bacon, p. 88.
3 Cokayne, vol. XII/1, p. 356. Mary had died before 21 July 1483, when her husband directed in his will that he be buried at Tintern Abbey 'where my dear and best beloved wife resteth buried'. Thomas, 'Herberts of Raglan', p. 296. MacGibbon, p. 224, gives her death date as 1481.
4 S.J. Gunn, 'Grey, George, second earl of Kent (*d.* 1503)', *ODNB*, September 2011.
5 Cokayne vol. 1, pp. 248–50.
6 *Materials for a Reign of Henry VII*, pp. 562–63; C 142/7/2.
7 E 315/486/7.
8 *Heralds' Memoir*, p. 102.
9 Currin, 'King's Army', esp. pp. 398, 400, 403.
10 *Heralds' Memoir*, p. 71, 81.
11 *CPR*, 1485–94, pp. 106, 278–79, 481, 494–95; PROME, November 1487 [opening].
12 TNA: C 142/7/2, C 142/7/39. For the will, see the Appendix.

13 *CPR*, 1485–94, p. 382.
14 See Appendix.
15 For what follows see *Royal Funerals*, pp. 4 n. 7, 66–74.
16 D. H. Thomas, 'Herberts of Raglan', pp. 278, 351.
17 TNA: PROB 11/10/401; Thomas, pp. 353–57.
18 Pugh, *Marcher Lordships of South Wales*, p. 241 n.5; Mary L. Robertson, 'Wingfield, Sir Richard (*b.* in or before 1469, *d.* 1525)', *ONDB*, October 2008.
19 Harris, *Edward Stafford*, p. 42.
20 Wingfield, p. 251.
21 C.S.L. Davies, 'Stafford, Henry, second duke of Buckingham (1455–1483)', *ONDB*, September 2011; Horrox, *Study in Service*, pp. 172, 264.
22 Pugh, *Marcher Lordships of South Wales*, p. 241 n.5.
23 Wingfield, ed., *Some Records of the Wingfield Family*, p. 223.

Index